BV
820
.B37
1994

Barbour, John D.

Versions of
  deconversion.

$35.00

DATE			

BAKER & TAYLOR

VERSIONS OF
DECONVERSION
Autobiography
and the Loss of Faith

JOHN D. BARBOUR

VERSIONS OF DECONVERSION

Autobiography
and the Loss of Faith

University Press of Virginia

Charlottesville and London

THE UNIVERSITY PRESS OF VIRGINIA
Copyright © 1994 by the Rector and Visitors
of the University of Virginia

First published 1994

Library of Congress Cataloging-in-Publication Data
Barbour, John D.
Versions of deconversion : autobiography and the loss of faith /
John D. Barbour
p.   cm. — (Studies in religion and culture)
Includes index.
ISBN 0-8139-1546-5
1. Ex-church members—Case studies.   2. Apostasy—Case
studies.   3. Apostasy—Comparative studies.   4. Autobiobgraphy
—Religious aspects—Christianity.   5. Autobiography—Religious
aspects.   I. Title.   II. Series: Studies in religion and culture
(Charlottesville, Va.)
BV820.B37   1994
280'.092'2—dc20
94-12207
CIP

Printed in the United States of America

for Blair, David,
and Heather

CONTENTS

ACKNOWLEDGMENTS

Herman Melville expressed well some of my feelings as I worked on this book: "God keep me from ever completing anything. This whole book is but a draught—nay, but the draught of a draught. Oh, Time, Strength, Cash, and Patience!"

Some of the time and cash necessary for this project were provided when St. Olaf College awarded me one semester's release from teaching. My strength and patience depended very much on family members, friends, and colleagues who encouraged me and responded to early drafts. The first two chapters were read by all of my colleagues in the Religion Department at St. Olaf, and later chapters by Randy Albers, Blair Barbour, Stuart Charmé, Gary Ebersole, Susan Henking, DeAne Lagerquist, Meg Ojala, Diana Postlethwaite, Barbara Reed, and Mary Titus. Ian and Deane Barbour read the entire manuscript and offered many helpful suggestions. Robert Scharlemann made valuable criticisms, and Cathie Brettschneider's advice facilitated the editorial process. Jody Greenslade's typing and computing skills made revisions much easier.

Thanks, too, to my immediate family members, Meg, Graham, and Reed, for showing their own forms of strength and patience. When I was stuck on how to conclude the book, four-year-old Reed advised me to "just say what you said in the beginning." Graham (age eight): "Yeah, like in the Jabberwocky." Their presences in my life have made a great difference in the writing of this book.

VERSIONS OF DECONVERSION

Autobiography
and the Loss of Faith

1

INTRODUCTION

THIS BOOK EXAMINES the reasons for which autobiographers have rejected their religious beliefs and analyzes the different ways in which they have interpreted a loss of faith. While there are innumerable studies of the conversion narrative as a shaping influence on autobiography, deconversion has not been addressed. Yet the loss of faith has often been as decisive an event in the lives of autobiographers as has religious conversion. Augustine, for instance, who is usually considered the fountainhead of Western autobiography, devotes much of his *Confessions* to explaining why it took him nearly ten years to free himself from the doctrines of the Manichees. The subject matter of this book encompasses writers whose deconversion leads eventually to another religious faith, those who embrace atheism or agnosticism, and autobiographers who use deconversion as a metaphor or analogy to interpret some other experience of personal transformation.

A religious conversion is a profound change in belief and action in relation to what a person conceives of as ultimate reality. *Conversion* was originally a term describing how the material of a work of art is transformed by the artist. The word was taken up by Christian tradition as a metaphor for how God remakes the believer who has faith. For instance, Augustine confesses to God: "You converted me to yourself, so that I no longer desired a wife or placed any hope in this world but stood firmly upon the rule of faith"(8.12).[1] The Latin root of the word *conversion* means to "turn around" or "transform," indicating the radical nature of this event. As used by scholars of religion since William James, *conversion* means the attainment of some form of belief, conscious adherence to new religious convictions.[2] The *Oxford English Dictionary* holds that the prefix *de-* before a noun will "deprive, divest, free from, or get rid of the thing in question." Accordingly, I shall use the term *deconversion* to designate a loss or deprivation of religious faith.

Just as scholars distinguish different types of conversion, I will discuss varieties of deconversion and therefore wish to leave the definition of this concept rather general, as simply loss of faith. A deconversion has four basic characteristics that different autobiographers may emphasize to a greater or lesser extent. Deconversion involves doubt or denial of the truth of a system of beliefs. Second, deconversion is characterized by moral criticism of not only particular actions or practices but an entire way of life. Third, the loss of faith brings emotional upheaval, especially such painful feelings as grief, guilt, loneliness, and despair. Finally, a person's deconversion is usually marked by the rejection of the community to which he or she belonged. Deconversion encompasses, then, intellectual doubt, moral criticism, emotional suffering, and disaffiliation from a community. Every autobiography discussed in this book involves at least three of these four dimensions of deconversion, although in particular cases one element may not be present. For instance, in *Grace Abounding* Bunyan does not reject a religious community, and the nature of his deconversion is rather different from Augustine's. In his *Apologia* John Henry Newman makes few moral criticisms of himself or his former faith as he precisely measures his increasing doubts about the Anglican church and, after considerable emotional suffering, joins the Roman Catholic Church.

A deconversion may involve a sudden dramatic reversal, or it may be a more protracted and even inconclusive process of doubt and uncertainty. I distinguish deconversion from *secularization* in terms of a person's self-consciousness about the choice to reject a faith. As a literary narrative, a version of deconversion represents a series of events arranged as a plot and a decision that the writer tries to justify. Secularization is a gradual fading away of beliefs, as religion simply ceases to inform a person's life, to make any real difference. In this century, secularization is probably the more common way that people lose their faith, but, in contrast to deconversion, it does not usually motivate or decisively shape the writing of autobiography. A version of deconversion involves the narration of the significant events that call a faith into question, an analysis of choices, and usually a rather dramatic reversal: One's former faith is presented as not just irrelevant but as wrong or misguided. Like most conversions, deconversions usually take a long time and are punctuated by crucial recognitions and decisions that structure the plot.[3] We shall see also that deconversions (again like conversions) rarely entail the total reversal stipulated by an ideal definition.

How central and dominant in an autobiography must an account of eroding faith be to merit consideration as a distinctive version of deconversion? In some of the texts to be discussed, deconversion is the central and dominating focus while others treat the loss of faith more casually, in passing. In many cases an author rejects only part of his former faith. Although Newman presents his shift of loyalties from Anglicanism to Roman Catholicism as an ordeal of doubt, loneliness, and suffering, he never loses his faith in God.

Can the interpretation of deconversion be separated from analysis of whatever beliefs replaced the lost ones? That is, can one discuss an author's loss of faith apart from his or her conversion to new values? In one sense, every conversion is a deconversion, and every deconversion a conversion. The "turning from" and "turning to" are alternative perspectives on the same process of personal metamorphosis, stressing either the rejected past of the old self or the present convictions of the reborn self. William James pointed out that in most conversions a person is preoccupied with a sinful past life, "so that conversion is 'a process of struggling away from sin rather than of striving towards righteousness.'"[4] While conversion and deconversion are inextricably linked in experience and in analysis, this book focuses on the loss of faith as an experience worth studying in its own right. In examining deconversions, I will analyze what a writer is "struggling away from" and explain how the depiction of such struggle reflects the author's ethical and religious concerns both in the past and at the time of writing. Approaching these narratives in terms of deconversion rather than the familiar conversion theme will throw new light both on particular texts and on the broader issue of how autobiography may express ethical and religious values. In each instance I will argue that analyzing the author's treatment of an experience of deconversion provides a useful and usually neglected hermeneutic lens for interpreting these texts.

This book focuses primarily on writers who lose faith in Christianity. Analogous sorts of disavowal and disaffiliation may occur in relation to other systems of belief and other religious communities, but deconversion in the context of Christianity takes distinctive forms and expressions. For instance, we will trace the persistence of such Christian motifs as a central event of crisis and an emphasis on the subjective experience of faith as critical for religious identity. In the final chapter I raise the question of the extent to which the concept of deconversion can be applied more broadly to other literatures and cultures.

The term *deconversion* is especially appropriate for the subject of this book because it suggests the paradoxical ways in which narratives of lost faith mirror conversion stories. Accounts of deconversion often use the same old wineskins for the new wine of unbelief. In their use of scriptural language, depiction of a central crisis scene, account of emotional upheaval, and overall narrative structure, many stories of the loss of faith mimic the classical Christian testimony of conversion. At the same time, both Christian and anti-Christian writers modify autobiographical conventions and devise innovative new forms in order to express distinctive aspects of their own spiritual struggles. One of my central interests is in how autobiographers try to break away not only from discredited religious beliefs but from the forms of narrative associated with those beliefs.

Among the reasons for which people reject a faith, I see ethical considerations as primary, determining not only when religious beliefs or practices are deemed to be harmful or hypocritical but when cognitive uncertainties or doubts become compelling grounds for deconversion. Autobiographers usually reject their religion for reasons of conscience, that is, because of a commitment to intellectual honesty or because they see certain beliefs as having a destructive effect on their society. Deconversion raises many of the issues involved in discussions about the "ethics of belief." While this topic is often discussed as an epistemological issue, it is also a moral problem, an affair of conscience. The debate is based on the assumption that every person has a moral responsibility to have sufficient evidence to support his or her beliefs. A conscientious and responsible account of one's life may need to explain not only adherence to new convictions but also shifts, erosions, and losses of belief.[5]

Deconversion may involve not only ethical concerns but also a religious dimension. An author may appeal to a religious community's own professed beliefs, criticizing a failure to "practice what you preach," or to a source of value transcending that community. Usually, although not always, an autobiographer explains what values replaced his lost faith. But even when writers focus only on the rejected faith, as do Edmund Gosse and Jean-Paul Sartre, and do not affirm an alternative vision of the truth, their basic convictions inevitably emerge in the analysis of mistaken beliefs. I will explore the ways in which an experience of deconversion shapes a person's later convictions, whether or not these involve affirmation of a new religious faith. The reaction against a mistaken belief has a tremendous influence on the way in which a person articulates fundamental values, often providing an image of the "other" against which present identity is contrasted. False faith is dialectically defined in relation either to true faith (for the believer) or responsible thinking (for the agnostic).

A person's deconversion raises the question of the standard by which a religious faith is judged to be wrong. Thus interpretation of deconversion narratives calls for explication of an author's most deeply held values and ultimate concerns. The religious dimension of autobiography is not simply located in an author's record of past loyalties but also in the "autobiographical act" (as critics term it)—in the author's process of writing, as the articulation of those central convictions that shape a perspective on the past. In assessing the motives and reasons for deconversion, the most profound autobiographies reveal their authors' ultimate concerns and fundamental convictions about human existence and destiny.

Deconversion raises other religious and theological issues, such as the relationship between faith and morality, for it often arises in a situation when their demands seem to conflict. Deconversion is theologically compelling, too, in that it illuminates tensions between faith and doubt in more ordinary religious experience.[6] Deconversion is the most radical consequence of the doubts and skepticism that I think many believers have about certain aspects of their religious tradition. Most persons have experienced some form of loss of faith, if not in God or an entire historical religious tradition, then at least in particular beliefs or doctrines, church practices, or institutions. Such experiences of disillusionment and rejection are not necessarily antireligious, in my view, but may express spiritual searching and development. To be truly vital, a person's religious faith and theology must be subject to revision, reinterpretation, and renewal in response to the challenges to religious faith posed by other religions and by secular culture.

The incentive for deconversion does not arise only from outside the demands of faith itself. Monotheistic faith has its own imperatives calling for the renunciation of idolatry, the rejection of false understandings of belief, and the criticism of hypocritical practices. The authentic spiritual life almost inevitably includes moments of disillusionment and even radical doubt or despair. Deconversion involves disillusionment: both the bitterness, nostalgia, and pain involved in losing the basis of one's confidence and comfort and the recognition that only when illusions are destroyed can reality be understood and a more authentic life be experienced. What is the meaning of such moments of crisis and their long-term significance in life? I hope that the study of deconversion in autobiography provides suggestive and instructive analogies to other forms of religious searching and offers the reader insights that apply to a broad range of experiences.

I submit that the field of religious studies has much to learn from the phenomenon of deconversion. Christian theology, too, should attend to autobiographers who have discerned God's work in their own experiences of deconversion. A self-critical Christian theology should also be informed by the testimony of those who have criticized or rejected its central beliefs. The insights of those who have conscientiously rejected Christian beliefs ought to play a role in Christian self-definition and in the apologetic task of interpreting the faith to nonbelievers.

Deconversion is especially interesting in light of the increasing challenges to traditional concepts of self and identity from many contemporary critical perspectives. The autobiographers examined here revise their fundamental beliefs about their identity as they change their convictions about God, truth, the moral good, and the best literary form for narrating their lives. These autobiographers do not view ideas of self, God, truth, goodness, and text as immutable or uncontested, yet they recognize that these concepts are indispensable both for understanding their own lives and for their various rhetorical purposes in relation to an audience. Both their challenges to, and their critical revisions of, these crucial concepts are instructive for contemporary debates in many academic disciplines.

I am interested in both the reasons for which a religious faith is rejected and the ways such stories are told, that is, in the "versions" of deconversion considered as narrative strategies. The autobiographer's task in interpreting deconversion involves finding metaphors and rhetorical strategies adequate to explain how the workings of conscience required the rejection of a former faith.

Autobiographers have explained a loss of faith in a fascinating variety of ways, usually by modifying or revising the conventions of previous writers. This literary innovation expresses a striving for honesty and new insight in exploring the meaning of deconversion. I will discuss the ways in which agnostics and Christians alike have sought to modify traditional forms of the conversion narrative to interpret their own lives as well as ways in which the experience of religious deconversion becomes a metaphor for other kinds of personal change. I will therefore outline and analyze patterns of continuity and of transformation in these versions of deconversion.

The vast philosophical literature of atheism ranges from such early materialists as Epicurus to the logical positivism of Alfred J. Ayer and the existentialism of Sartre.[7] There are innumerable analytic critiques of particular systems of belief and countless philosophical arguments for atheism or agnosticism, but such works rarely involve sustained recourse to narrative. I confine my subject matter to autobiographical narratives, which usually sketch philosophical debates only insofar as they have direct bearing on the author's own loss of faith. In my view most philosophical and theological arguments against theism are too abstract to explain the real reasons why most people lose faith. In contrast, autobiographical narratives express the interplay of cognitive, volitional, and emotional factors within the individual and the writer's commitments within a particular society and broader cultural context.

Expressions of the loss of faith can be found in many literary genres, ranging from biblical wisdom literature such as Ecclesiastes to contemporary lyrical poetry. This book treats only autobiographical narratives in prose, although there are many other literary texts that might be interpreted in relation to my theme, for instance such poetry as Tennyson's *In Memoriam* or Melville's verse, and such novels as Hardy's *Jude the Obscure* or Forster's *A Passage to India*. I will consider autobiography, with Philippe Lejeune, to be "a retrospective prose narrative that someone writes concerning his own existence, where the focus is the individual life, in particular the story of his personality."[8] In distinguishing autobiography and fiction, I follow Lejeune's concept of the autobiographical pact, which is based on the identity of the proper name shared by a work's protagonist, narrator, and author. This evidence within the text, not dependent on biographical evidence, indicates an author's intention to render his or her own experience. Lejeune's ideas have been criticized by other scholars of autobiography, and there are ambiguous borderline cases, but his is still the best theoretical account of the difference between auto-biography and fiction.[9]

By surveying a range of texts by authors of very different religious and antireligious convictions, I hope to provide a broad overview as well as some detailed analyses of particular cases and to explore the most significant literary and religious issues raised by narratives of deconversion. The texts selected for analysis are all works in which the loss of faith is a crucially important event that decisively shapes the autobiographer's perspective. Each chapter is organized in terms of some central theme or issue common to several autobiographies, for instance the examination of racial prejudice, the analysis of religious hypocrisy, and the interpretation of a deconversion as apostasy from Christian faith.

My approach involves an interdisciplinary attempt to integrate the insights of literary criticism with ethical theory and religious reflection. Literary and religious concerns are inextricably linked in these autobiographical texts, as they should be in critical analysis. Literary critics have usually not addressed the spiritual searching expressed in accounts of losing faith. Nor have theologians or scholars of religion discerned the significance for their fields of the literary innovation and creativity involved in versions of deconversion. I hope to show how autobiographical theory and critical studies of specific texts can provide valuable resources for ethical and religious reflection. The book will demonstrate, too, the centrality of issues of conscience, integrity, and the justifiability of religious faith as these arise both in the writing of autobiography and in critical interpretation of these narratives, including the ones that reject orthodox or institutional expressions of Christianity.

The subsequent chapters are organized as follows. Chapter 2 explores the ways in which Augustine, John Bunyan, and John Henry Newman describe their experiences of losing faith before they come to what each one sees as authentic Christianity. Chapter 3 analyzes how Thomas Carlyle, John Stuart Mill, and later autobiographers have interpreted various forms of personal crisis as analogous to a loss of religious faith. In chapter 4 I discuss Victorian crises of faith, focusing on John Ruskin's *Praeterita* and Edmund Gosse's *Father and Son*. This chapter examines the "aesthetic critique" of Protestantism and explains how the form of a traditional Christian conversion narrative shapes agnostics' depictions of that pivotal moment of their lives when they reject religious faith. Chapter 5 explores how Native Americans and African Americans have criticized whites' uses of Christianity to justify power and privilege over people of color. Writers as diverse as Frederick Douglass, Charles Eastman, Malcolm X, and Lame Deer have sought to deconvert white readers from various false understandings of Christianity that sanction such injustices.

In the sixth chapter I analyze how issues of cognitive uncertainty and doubt place Mary McCarthy and Anthony Kenny in a situation of hypocrisy that each resolves by rejecting Roman Catholicism. The subject of chapter 7 is Sartre's pervasive use of the theme of deconversion in *The Words* to interpret his literary career. Chapter 8 delineates a pattern whereby Christian autobiographers (Dorothy Day, C. S. Lewis, Langdon Gilkey, and Edwin Muir) present an earlier loss of faith as apostasy, or rebellion against God, and use this experience as the basis for an apologetic argument for the validity of a reinterpreted Christian faith. Chapter 9 explores the reasons for and rhetoric of deconversion from several religious cults in the United States during the 1970s. In chapter 10 I reflect on how issues of gender identity can influence the depiction of the loss of faith, focusing on five recent works by American women. The final chapter summarizes my understanding of the literary and religious significance of narratives of deconversion.

2

THREE CHRISTIAN
VERSIONS OF
DECONVERSION

Augustine, Bunyan,
and Newman

AUGUSTINE'S STORY OF his conversion to Christianity has had an enormous influence on the writing of autobiography in both its explicitly religious forms and its secular varieties. The *Confessions* is also a story of deconversion, of a loss of faith and decade-long struggle to break away from the influence of Manicheism. Augustine was the first person to describe in detail his own loss of faith, and his autobiography is a paradigmatic account of deconversion. At the same time that later autobiographers have been influenced by Augustine's story, they have created new versions of deconversion, interpreting the loss of faith with fresh metaphors and alternative hermeneutic strategies. In this chapter I trace patterns of continuity and innovation in the intellectual and moral concerns, metaphors, and narrative patterns in Christian autobiographies recounting a deconversion, focusing on those by Augustine, John Bunyan, and John Henry Newman. I examine both the reasons these autobiographers lose faith and the ways in which they interpret their deconversions.

Turning away from an ultimate concern takes two forms in early Christian thinking. The approved type of deconversion was the rejection of idols prerequisite to genuine turning to God. The biblical idea of exclusivity in religious commitment, the Old Testament prophetic attack on idolatry, and the necessity of moral repentance in responding to God all influenced Augustine's portrayal of a deliberate turning away from his former sinful life. A similar view of deconversion was involved in the ideal of commitment to philosophy. Seeking wisdom was a disciplined way of life that demanded a total break with one's former worldly pursuits. Augustine says that his new love of wisdom after reading Cicero brought disillusionment with his previous life: "All my empty dreams suddenly lost their charm and my heart began to throb with a bewildering passion for the wisdom of eternal truth" (3.4). The philosopher's rejection of worldly life in favor of contemplation lacks the idea of repentance for sin, but it overlaps with the Christian ideal of withdrawal from the cares of the world. These two views of deconversion as a desireable break with one's former life converge in Augustine's retreat to Cassiciacum after his experience in the garden.

Christians have always distinguished the right kind of loss of faith from the wrong type: apostasy. Apostasy, denoting rebellion, insurrection, or secession, means the public abandonment of Christianity for another institutionalized religion.[1] Augustine's defection from his childhood training in Christianity, although not proclaimed publicly, meant that he was virtually an apostate for many years. Thus the *Confessions* exemplifies both types of religious deconversion, the rejection of false beliefs (and worldly attachments) and the apostate's rejection of Christianity. For my purposes, the essential distinction is based on the autobiographer's perspective: that is, whether he continues to reject or has come to affirm the religious faith he once denied. In this book, deconversion is a broad concept that refers to any loss of faith, while "apostasy" is limited to those deconversions that an autobiographer later reverses and comes to see as a great mistake. In this chapter I discuss Augustine's deconversion from Manicheism, examining how he treats his loss of faith in beliefs that he continues to see as false from his present perspective. In chapter 8 I will return to Augustine's example in considering how Christian autobiographers have portrayed an earlier loss of Christian faith as the act of apostasy.

I will interpret the works of Augustine and later autobiographers in terms of four basic rubrics. The first two are the basic reasons for the loss of faith, which may be summarized as intellectual doubt and moral criticism. Crucial in Augustine's deconversion is his experience of epistemological uncertainty and intellectual doubt. Augustine was skeptical about the extraordinary myths and theories of Manicheism and troubled by discrepancies between Manichee doctrines and known astronomical facts. In retrospect he saw that the root cause of his prolonged difficulty in thinking his way out of this religion was a conceptual difficulty, the inability to conceive of God as a spiritual substance (5.14). After Augustine left the Manichees, he went through a period of skepticism when he could not believe any doctrine. "I began to think that the philosophers known as Academics were wiser than the rest, because they held that everything was a matter of doubt and asserted that man can know nothing for certain" (5.10). There is no need to rehearse here the stages of Augustine's intellectual movement away from Manicheism through Neoplatonism toward Christian faith. What is most significant for our analysis is his vivid description of how epistemological uncertainty can preclude religious belief and his example of intellectual honesty, integrity, and courage in rejecting the claims of religious doctrine even when he was not certain of a better alternative. Augustine demonstrated how these virtues may be expressed in the experience of intellectual doubt. He is more often a model for secular autobiographers in this regard than in his insistence that certain truths can be known only through faith.

A second essential component of Augustine's narrative of deconversion is moral criticism of both the Manichee way of life and his own efforts to practice it. At the heart of Manicheism's appeal to Augustine was its dualistic explanation of evil as something the spirit suffered when it became trapped in matter. This explanation of evil allowed Augustine to avoid taking responsibility for his sins: "I still thought that it is not we who sin but some other nature that sins within us. It flattered my pride to think that I incurred no guilt and, when I did wrong, not to confess it so that you might bring healing to a soul that had sinned against you. I preferred to excuse myself and blame this unknown thing which was in me but was not part of me" (5.10). We would now call this motivation for holding to Manichee doctrine a case of self-deception. Augustine's *Confessions* is the first extended first-person account of how a religious faith can systematically entrap a believer in a pattern of thought and action that is not only deemed immoral but threatens to undermine the sense of moral responsibility itself. Augustine's deconversion depended partly on his learning to recognize and take responsiblity for his misuses of freedom, though a full understanding of sin came only after he became a Christian. Repugnance at the ethical implications of a religion is usually the most powerful incentive for a story of deconversion, and the writer's dramatization of the struggle to be morally responsible structures the plot of many such works. Moral critique—of both a writer's former religious beliefs and his motivation for believing them—is usually the primary agenda shaping versions of deconversion.

The third and fourth features of Augustine's *Confessions* that shape later versions of deconversion concern not the reasons for the loss of faith but the way the story is told. I will discuss first Augustinian metaphors for the experience of deconversion and then his overall narrative structure. Augustine provided a rich fund of emotionally charged metaphors for later writers describing a loss of faith. Although these metaphors are not always tightly linked, their cumulative effect is highly evocative of the emotions produced by deconversion: "I was walking on a treacherous path, in darkness. I was looking for you outside myself and I did not find the God of my own heart. I had reached the depths of the ocean. I had lost all faith and was in despair of finding the truth" (6.1). For Augustine the loss of faith is not simply a matter of intellectual development; deconversion is an existential transformation, a radical alteration of his deepest fears, passions, and hopes. Augustine feels that he has lost control of his will, that he is utterly alone, and that he is experiencing a form of suffering that afflicts every level of his being. Metaphors of thirst and hunger, bondage, mental confusion, bodily disease, and physical motion (wandering, distance from God, rising and sinking) vividly render the ordeal of a soul that has turned away from its ultimate loyalty.

Among these metaphors Augustine highlights an analogy between deconversion and illness. After explaining how Ambrose helped bring him "into a state of wavering uncertainty," Augustine records his mother's spiritual diagnosis: "She had no doubt that I must pass through this condition, which would lead me from sickness to health, but not before I had surmounted a still graver danger, much like that which doctors call the crisis" (6.1).

In book 8 (ch. 11) his account of "the nature of my sickness" reaches the turning point, the "crisis," and the patient begins to heal. Augustine's medical imagery of fever, pain, and chilling and the analogy of an illness dramatically resolved in a crisis shape innumerable later narratives of deconversion and conversion. Augustine's deeply evocative writing was a constant reminder that loss of faith is not only a matter of intellectual realignment and of behavioral reform but also results in the most wrenching and uncontrollable emotions. Thought, volition, and affections are all transformed.

The New Testament describes the experience of metanoia, or turning to God, with a rich variety of metaphors and symbols, including movement from darkness to light, the restoration of purity, imagery of death and birth or rebirth, new creation, dying to self and rising in Christ, release from captivity, refusal of harlotry and marriage to the beloved, and rejection of Satan along with reconciliation with God. Each of these metaphors suggests an interpretation of the loss of faith as well as conversion to God. Augustine was not the first Christian to apply these figures to his own life, but he did so with unprecedented detail, scope, and intensity. He was the first writer to comprehend so broad and deep a range of personal experience in terms of biblical events and images. In particular, Augustine adapted the example of Paul's sudden conversion as a model for his own transformation, which probably took much longer in actuality than the celebrated scene in the garden in book 8. Augustine's use of biblical typology became a model for later Christian writing about the self, as autobiographers took characters and incidents in the Bible to figure their own lives. When the bishop of Hippo adapted the Prodigal Son's profligacy, Israel's wandering in the wilderness, and Paul's captivity to the flesh as metaphors for his own condition, he originated the analogies that governed spiritual autobiography for many centuries. The specific metaphors Augustine chose to describe deconversion, especially the particular biblical figures he selected and his vivid descriptions of physical, mental, and spriritual suffering, reappear constantly in later writing. Even more significantly, Augustine established the essential hermeneutic method of self-interpretation: "He is not the inventor of autobiography but the master of autobiographical figuration, and his authority lies less in determining the choice of figures than in demonstrating the art of figurative self-writing."[2] Augustine showed how particular metaphors and biblical figures could make a story of waning faith powerfully moving and significant.

The fourth aspect of Augustine's paradigm of lost faith is the overall form of his narrative, in particular his dramatization of how deconversion leads to a reconversion. Augustine's story of deconversion, like all Christian versions of the loss of faith, is based on a teleology of the soul. Christian narratives depend on an anticipated ending: the attainment of true faith in God. This implied ending structures the plot of Christian stories of deconversion from the work's beginning. The culmination and closure of Augustine's story is part of readers' expectations from the very outset: "You made us for yourself and our hearts find no peace until they rest in you" (1.1). All his metaphors for deconversion imply a later stage of religious salvation: Israel's wandering will lead to the Promised Land, the Prodigal Son will return home, hunger and thirst demand satisfaction, and an invalid will either recover his health or die. Given Augustine's belief that the soul will be destroyed if it does not finally rest in God and given his view of God's providential guidance of his life, there is a constant irony about his deconversion. For—to take the medical analogy—Augustine's loss of faith is a sickness that leads to renewed health. What feels like the agony of dying in fact produces spiritual rebirth. His wandering and rootless existence after he breaks with the Manichees slowly brings him closer to God.

For Augustine deconversion is necessarily only a stage in a longer process, since human beings long to trust and believe in something beyond themselves. One cannot rest in deconversion; the heart and mind and soul will search restlessly for a new center of devotion, trust, and love. Placing one's faith in anything other than God inevitably leads to disappointment. The *Confessions* describes not only a deconversion from Manicheism and conversion to Christianity but a series of conversions to and deconversions from various other objects of Augustine's ultimate concern: philosophy, the unnamed friend who dies, the orator's career, Neoplatonic wisdom, and the pleasures of "woman's love." In his descriptions of attachments to and revulsions from these "lesser goods" or worldly values, Augustine prefigures autobiographers such as those discussed in the next chapter, who use deconversion from religious faith as a metaphor for other kinds of renunciations. For most of these writers—certainly for the Christians among them—deconversion cannot be explained apart from the norms of true faith. As in the *Confessions,* most accounts of deconversion are inextricably intertwined with the steps of conversion that lead the authors to God or to whatever they hold most valuable as they write. As we shall see in chapter 4, it was only in the late nineteenth century that it became possible to focus a narrative on deconversion itself, and to attempt to consider it in isolation from the autobiographer's faith at the time of writing.

Augustine's *Confessions* is the source of the tradition of deconversion narratives and a paradigmatic Christian version. This book's depiction of a crisis scene and its closure in the attainment of a new faith are the two most enduring literary features of versions of deconversion. Yet the Christian tradition contains numerous versions of deconversion, and some later writers modify, adapt, or reject certain features of the Augustinian model. Other autobiographers were not directly influenced by the *Confessions* and devised alternative forms to express their different understandings of the loss of faith. For example, British spiritual autobiographers of the seventeenth century "returned to the fountainhead of the Pauline epistles and, with a few exceptions, were remarkably little influenced by the *Confessions.*"[3]

In the early English and American traditions of spiritual autobiography, John Bunyan's *Grace Abounding to the Chief of Sinners* (1666) became a more influential model of the loss of faith than Augustine's *Confessions.* To speak of deconversion and conversion in the context of Bunyan's experience is not, as with Augustine, to trace the movement of an individual from one tradition to another. We are dealing not with what scholars of conversion call tradition transition but with "intensification": "the revitalized commitment to a faith with which converts have had a previous affiliation, formal or informal. It occurs when nominal members of a religious institution make their belief and commitment a central focus in their lives, or when people deepen and intensify involvement through profound religious experience and / or explosive new insights."[4] Of the four characteristic elements of deconversion, Bunyan's case does not involve a rejection of a religious community. He does experience the other three elements: intellectual doubt, moral revulsion from a former way of life, and emotional suffering.

As conversion means something different in Bunyan's world from Augustine's, so, too, must the meaning of deconversion be defined in terms of Bunyan's Puritan context. Bunyan does not reject another religious tradition but struggles to become more than a superficial Christian and to experience personally the assurance of God's salvation. Being a Christian means more than practicing good morality; it means knowledge of one's utter dependence on God. When Bunyan began to reform his outward conduct his "neighbors did take me to be a very godly man, a new and religious man." They were misled, for as yet "I knew not Christ, nor grace, nor faith, nor hope. . . . as yet, I was nothing but a poor painted hypocrite."[5] Conversion in the Puritan movement means an intense emotional experience born out of confrontation with the Holy Spirit and arising out of one's encounter with the Word. Conversion brings the assurance that one is saved, that one is a member of the Elect delivered from sin into the Kingdom of Heaven. Essential to the Puritan psychology of conversion is a prior painful experience of desperation and despair, when the believer realizes the futility of his or her attempts to earn salvation by human efforts. In theological terms, this means that an understanding of God's wrath toward human sin is necessary before one can understand God's mercy. Puritans usually call conversion "turning," and what one turns away from is confidence in one's own ability to achieve moral perfection. The Puritan loses faith not in God or Christ but in his or her own salvation. It is this form of "turning away," the "death" preceding the "new birth," that I will consider as the Puritan version of deconversion exemplified by Bunyan's *Grace Abounding*.

Bunyan never abandons Christianity. He takes consolation from the warning about apostasy in Hebrews 6, which allows him to distinguish his own mere "falling" from "falling *quite away*":

> First, I confessed I was fallen, but not fallen away, that is, from the profession of faith in Jesus unto eternal life. Secondly, I confessed that I had put Jesus Christ to shame by my sin, but not to open shame. I did not deny him before men, nor condemn him as a fruitless one before the world.
>
> Thirdly, nor did I find that God had shut me up, or denied me to come, though I found it hard work indeed to come to him by sorrow and repentance; blessed be God for unsearchable grace. (57–58)

Bunyan's deconversion is not public apostasy culminating in "blindness, hardness, and impenitency." He distinguishes between the apostate's utter rejection of the faith and that temporary experience of abandonment and despair that is an accepted, even an essential, part of the Christian life. This form of deconversion, involving temptation, a fall, and repentance, is as integral to Puritan experience as the assurance of salvation. In Bunyan's work we can discern again the mutual dependence of deconversion and conversion: "You may perceive my castings down, and raisings up: for he woundeth and his hands make whole" (2). In a way different from Augustine, Bunyan makes deconversion an essential part of the normative structure of Christian experience.

In this Calvinist version of deconversion, intellectual doubt centers on the question of whether one is a member of the Elect. Bunyan cannot decide which biblical types apply to his condition. Is he like the rejected Esau, or do the Bible's hopeful promises of salvation prefigure his destiny? Intellectual doubt takes the form of an agony of hermeneutic uncertainty. Conflicting biblical passages produce Bunyan's paralyzed anxiety: "My peace would be in and out sometimes twenty times a day: comfort now, and trouble presently; peace now, and before I could go a furlong, as full of fear and guilt as ever heart could hold; and this was not only now and then, but my whole seven weeks' experience; for this about the sufficiency of grace, and that of Esau's parting with his birthright, would be like a pair of scales within my mind" (53). Bunyan also wrestles with doubts about the Bible's reliability, questions whether Jews and Moslems have a true religion, and worries about whether Satan is responsible for his moments of reassurance. Conversion is supposed to bring asssurance that the grace of God does indeed apply to and suffice for one's condition and confidence that one is a member of the Elect. Yet although Bunyan believes that he should be released from all his doubts when he turns wholly to God, the temptation "to question the being of God, and the truth of his gospel" (83) persists even to "The Conclusion."

Bunyan's descriptions of his intellectual doubts as temptations shows, as clearly as in Augustine, the inseparability of questions of knowledge and questions of ethics. A striking moral dimension of Bunyan's narrative is the constant struggle of his scrupulous conscience against a series of temptations. While the more sensual forms of sin receive their share of condemnation in Puritan preaching and writing, Grace Abounding focuses on more subtle and spiritual forms of sin. Bunyan wrestles with temptations to break off his prayers prematurely, to blaspheme when he is preaching, and to yield to Satan's many devices for "chilling your heart" (30). It is not only matters of conduct but anything less than complete love and trust in God that provokes remorse and guilt. Distraction, forgetfulness, and perfunctory performance become occasions for intense self-loathing.

In defining deconversion, I said that a primary characteristic is moral revulsion from one's former way of life. In Bunyan's work this takes the form of his struggle away from sin, that is, the process of repentance. Bunyan is the classic model of Protestant autobiography, demonstrating in narrative form what Luther elaborates as a two-stage theory of repentence under the work of the law and acceptance of grace upon hearing the gospel's promise. This view of conversion accentuates the absolute necessity of conviction of sin prior to acceptance of the promise of God's forgiveness. The form that "turning away" takes in this Protestant deconversion is revulsion from one's sins, especially the proud self-sufficiency of trusting in one's own moral righteousness. From the point of view of the autobiographer looking back, this way of life is tantamount to a form of faith that must be renounced.

Sin also takes more worldly forms. The moral dimension of deconversion for Bunyan therefore encompasses his constant battle against temptations to love this world too much. In a vision Bunyan sees a wall with a narrow gap through which he must pass. The wall separates Christians and the world, and the narrow way through is Jesus Christ; none could enter unless "they left this wicked world behind them; for here was only room for body and soul, but not for body and soul, and sin" (18). The internal moral struggle is a conflict between the old sinful self and the slowly emerging man of faith, but evil is often projected outwards onto various tempters, especially Satan, who Bunyan fears may even suggest the terrifying biblical texts that spring unsolicited into his mind. As in Augustine's *Confessions,* the greatest goods in the temporal world are perceived as seductive dangers to the soul. One of the most moving passages in *Grace Abounding* speaks of "parting with my wife and poor children" as "the pulling the flesh from my bones" (80). Bunyan lingers over the image of the blind child who would be abandoned if he were imprisoned for preaching the gospel: "Poor child! thought I, what sorrow art thou like to have for thy portion in this world? Thou must be beaten, must beg, suffer hunger, cold, nakedness, and a thousand calamities, though I cannot now endure the wind should blow upon thee: but yet recalling myself, thought I, I must venture you all with God, though it goeth to the quick to leave you: O I saw in this condition I was as a man who was pulling down his house upon the head of his wife and children; yet thought I, I must do it, I must do it." (80) The image of leavetaking from one's family, with which Bunyan begins Christian's journeying in *Pilgrim's Progress*, is his central metaphor for the necessary parting from the world that accompanies deconversion.

Bunyan is as creative as Augustine in his use of biblical typology and contemporary metaphors to interpret his deconversion. He explores analogies between himself and David, Solomon, Peter, and Judas, all of whom were guilty of terrible sins against God. Bunyan assumes that every psalm and every cry of despair or consolation prefigures his own experience. He uses so many biblical figures that some scholars have denied that he really manifests the consistency of self-interpretation characteristic of the typological method: "His biblical citations are interlinear, so to speak, rather than structural, and his identification with biblical personages is locally illuminating rather than typologically identifying him in a universal role or shaping the stages of his life."[6] However, I submit that Bunyan's self-conception is most decisively shaped by two groups of biblical allusions, those dealing with Israel's wilderness wanderings and those involving Paul's struggles against both human adversaries and "the law," which for Bunyan means the understanding of Christianity as merely a matter of good conduct. In the Preface, Bunyan introduces these two biblical analogies as models for the remembrance of acts of grace: "It was Paul's accustomed manner (Acts 22), and that when tried for his life (Acts 24), even to open before his judges the manner of his conversion: he would think of that day and that hour, in the which he first did meet with grace: for he found it support unto him. When God had brought the children of Israel through the Red Sea, far into the wilderness; yet they must turn quite about thither again, to remember the drowning of their enemies there (Num. 14:25), for though they sang his praise before, yet they soon forgot his works" (2). Although nearly any biblical event or character involving an important decision can become a trope for Bunyan's struggle to determine whether he is one of the Elect, Paul's experience and the wilderness events are most central for his self-understanding. Bunyan's choice of these biblical types and his view of their relevance to his life justifies his painstaking analysis of his vacillating fears and hopes, and they soon become conventions of spiritual autobiography. The writer's turning "quite about thither again" to remember his deconversion and conversion models an essential act of the Christian life, orienting the soul and reconfirming its faith. Bunyan uses many of the same biblical metaphors for spiritual suffering as Augustine, as well as new ones drawn from his own time, such as being "racked upon the wheel" (39) of torture at the thought of remaining without grace.

In terms of plot structure, Bunyan's version of deconversion constitutes a striking development. Like Augustine, Bunyan sees his spiritual ordeals and repentance as prefatory to salvation: "Turning away" from the world and then "turning to" Christ and God structure the plot. But he does not present one climactic moment of conversion such as Augustine describes in book 8. Conversion is a long and arduous struggle—a pilgrim's progress—rather than an abrupt transformation of the soul. *Grace Abounding* places the most vivid assurance of salvation near the beginning of the spiritual journey, not toward the end—at the point when Bunyan receives "an evidence, as I thought, of my salvation from Heaven, with many golden seals thereon, all hanging in my sight" (34). After this first assurance Bunyan undergoes an increasingly severe series of temptations to blaspheme and to "sell Christ." Although Bunyan scholars have advanced differing theories of where the decisive turning point should be located, this inconclusive debate demonstrates that in fact his story has no single climax such as the one Augustine dramatized so memorably.

Grace Abounding is better interpreted as an example of what William James called "gradual" conversion than as conforming to the Augustinian model of a sudden conversion.[7] Instead of a central climax of crisis and redemption Bunyan presents many scenes in which he doubts his election and then is temporarily reassured. No one event permanently resolves Bunyan's doubts, and his anxiety about salvation continually reasserts itself. The form of *Grace Abounding* thus resembles a series of episodes each describing a drama of anxiety and reassurance. Bunyan's version of deconversion, like Augustine's, presupposes a resolution in Christian faith, but the process is recapitulated again and again in a series of episodes showing the nature of Christian life as an ongoing process of turning away from the world's temptations and from doubts about one's election. Just as in the *Confessions*, deconversion necessarily leads to conversion, as anxiety gives way to assurance. But for Bunyan every conversion is temporary; doubt and temptation recur, and the cycle commences again. Even in the Conclusion Bunyan finds "to this day seven abominations in my heart" that make him feel "afflicted and oppressed" (83). His work exudes little sense of lasting assurance or confidence, and one senses the writer preparing for another downward spiral. Though book 10 (chapters 28–42) of Augustine's *Confessions* does show the postconversion Christian life as a continual battle with temptation, Bunyan's model accentuates much more forcefully the constant necessity of deconversion and conversion as a permanent aspect of Christian existence, as the believer turns away—again and again—from the world and from anxieties about salvation.

This pattern of repeated deconversion and conversion throughout life is characteristic of Puritan religious experience. Seventeenth-century doctrine and preaching stressed the need for believers to imaginatively reenact their intitial conversion in order to revitalize their faith: "The Elect defend against spiritual deadness and raise their faith to consistently higher levels by re-enacting the actions and affections associated with coming to believe. The experience of conversion takes place repeatedly, a circumstance alluded to by the phrase 'first conversion' to designate the inceptive happening. . . . Reliving the humiliation and desire that accompany infusion of the habit augments faith. [Thomas] Shepard told his congregation not to rest smugly on faith attained: 'Be always converting, and be always converted.'"[8] Puritan piety requires not simply conversion, but repeated reconversion. Repentance is the crucial point that initiates this process, preparing the Puritan to turn outside the self for the peaceful conscience and spiritual power that could never be produced by an act of will. "The experience of repentance duplicates the first part of the affective cycle of conversion (repeated in reconversion), for it parallels the same downward spiral from sorrow to humiliation that heralds the infusion of faith."[9] The Puritan way of salvation generated a continuing cycle of deconversions and reconversions, as each moment of confidence and assurance yielded, slowly and subtly, to presumption, pride, or complacency. Noted by the Puritan's scrupulous conscience, one's very assurance caused a new round of despair about one's moral condition and doubts about one's election, precipitating a new need for deconversion in the form of repentance and struggling away from sin. Whether one regards this negatively as a classic double bind or vicious cycle, or positively as a profound means of revitalizing the basis of religious commitment and regeneration, the Puritans forged a tight bond between the cycles of deconversion and conversion. Believers were encouraged to go through these cycles of reconversion, often called "renewing the covenant," throughout their lives.[10]

In summary, Augustine's and Bunyan's versions of deconversion share a narrative form structured in relation to the soul's final destiny, salvation. As stories of a loss of faith they differ primarily in that the basic plot of Augustine's story involves a long process of deconversion from Manicheism, learning about Christianity, and a sudden climactic conversion that results in commitment to the church. For Bunyan conversion is a lifelong struggle of intensification, and deconversion is best understood as the Christian's periods of repentance for doubt; despair, or what eighteenth-century Methodists came to call "backsliding." These two narrative patterns of deconversion and conversion each reflect important insights into Christian experience. Augustine's pattern of sudden conversion dramatically accents the unpredictable power of God's grace, while Bunyan's model stresses the necessity of constant moral struggle away from sin within the lives of the redeemed. In both works, the "turning away" is as closely and carefully delineated as the final steps of conversion.

Many Christian autobiographies before the twentieth century follow one of these two patterns of deconversion and conversion. There are, however, many different types of spiritual autobiography, and scholars have analyzed the differences between the Puritan form and those devised by Quakers, Anglicans, Catholics, and secular writers. Some scholars hold that these latter autobiographies have a predictable form and content, avoid deep inner conflicts, and do not constitute a compelling alternative to the Puritan form. Paul Delany asserts that Catholic and Quaker autobiographies are largely devoted to circumstantial accounts of journeys and struggles against persecution, while Anglicans and aristocratic writers suffer from what he calls the "stiff upper lip" convention.[11] In contrast to this view, however, Owen Watkins's analysis of Quaker testimonies suggests a distinctive Quaker version of deconversion.[12] The Quaker turns inward to the Light, away from fruitless searching for the truth in other sects, away from excessive concern with the forms of ritual worship and formulas of intellectual belief. For the Quakers George Fox and John Woolman, deconversion means abandoning the outward rites and established organization of the church, and conversion means attending to the Inner Light, as well as testing spiritual insights by their practical outcome in a responsibly lived life in the world.

Puritan autobiographies are not a homogeneous body of texts, and it is no longer possible to "treat 'Puritan spiritual autobiography' (or any subgenre of it) as a monolithic, predictable body of expression."[13] There were significant variations, for instance, be-

tween the conversion narratives of English and early American
Puritans. Patricia Caldwell interprets fifty-one "confessions" recorded by Thomas Shepard between 1637 and 1645 by members
of his congregation in Cambridge, Massachusetts. These narratives record public confessions required for admission into the
church, a practice widely adopted in New England. The process
was highly ritualized, and the resulting narratives use predictable
conventions, yet some persons mark their records with their own
individualities. Caldwell's study shows how these accounts of deconversion and conversion result from ritualized public events,
use a vocabulary prescribed by preachers, and work within a set
of formulaic expressions, even as they improvise. Of particular
interest is Caldwell's assertion that it was the believer's articulation of repentance that was the crucial test of whether conversion
had become more than mere adherence to doctrine: "Over the
years, it was taken more and more for granted that a profession
of repentance, above and beyond the profession of faith, was the
distinguishing factor that made a conversion narrative personally
felt and experiential, rather than merely 'objective.' "[14] A version
of deconversion in the form of a narrative recounting the loss of
faith in one's own moral worth was as important in this species of
Puritan religious piety as was the description of how one accepted
God's grace.

In America, Christian autobiographers adopted new metaphors
to describe spiritual development, thereby suggesting fresh perspectives on deconversion. For several generations emigration
from the Old World served as a trope for the old self that must
be left behind, and the book of Exodus found new relevance. The
language of mercantile accounting and bourgeois economic practice was adapted to keep track of debts, losses, or errors in one's
spiritual account, in the manner of Benjamin Franklin. It would
be stretching things to force Franklin's autobiography onto a Pro-
crustean bed, trying to interpret it as a Christian account of deconversion and conversion.[15] Still, we can see a pale reflection of
the Christian pattern in his "turning away" from all the corrupting
influences that threaten his scheme for moral perfection. These
temptations are portrayed as outside himself, however, in alcohol
or wayward women or slothful companions; he has moved a long
way from the Puritan awareness of human depravity. Franklin does
explain why he lost interest in disputes over religious doctrine
and instead devoted his energies to practical concerns. However,
Franklin does not really reject his former faith; he moves toward

an attenuated deism without reckoning how much of Christianity
he has discarded. He does not present his changing beliefs as a loss
of faith but simply shows how theological doctrines and denomi-
national differences came to seem to him irrelevant distractions
from the important tasks in life. Because Franklin does not devote
a great deal of attention to religious matters, I see his autobiography as a classic document revealing the process of secularization rather than an innovative account of lost faith—unless we
consider the portrayal of secularization as itself a new version of
deconversion.

A significantly different Christian version of deconversion is John
Henry Newman's *Apologia Pro Vita Sua*. Newman records the
kind of conversion classified sociologically as "institutional transition": an individual's change from one community to another
within a major religious tradition, or "denomination switching."[16]
It is not the relative merits of the Anglican and Roman Catholic
churches as functioning communities that determine Newman's
allegiance but his analysis of their theological positions. The form
deconversion takes in this "history of my religious opinions" is
Newman's slow realization of the intellectual bankruptcy of the
Anglican tradition's claim to represent the via media, a compromise between the extremes of Rome and the Protestant Reforma-
tion.

The plot of this version of deconversion is not, like Augustine's,
the story of a long struggle to leave another religion and attain
Christian faith, nor does it resemble Bunyan's record of repeated
"castings down and raisings up." Newman's narrative of deconversion is instead presented as a movement away from doctrinal
heresy to Christian orthodoxy. The *Apologia*'s plot is structured
from the outset by the author's overriding commitment to correct doctrinal belief. Newman's record of his "religious opinions"
omits many concerns and experiences about which we would like
to know more. It documents primarily the author's conscious
adherence to particular Christian doctrines: final perseverance,
eternal punishment, baptismal regeneration, and others. Newman
never loses his faith in God and remains fully committed to the
Christian Church; his rejection of the Anglican tradition occurs
as soon as he becomes convinced that its beliefs make him a
heretic. As did Augustine, Newman slowly realizes that his past
understanding of the true Catholic faith was a caricature. In contrast to Augustine, however, Newman's autobiography presents

his deconversion and conversion as primarily a matter of doctrinal orthodoxy; matters of emotion, relationships with others, and vocational choices are discussed only insofar as they bear on this overriding concern.

Newman's version of deconversion strongly accentuates the element of intellectual doubt and de-emphasizes the moral interests associated with both Augustine and Protestant autobiography. He virtually defines his autobiography as a history of intellectual doubt: "Certitude of course is a point, but doubt is a progress; I was not near certitude yet. Certitude is a reflex action; it is to know that one knows. Of that I believe I was not possessed, till close upon my reception into the Catholic Church. Again, a practical, effective doubt is a point too, but who can easily ascertain it for himself? Who can determine when it is, that the scales in the balance of opinion begin to turn, and what was a greater probability in behalf of a belief becomes a positive doubt against it?"[17] This would be an apt subtitle for Newman's version of deconversion: "a record of the progress of a doubt." Since certitude is but a "point," the narrative account of Newman's spiritual journey is best construed as the record of the waxing and waning of doubt. To answer Charles Kingsley's accusations of untruthfulness and to show that during his Tractarian period he was not already secretly converted to Catholicism, Newman elaborates the temporal progress of his deconversion, tracing its progress over a number of years. Since "great acts take time" (136), the chronology of his loss of faith in Anglican Christianity must be documented in precise and punctilious detail.

The question of how a person is to achieve certainty in religious knowledge is a central preoccupation of Newman's theological writing, and his ideas are developed most fully in *A Grammar of Assent*, written immediately after the *Apologia*. Newman's autobiography exemplifies many of his ideas about doubt, assent, and certitude. Critics have traced how the *Apologia* illustrates the seven stages of what Newman calls his "graduated scale of assent": denunciation, rejection, toleration, surmise, opinion, belief, and certitude.[18] Yet the *Apologia* is not simply an illustration of this theory, for it shows how Newman's change of religious belief and community transformed his thinking, conscience, feeling, and imagination in complex ways that took him years to understand. The *Apologia* is a scrupulous and relentless analysis of the development of Newman's ideas, and yet it is a work of great emotional power, showing how "the whole man moves; paper logic is but the record of it" (136).

Newman explores one of the most difficult problems for the autobiographer who has been through a deconversion: attaining and expressing confidence that one's present convictions will stand the test of time. Having lost faith once, how can an autobiographer be sure he will not undergo another reversal or revolution of fundamental beliefs? When Newman published Tract 90, in which he interpreted some of the Thirty-nine Articles of the Church of England in a Catholic sense, he was called many "hard names." But Newman asserts that he was not as disturbed by the public's loss of confidence in him as he was by his own self-doubts: "Confidence in me was lost;—but I had already lost full confidence in myself. . . . How was I any more to have absolute confidence in myself? / how was I to have confidence in my present confidence? how was I to be sure that I should always think as I thought now?" (79). An ordeal of prolonged intellectual doubt may foster a lingering sense of skepticism about an autobiographer's present convictions, both in his own mind and in his readers.

Newman therefore needs to clarify for himself and his audience why his present religious beliefs have more substantial and lasting authority than the superseded ones. In the final chapter of the *Apologia*, "Position of My Mind since 1845," he asserts that since conversion he has experienced no more intellectual uncertainty or doubt: "From the time that I became a Catholic, of course I have no further history of my religious opinions to narrate. In saying this, I do not mean to say that my mind has been idle, or that I have given up thinking on theological subjects, but that I have had no variations to record, and have had no anxiety of heart whatever. I have been in perfect peace and contentment; I never have had one doubt" (184). The portrayal of his "intellectual satisfaction and repose" as a Roman Catholic demonstrates one of the conditions of certitude defined in the *Grammar of Assent*. Although he admits that there are still difficulties besetting "every article of the Christian creed," and devotes most of chapter 5 to systematically addressing criticisms of Catholicism, yet "ten thousand difficulties do not make one doubt" (184). The account of his loss of faith in the Anglican church and theology is essential in Newman's overall rhetorical strategy, as he contrasts the agonized perplexity and vacillation of his long deconversion with his peaceful mind and conscience since becoming a Roman Catholic. Conversion is "like coming into port after a rough sea; and my happiness on that score remains to this day without interruption" (184).

Newman avoids the conventions of the Protestant "chief of sinners" genre, redefining the moral purpose of a spiritual autobiography. His *Apologia* is an attempt to vindicate his truthfulness against Kingsley's accusations that Newman "did not care for truth for its own sake, or teach his disciples to regard it as a virtue" (3). The form Newman's defense takes is not simply explanation but justification of what he believed from 1833 to 1845 and of why he made his opinions public when he did. He must defend himself against the appearance of intellectual hypocrisy: "this reticence, and half-speaking, and apparent indecision" (9). So Newman's version of deconversion is not simply an account of changed belief but a demonstration of his moral honesty and courage as he slowly reached the conclusion that the Anglican theory lacked validity. The *Apologia* traces not only the history of his religious opinions but the workings of the author's conscience during the time of deconversion. The *Apologia* represents, as well, an exercise of conscience for Newman as he writes: a self-assessment in terms of the ethics of belief that guide both what he believes and how he articulates that to others.

Augustine and Newman believe in the rightness of their deconversions and show the importance of intellectual integrity and moral courage in breaking with an inadequate system of religious doctrine. Yet Augustine continually accuses himself of self-deception and confesses remorse for his inability to understand Christian doctrine for so long. In contrast to Augustine's frequent expressions of chagrin, Newman's apology defends his moral rectitude during the years he was losing faith. He expresses little remorse or moral condemnation of his earlier life. Newman's moral indignation is directed at Kingsley, although he maintains a tone of lofty superiority over personal animosity: "I am in warfare with him, but I wish him no ill" (5). Newman's moral perspective on the past contrasts markedly with Augustine's or Bunyan's. All three autobiographers experience radical doubts that undermine their faith, but only Newman presents doubt—confined to certain articles of doctrine, not the existence of God—as a morally approved and courageous, even heroic, action. Newman asserts that his conscience vindicates him and that the reader, too, should approve of his intellectual integrity and scrupulous concern for the ethics of belief. Newman's basic decision to write an apology thus shapes a very different moral stance in his version of deconversion.

Because of his particular theological concerns, Newman's use of metaphor and analogy differs from the dominant English tradition of autobiography. Linda Peterson has argued that most of the great Victorian autobiographers, including Newman, Ruskin, Martineau, and Gosse, objected both to the view of the self in the Protestant tradition of spiritual autobiography and to the typological hermeneutics that was its basic method of self-interpretation. Because evangelical Protestants made the Bible the ultimate authority for life and thought, the tradition of spiritual autobiography deriving from Bunyan was intimately associated with the typological method. Newman rejected this evangelical pattern of autobiography:

> It was probably the excessiveness of the evangelical imagination . . . that made Newman shun typology as his mode of interpretation in the *Apologia*—that and its cause, the Protestant dependence on private judgment and on what was known in matters of biblical interpretation as "the inspiration of the Holy Spirit." Newman did not object to typological interpretation in itself. . . . In the nineteenth century, however, typology was so intricately bound to the tradition of the evangelical conversion narrative that Newman could not have used it without seeming to acquiesce in the theology with which it was associated.[19]

The few biblical allusions in the *Apologia* illustrate Newman's state of mind at a particular point but do not represent a consistent method of self-interpretation. The purpose of such allusions is, in Peterson's words, "primarily rhetorical, not hermeneutic."[20]

Instead of interpreting his deconversion in terms of a wilderness wandering or a period of temptation, Newman takes as his central metaphor an incident in fifth-century Christian history, the controversy among Chalcedonian Catholics, Alexandrian Monophysites, and the Eutychians. Newman realized that the supposedly moderate Monophysites were no less heretical than the Eutychians and that the contemporary claim of the Anglican church to represent a via media placed it in a position similar to that of the Monophysites: "In the middle of the fifth century, I found, as it seemed to me, Christendom of the sixteenth and the nineteenth centuries reflected. I saw my face in that mirror, and I was a Monophysite. The Church of the *Via Media* was in the position of the Oriental communion, Rome was, where she now is; and the Protestants were the Eutychians" (96). The clinching argument is Newman's discovery of Augustine's admonition to the Donatists: "The world judges with assurance that they are not good men who, in whatever part of the world, separate themselves from the rest of the world" (98).[21] Newman applies these words to the position of the Anglican church and concludes that he is a heretic. He correlates Augustine's decisive words with the child's words in the climactic scene of Augustine's own conversion narrative: "Who can account for the impressions which are made upon him? For a mere sentence, the words of St. Augustine, struck me with a power which I never had felt from any words before. . . . they were like the 'Tolle, lege,—Tolle, lege,' of the child, which converted St. Augustine himself" (98–99). This is a moment of epiphany for Newman—or rather one of negative epiphany, for a crucial theological belief is not manifested but vanishes. "The theory of the *via media* was absolutely pulverized." Newman's significant decision to draw his primary metaphor for deconversion from the tradition of the early church rather than from the Bible reflects his transformed understanding of Christian faith, especially his Catholic view of the proper source of authority for the believer.

In many ways Newman's primary metaphorical figure for self-interpretation is Augustine himself—that is, Augustine *as* self-interpreter. Until the 1830s, when Newman reintroduced Augustine's *Confessions* (translated by Edward Pusey) to the English public, it was the Protestant tradition of spiritual autobiography, especially the works of Bunyan and Fox, that most influenced writing about the self. Newman's autobiography "reminded English autobiographers of the Augustinian figures and form they might use as alternatives to Bunyanesque patterns."[22] For instance, Peterson argues that Newman's *Apologia* adopts Augustine's use of medical imagery for the "deathbed" period of hovering between the old faith and the new and that Newman's elegiac closing, a dedication to his brother priests, stresses the communion of saints rather than the salvation of the individual soul. Newman's fifth chapter—"Position of My Mind since 1845"—corresponds to Augustine's books 10–13, serving as the doctrinal confession following experiential confession of the steps that lead to conversion. Like Augustine, Newman integrates narration of personal experience with theoretical exposition clarifying the proper hermeneutic principles for self-interpretation. In all of these ways, he recalls Augustine's *Confessions* partly in order to counter the prevailing English mode of spiritual autobiography.

Although in these ways he depends on Augustine as an authoritative model, Newman develops a radically different narrative pattern for spiritual autobiography. The plot of the *Apologia* is constructed to emphasize the gradual nature of conversion rather than a sudden climactic event. There are three reasons for this emphasis. First, Newman asserts that "I determined to be guided, not by my imagination, but by my reason. . . . Had it not been for this severe resolve, I should have been a Catholic sooner than I was" (100). Reason acted as a brake, slowing down his inclination to act in accord with his "secret longing love of Rome the Mother of English Christianity" (133). Second, Newman presents his personal religious growth as analogous to the history of the Roman Catholic Church's doctrinal development. In writing his *Essay on the Development of Christian Doctrine,* which he published in 1845, Newman concluded that the church's understanding of doctrine was not arrested at the point of the early apostles but undergoes a continual process of development. This understanding was crucial in helping him finally to commit himself to Roman Catholicism. The history of his own intellectual development and the history of the church's doctrinal development are both matters of steady growth or of a natural unfolding, not a deformation or loss of an original purity or perfection.

Third, Newman renders his spiritual transformation as slow, steady development because he wishes to stress continuity with the original nucleus of his theological beliefs, which in chapter 2 he formulates as the Principle of Dogma, the Visible Church, and the Apostolic Succession. He tries to show that his conversion to Roman Catholicism is not inconsistent with his deepest and original religious convictions but a better expression of them than the Anglican church could provide. There is thus an interesting tension within the *Apologia* between Newman's suggestion that he does not really undergo a radical transformation but remains true to his original beliefs and his need to show that he *has* changed and was not secretly a Catholic during the Tractarian controversy. He resolves this tension by structuring the plot of his deconversion and conversion as a matter of tiny increments of change in the degrees of doubt and assent.

The narrative structure of the *Apologia* is also strikingly original in that Newman makes not conversion but deconversion the dramatic climax of the book. The shattering of his faith is the occasion for God's grace. Newman passes over in silence the moment of his entrance into the Roman Catholic Church. It is his loss of faith in the Anglican tradition, rather than his secure grasping of true belief, that is the turning point and the most vividly rendered scene. Ominous spectral imagery marks this event: "I had seen the shadow of a hand upon the wall. . . . He who has seen a ghost, cannot be as if he had never seen it" (99). Again, when Newman was studying the Arian controversy, "the ghost had come a second time" (114). It was God's hand, not a ghost's, that Newman saw. The "pulverizing" of his ecclesiastical loyalty, with its shattering implications for Newman's sense of identity and vocation, was a genuine revelation, although Newman could not yet see where his true calling lay. "The heavens had opened and closed again" (99). In the *Apologia* it is the movement of deconversion, not conversion to orthodoxy, that is given prominence and the most memorable metaphoric equivalents: the vision of his face in a mirror as a despised and rejected double, a vision of a ghostly hand upon a wall, and the description of his waning faith in the Anglican church's theology as akin to a deathbed illness, "with seasons of rallying and seasons of falling back" (121). In contrast, the moment of commitment to Roman Catholicism is only noted in passing.

Whereas Augustine's rhetorical strategy focuses on differences between the Christian and Manichean views of evil and the created world and Bunyan addresses the anxiety about their election shared by fellow Calvinists, Newman appeals to an aversion to heresy and a concern for orthodox belief that he assumes his Christian audience shares. He also addresses his broader audience's ideas about integrity and the ethics of belief, issues of concern to Catholic, Protestant, and non-Christian readers alike. Newman presents his deconversion and conversion as the intellectual development—following the guiding light of God—that saved him from heresy and restored him to the authentic doctrine of the church. In each case, the writer's depiction of deconversion is inextricably related to his portrayal of conversion. The autobiographer's depiction of his turning away from a particular form of faith influences not only the way he interprets his own life but his presentation of the nature of authentic Christian belief and practice.

These three Christian versions of deconversion show each autobiographer assessing the reasons for a loss of faith and creating a compelling literary form to articulate this assessment. Each narrative explores intellectual doubts and moral criticisms of a former religious position. Each version selects significant metaphors and analogies from the Bible (and, in Newman's case, the fathers of theological orthodoxy) and from contemporary experience and uses these key metaphors to interpret the emotional and intellectual transformations involved in a loss of faith. The plot of each Christian version of deconversion is patterned by the expectation that deconversion will eventually be followed by conversion to the one true faith. These three works vary in significant ways in presenting a loss of faith, in accord with each writer's particular aims and concerns. Christian autobiographies will have a shaping influence on later portrayals of losing faith, even when writers reject or revise their predecessors' versions of deconversion.

3

DECONVERSION
AS A METAPHOR
FOR PERSONAL
TRANSFORMATION

AUGUSTINE SHOWED HOW a Christian autobiographer could present his own past loyalties and affections as, in effect, secular forms of faith, as ultimate concerns. In retrospect Augustine sees his love for his unnamed friend in this way. His grief when his friend dies brings home to him his misplaced trust: "What madness, to love a man as something more than human! . . . For the grief I felt for the loss of my friend had struck so easily into my inmost heart simply because I had poured out my soul upon him, like water upon sand, loving a man who was mortal as though he were never to die" (4.7–8). Many Christian autobiographers portray their pre-Christian loyalties as idolatrous substitutes for God. Yet before the nineteenth century the loss of faith is usually presented as but a preliminary step in the conversion process, and it is interpreted from the normative perspective of Christianity. A new version of deconversion is created when the loss of faith is used as a metaphor for interpreting other kinds of personal transformation than conversion to Christian faith. This chapter explores how deconversion became a crucial hermeneutical lens for autobiographers in understanding and representing radical changes of identity and character.

In looking at deconversion as a metaphor for personal transformation, I follow the example of William James, who presented conversion not as an exclusively religious phenomenon but as a process with secular equivalents. Like conversion, deconversion is an experience interpreted with distinctively Christian symbols and narrative structures; like conversion, too, the loss of faith becomes a metaphor in Western culture for analogous experiences of change involving radical doubt, moral revulsion from a way of life, emotional upheaval, and rejection of a community.

In the late eighteenth and early nineteenth centuries, writers began to use the traditional symbols and structure of spiritual autobiography to interpret changes without specific Christian content. The concern of explicitly spiritual narratives with the soul's pilgrimage strongly shaped the work of defining the self in "secular" autobiography: " 'Self' is the modern word for 'soul.' "[1] Rousseau demonstrates the change when he describes two very different sorts of conversion in books 2 and 8 of his *Confessions* (completed in 1765 and published in 1781). In Turin in 1728 Rousseau renounced his Protestant background and converted to Catholicism, or "papism." Having discussed religious matters while being wined and dined by several priests, Rousseau entered a hostel for the preparation of converts, "there to be instructed in the faith which was the price of my subsistence."[2] At the hospice were several "scoundrels" who were, in effect, professional apostates, "embracing Christianity and having themselves baptized wherever the rewards were sufficiently tempting." Rousseau's own conduct is hardly superior, for he finds himself going through the motions of a conversion:

> I had allowed myself quite easily to be fooled. Envisaging popery only in relation to feasting and good cheer, I had easily accustomed myself to the idea of being a Catholic. But the thought of solemnly entering that faith had only occurred to me fugitively and as something in the distant future. But at this moment there was no deceiving myself; I saw with the liveliest horror the sort of obligation I had incurred and its inevitable results. . . . I knew that, whichever were the true religion, I was going to sell my own, and that even if I were making the right choice I should in the depths of my heart be lying to the Holy Ghost, and should deserve the contempt of humankind.[3]

Rousseau empties this event of its traditional Christian meaning and makes it an instance of the corrupting influence of society and an occasion of youthful folly. After his "solemn abjuration" of his Protestant upbringing, Rousseau is turned out of the hospice with twenty francs. He immediately resumes his wanderings with no immediate consequences of his act: "All that had accrued from the self-interested step I had just taken was the memory of having become simultaneously an apostate and a dupe."[4]

In contrast with this foolish pseudoconversion, whose significance is primarily an occasion for Rousseau to excuse himself, book 8 recounts an unconventional yet genuine conversion, in the sense of a fundamental turning point of his life. During the summer of 1749 he happened to read the prize question proposed by the Dijon Academy: "Has the progress of the sciences and arts done more to corrupt morals or improve them?"[5] The effect is instantaneous: "The moment I read this I beheld another universe and became another man." Rousseau's description of the scene parallels the conversion of Augustine: Both men are radically transformed by chance discoveries of a written text while alone in a natural setting. Rousseau's experience led to the writing of his *Discourse on the Moral Effects of the Arts and Sciences*, so this incident marks the origin of his literary career. Ironically, the conversion brought him nothing but misunderstanding, persecution, and bitterness: "From that moment I was lost. All the rest of my life and of my misfortunes followed inevitably as a result of that moment's madness."[6] In book 8 Rousseau uses motifs from the tradition of conversion narratives to describe a radical transformation of his life that is very different from Christian conversion to God. Rousseau demonstrated how the conversion narrative could be secularized so that elements from the Christian literary tradition were incorporated to interpret crucial turning points in a much larger autobiographical narrative. Motifs from the conversion narrative associated with the attainment of Christian faith figure his discovery of his life's primary commitment. However, deconversion—the turning away from a former faith—is not one of the elements Rousseau adapts in book 8, while in book 2 he treats his "solemn abjuration" as low comedy, as a farce.

M. H. Abrams has explored the secularization of spiritual autobiography during the romantic period and the emergence of a new form of autobiographical writing that traces the development of an author's identity and sense of vocation as a writer. Focusing on English works (and omitting Rousseau), Abrams presents Wordsworth's *The Prelude* as the first of the great "creative autobiographies," a genre including Keats's *Fall of Hyperion*, Carlyle's *Sartor Resartus*, John Stuart Mill's *Autobiography*, and many other

modern works, written in poetry as well as in prose, and vary-
ing in their degree of fictionality. Abrams discusses the "crisis-
autobiography" of the artist as a "more-or-less fictional work of art
about the development of the artist himself, which is preoccupied
with memory, time, and the relations of what is passing to what
is eternal; is punctuated by illuminated moments, or 'epiphanies';
turns on a crisis that involves the question of the meaning of the
author's life and the purpose of his sufferings; is resolved by the
author's discovery of his literary identity and vocation and the
attendant need to give up worldly involvement for artistic detachment; and includes its own poetic, and sometimes the circumstances of its own genesis."[7] In this form of semifictional autobiography, Christian theological beliefs are translated into a secular pattern as the traditional plot of salvation is replaced by the
progressive education of the writer's mind. The author's discovery
of his identity and vocation in the world displaces commitment
to God and the church. Change is wrought not by providential
action but by the individual who achieves maturity through finding meaning in suffering. A "biodicy" or "theodicy of the private
life" is central to romantic autobiographical writing; Wordsworth
and those for whom he becomes a model translate "the painful
process of Christian conversion and redemption into a painful
process of self-formation, crisis, and self-recognition, which culminates in a stage of self-coherence, self-awareness, and assured
power that is its own reward."[8]

This form of autobiographical writing turns upon a "crisis" that
corresponds to the traditional climax of a conversion narrative
such as Augustine's *Confessions*. This crisis is a reorientation of
the author's life, a secular adaptation of the deconversion and conversion involved in the Christian's turning away from the world
to God. The "crisis-autobiography" of the creative individual often
uses the loss of faith as an interpretive framework for figuring the
initial stages of personal change. The vocabulary and conventions
used to describe deconversion are applied to the experiences that
precipitate a writer's loss of confidence and purpose, for example
the grim consequences of the French Revolution, the impairment
of imaginative power, or the lack of meaningful work. Let us look
more closely at how two key figures employ the loss of religious
faith as a metaphor to interpret a crisis. Thomas Carlyle and John
Stuart Mill show how traditional ways of describing the loss of
faith could be put to new uses and suggest how deconversion may
function as a metaphor for other kinds of personal transformation.

Sartor Resartus is an autobiographical work in that portions of book 2, the biography of Teufelsdröckh, reflect aspects of Carlyle's experience, and the "philosophy of clothes" records most of Carlyle's deepest convictions. However, the experiences of Teufelsdröckh were "symbolical myth all," wrote Carlyle, except for one significant event: the central incident of deconversion. "The incident in the Rue St. Thomas de l'Enfer . . . occurred quite literally to myself in Leith Walk [Edinburgh], during three weeks of total sleeplessness, in which almost my one solace was that of a daily bathe on the sands between Leith and Portobello."[9] This incident was the seed for the chapter "The Everlasting No," the depiction of deconversion preceding the later stages of conversion in "Centre of Indifference" and "The Everlasting Yea."

Before his crisis Teufelsdröckh had spent a number of years wandering aimlessly, lacking any sense of meaning or purpose in either his own life or the universe. "Doubt had darkened into unbelief" (159) as he brooded over the possibilities of atheism or of a deistic God indifferent to his creation: "Is there no God, then; but at best an absentee God, sitting idle, ever since the first Sabbath, at the outside of his Universe, and seeing it go?" (159).[10] Carlyle's hero is demoralized by the utilitarianism, skepticism, and materialism of the times. These naturalistic philosophies, with their view of a soul-less, mechanical universe, ultimately undermine all sense of self-worth: "The fearful Unbelief is unbelief in yourself; and how could I believe. . . . To me the Universe was all void of Life, of Purpose, of Volition, even of Hostility: it was one huge, dead, immeasurable Steam-engine, rolling on, in its dead indifference, to grind me limb from limb" (163–64). In the midst of depression and despair, Teufelsdröckh one day asserts his famous protest against "the Everlasting No." This passage deserves generous quotation, for it set the pattern for many Victorian accounts of deconversion.

> All at once, there rose a Thought in me, and I asked myself: "What *art* thou afraid of? . . . What is the sum-total of the worst that lies before thee? Death? Well, Death; and say the pangs of Tophet too, and all that the Devil and Man may, will or can do against thee! Hast thou not a heart; canst thou not suffer whasoever it be; and, as a Child of Freedom, though outcast, trample Tophet itself under thy feet, while it consumes thee? Let it come, then; I will meet it and defy it!" And as I so thought, there rushed like a stream of fire over my whole soul; and I shook base Fear away from me forever. I was strong, of unknown strength; a spirit, almost a god. Ever from that time, the temper of my misery was changed: not Fear or whining Sorrow was it, but Indignation and grim fire-eyed Defiance.

Thus had the EVERLASTING NO (*das ewige Nein*) pealed authorita-
tively through all the recesses of my Being, of my ME; and then it
was that my whole ME stood up, in native God-created majesty, and
with emphasis recorded its Protest. Such a Protest, the most important transaction in Life, may that same Indignation and Defiance,
in a psychological point of view, be fitly called. (166–67)[11]

The positive content of Teufelsdröckh's beliefs is worked out
in the succeeding phases of his conversion. These beliefs center
around the ideas that the universe is not mechanical but the
"living garment of God"; that the human spirit is free when it renounces pleasure as the goal of life; and that the meaning of life
can be found only through action and doing "the Duty which lies
nearest thee" (196).

Scholars differ on whether Teufelsdröckh's experience represents a Christian pattern of conversion. C. F. Harrold argues
that the heritage of Calvinism provides a "sub-pattern" of ideas
that Carlyle translated into German terms under the influence of
Goethe and German romantics.[12] Other commentators, however,
point out differences between the traditional idea of conversion
and Carlyle's version, which involves "no contrition, no reliance
upon grace or redeeming love, but on the contrary, much proud
and passionate self-assertion. The emotion that follows release is
hatred and defiance of the Devil, rather than love and gratitude
towards God."[13] Some critics deny that Carlyle ever affirmed anything beyond the "Everlasting No."[14] The issue is complicated by
the fact that *Sartor* does not give us Teufelsdröckh's beliefs un-
mediated but through the work of an editor who in the course of
the work gradually becomes "converted" to his hero's beliefs and
indistinguishable from Teufelsdröckh.[15] The difficulty of determining Carlyle's attitude to Christianity makes *Sartor Resartus* a
fascinating and ambiguous transitional work in the development
of versions of deconversion. To what extent is Carlyle describing a
traditional Christian experience of deconversion and conversion,
and to what extent is he using the familiar pattern as a metaphoric
vehicle for exploring a different kind of transformation?

Though both the substance and the narrative form of Teufelsdröckh's transformation are indebted to Christian sources, Carlyle describes a rather different kind of change from those traced
by Augustine, Bunyan, and Newman. What Carlyle turns away
from—the content of his deconversion—is quite distinct from
earlier versions of lost faith. At the time of the "Eternal No,"

Teufelsdröckh has long since lost his religious faith. The traditional Christian moral code, too, has a tired and weakening hold on him, as can be seen when Teufelsdröckh holds that "from suicide a certain aftershine (Nachschein) of Christianity withheld me: perhaps also a certain indolence of character" (165). During his crisis Teufelsdröckh does not turn away from another religious system or from the world but rather from several interrelated things: his own self-doubt and despair, his fear that the universe is a meaningless machine, and certain soul-destroying modern philosophies. Carlyle uses the traditional Christian pattern to express his ideas about the birth of the creative imagination and moral renewal. The vice Teufelsdröckh most wishes to eradicate is not sin against God but weakness of will and indecisiveness. He is more concerned to become a hero than to be a faithful Christian. There are parallels with Wordsworth's experience, though Carlyle is more insistent on strenuous activity to translate visionary experience into social terms: "Produce! Produce! . . . Work while it is called Today; for the Night cometh, wherein no man can work" (197).

Carlyle calls conversion "a spiritual attainment peculiar to the modern Era," by which he apparently means the Protestant era: "It was a new-attained progress in the Moral Development of man: hereby has the Highest come home to the bosoms of the most Limited; what to Plato was a hallucination, and to Socrates a Chimera, is now clear and certain to your Zinzendorfs, your Wesleys, and the poorest of their Pietists and Methodists" (198). Carlyle changes the traditional meaning of conversion by making it a potentially universal process, the crucial transition "in the Moral Development of Man." Christian language is for him one among many ways of explaining a spiritual process that is not limited to orthodox believers. The crisis experience is not confined to Christians but marks a person's passage into "spiritual majority" (199). It is thus a universal aspect of all spiritual development, an accession of self-confidence, coherence, and energy.

Deconversion in Carlyle's scheme, accordingly, means turning away from all those contemporary influences that he believed vitiated or corrupted the innate powers of humanity. The "Everlasting No" is Teufelsdröckh's rejection of contemporary philosophies that led him to doubt not only the existence of God but his own purpose in life and the possible meaningfulness of any human action in the world. In this version of deconversion, intellectual doubt centers on the rationalistic and materialistic philosophies that undermined Teufelsdröckh's self-confidence and energy. His moral criticism is leveled against the understanding of human nature implied by materialistic worldviews, which confine human energies to mundane concerns and neglect community and the spiritual life. Thus the meaning of deconversion is rather different in *Sartor* from previous autobiographies. The loss of faith has become a metaphor for another kind of personal change. Intellectual doubt and moral critique are not directed toward a traditional religious system or the world but toward a reductive philosophy that claims to explain the universe exhaustively. At the same time there is continuity between Carlyle's rejection of mundane preoccupations and the rejection of the world by Augustine and Bunyan. Deconversion in *Sartor Resartus* means turning away from all in the modern world that conspires to reduce the individual to an insignificant particle in a mechanical universe. Specifically, this means rejecting materialism, utilitarianism, and Enlightenment skepticism.

The form of deconversion in *Sartor* is equally innovative, even as it draws on Christian tradition. Carlyle uses many traditional biblical figures to interpret his hero's crisis, especially the Exodus account of the wilderness wandering and Christ's temptations. But his use of these figures differs from the tradition of typological reading epitomized by Bunyan. Carlyle uses biblical analogies along with literary and mythological figures who endured periods of doubt, exile, or wandering, such as Goethe, Prometheus, and Faust. A biblical reference is not a direct revelation from God as to a person's condition but one among many metaphors used to illuminate Teufelsdröckh's suffering. The figure of Cain has no greater authority or priority than a modern legend or the example of Carlyle's favorite writer: "Thus must he, in the temper of ancient Cain, or of the modern Wandering Jew,—save only that he feels himself not guilty and but suffering the pains of guilt,— wend to and fro with aimless speed. Thus must he, over the whole surface of the Earth (by footprints), write his *Sorrows of Teufelsdröckh*; even as the great Goethe, in passionate words, had to write his *Sorrows of Werter*, before the spirit freed herself, and he could become a Man" (156). Carlyle's account of deconversion is a tissue of biblical figures, but he shows an unprecedented self-consciousness about their metaphorical status and their grounding only in an author's judgment about their capacity to illuminate his experience.

Carlyle presents Christian language as "clothing" with which one culture has interpreted the process of spiritual development. Carlyle's commitment to the Christian pattern of conversion is so ambiguous partly because of his understanding of religious language as inherently symbolic: "It is in and through Symbols that man, consciously and unconsciously, lives, works, and has his being" (222). Moreover, Carlyle insists that superannuated symbols need to be dispensed with. His own attitude toward Christian symbols reflects his consciousness that these "old clothes" no longer retain all of their revelatory and authoritative power. Carlyle calls attention to his use of Christian images of conversion *as* metaphors, as one language among others for talking about spiritual realities, rather than as the normative discourse of a committed believer.

The plot of Teufelsdröckh's story follows the traditional pattern: Deconversion is succeeded by conversion. But Carlyle introduces an intermediate stage: " 'This,' says our Professor, 'was the CENTRE OF INDIFFERENCE I had now reached; through which whoso travels from the Negative Pole to the Positive must necessarily pass" (182). The Centre of Indifference is a period of testing and rejecting various alternative philosophies. Teufelsdröckh encounters a number of dramatic scenes and heroic individuals in his search for meaning outside himself: "He is now, if not ceasing, yet intermitting to 'eat out his own heart'; and clutches round him outwardly on the NOT-ME for wholesomer food" (170). He must reject all "products of the past" as inadequate before he can work out his own metaphysic and ethic in "the everlasting yea." According to one scholar, this chapter represents the years from 1822, when Carlyle had the Leith Walk experience, to about 1830, when he began to write *Sartor:* " 'The Centre of Indifference,' while 'symbolical myth all,' symbolized truly enough the eight-year period in which, after the first awakenings, he slowly evolved and consolidated his *Weltanschauung,* his message, the Everlasting Yea, and completed the conversion that had begun so long before." [16]

Carlyle's notion of a center of indifference complicates the traditional pattern, interjecting an intermediate period into what had been a two-stage model of conversion. Now a time and space of indifference, characterized by both intellectual indecision and apathy, mediates between the period of waning confidence and the positive feelings and beliefs involved in conversion. This aspect of *Sartor* shaped William James's notion of a "state of temporary exhaustion" prior to the self-surrender of conversion; he cites

Teufelsdröckh's experience as paradigmatic.[17] Carlyle formulates explicitly a pattern latent in Augustine's *Confessions;* Teufelsdröckh's indifference corresponds to Augustine's description of a long deathbed period when he had lost faith in Manicheism but not yet embraced Christian belief in God. This adaptation and elaboration of an element of the traditional conversion pattern for his own original purposes is characteristic of Carlyle's entire relationship to Christianity and typifies the ways in which his version of deconversion is both continuous and discontinuous with past versions.

In sum, the significance of *Sartor Resartus* lies in its innovative use of the loss of faith as an interpretive paradigm for the transformation of identity. Carlyle adapts the traditional Christian pattern of deconversion and conversion to figure his model of self-formation, which climaxes in a crisis of identity and vocation. Both the content and the form of his crisis show Carlyle to be an innovator who uses religious deconversion as a metaphor for the death and rebirth of an individual's imagination and moral energy. The content of Teufelsdröckh's lost faith—what he turns away from—is a secular philosophy rather than an organized religion or the world, even though Carlyle's condemnation of worldliness reveals his indebtedness to Christian tradition. The agency of redemption that resolves the crisis is not God's grace but willpower; Teufelsdröckh is not turned around but turns himself in a radically new direction. Formally, *Sartor* shows unprecedented self-consciousness about the adoption of Christian rhetoric as clothing, as symbolic language for speaking of a natural process of human development. The form spiritual development takes in the narrative of deconversion now requires a more elaborate plot, as a center of indifference mediates between "turning from" and "turning to."

That John Stuart Mill interpreted his crisis in terms of the metaphor of deconversion is evident in his description of his condition in 1826 as akin to the "conviction of sin" preceding conversion: "I was in a dull state of nerves, such as everybody is occasionally liable to; unsusceptible to enjoyment or pleasurable excitement; one of those moods when what is pleasant at other times, becomes insipid or indifferent; the state, I should think, in which converts to Methodism usually are, when smitten by their first 'conviction of sin.'"[18] The choice of this analogy is especially striking and significant given that Mill was virtually unique among the autobiographers examined in this book in having no childhood religious training.

For five years before this crisis, since his reading of Bentham's philosophy, Mill's life had had a sense of purpose and satisfaction. "I had what might truly be called an object in life; to be a reformer of the world. My conception of my own happiness was entirely identified with this object" (93). Mill "awakened from this as from a dream" when he asked himself whether the achievement of his goals of reform would bring him happiness: " 'Suppose that all your objects in life were realized; that all the changes in institutions and opinions which you are looking forward to, could be completely effected at this very instant: would this be a great joy and happiness to you?' And an irrepressible self-consciousness distinctly answered, 'No!' At this my heart sank within me: the whole foundation on which my life was constructed fell down" (94). Mill realized that much of his distress could be attributed to his education, which had precociously developed his intellect at the expense of the affections. "The habit of analysis has a tendency to wear away the feelings" (96), and to undermine the capacity to take pleasure in one's desires. According to Mill's theory of association, feelings arise "through the clinging of pleasurable or painful ideas to . . . things, from the effect of education or of experience" (96). Because his education had failed to create pleasurable associations, he believed, it was too late to change his character. Mill felt that no one could help or even understand his distress, and that there was no possible alleviation of it because the foundations of his character were laid in childhood.

Mill uses deconversion as one metaphor among others to describe his condition of doubt and emotional apathy. He uses quotation marks—"conviction of sin"—when he compares himself to religious converts, putting some tentativeness into this comparison. In contrast, lines from Coleridge's "Dejection" are said to "exactly describe my case" (94). The reference to conversion is more than just a passing remark, however; Mill's crisis reflects several elements of the traditional pattern of loss of faith and spiritual rebirth. For instance, reading an autobiographical work by Marmontel releases a flood of emotion highly reminiscent of Augustine's conversion through the words of scripture: "I was reading, accidentally, Marmontel's 'Memoires,' and came to the passage which relates his father's death, the distressed position of the family, and the sudden inspiration by which he, then a mere boy, felt and made them feel that he would be everything to them—would supply the place of all that they had lost. A vivid conception of the scene and its feelings came over me, and I was moved to tears. From this moment my burthen grew lighter. The oppression of the thought that all feeling was dead within me, was gone" (99). In this moment of epiphany Mill realizes that he still has the capacity for deep feeling. He begins to cultivate his emotional life by reading Wordsworth and soon redefines his conception of human felicity: "I seemed to draw from a source of inward joy, of sympathetic and imaginative pleasure, which could be shared in by all human beings. . . . I seemed to learn what would be the perennial sources of happiness, when all the greater evils of life shall have been removed" (104). Mill's crisis experience affected his intellectual development by expanding his idea of happiness beyond the confines of strict Benthamism.

Mill's change of beliefs is ambiguously presented as both a dramatic transformation and as only a modification of his father's doctrines. This ambivalence needs interpretation. There is no explicit rejection of early utilitarian and associationist theory, and his loss of faith in these ideas is only suggested. The "turning from" aspect of Mill's transformation is muted and expressed metaphorically rather than in terms of philosophical doctrine. Mill did not reject the utilitarian outlook or his father's basic goals of social reform but rather supplemented and enriched them with a new appreciation of the importance of the internal culture of the imagination and the affections. His views changed less than is suggested when he later calls his transition "the only actual revolution which has ever taken place in my modes of thinking" (133). Mill only partly represents the nature of the transformation he went through, confessing his sense of radical change but minimizing its impact on his ideas. The real significance of his personal crisis, and a crucial reason why he interprets it using the metaphor of deconversion, lies more in his discovery of affective and volitional aspects of his character than in new philosophical theories. His wish to restore the place of emotion and freedom is not simply a supplement to his earlier theory, however, for his revision of his father's doctrines constitutes a very different picture of human life and of the individual's duties. The presentation of his crisis conveys in dramatic form what he does not avow explicitly: that his father's philosophy was inadequate and even harmful and that his recovery of his own emotional capacity and his sense of freedom to reshape his character was experienced as a radical transformation.

The deconversion metaphor is an appropriate one for Mill's crisis because it highlights the way that personal transformation is not simply cognitive but involves a new center of loyalty and a reawakening of the emotions. As a result of his crisis, Mill altered his convictions, his affections, and his commitment to a commanding authority figure. His allegiances to two persons, his father and his wife, Harriet Taylor, dominate his autobiography. His characterization of each of them is highly selective and represents a conception of the meaning of life. Mill's autobiography is essentially the story of his deconversion from his father's ideals and authority and of a conversion to all that was symbolized for him by the person of Harriet Taylor. Mill came to doubt his father's view of the purpose of life: that individuals should work tirelessly and exclusively to develop their intellects so as to educate and reform society. Harriet Taylor represents for Mill, in contrast, the perfect balance of intellect, feeling, and idealism. Mill's personification of his wife as the embodiment of the chief human virtues verges on deification; indeed, he acknowledges that "her memory is to me a religion, and her approbation the standard by which, summing up as it does all worthiness, I endeavor to regulate my life" (170).

Mill's uncritical adulation, especially his claim that all his published writings "were as much my wife's work as mine" (171), has aroused nearly universal skepticism. I am interested, however, not in the accuracy of his claims about Taylor but in the reasons for Mill's manner of presenting her and his father. James Mill and Harriet Taylor are "mythologized" as "two deities," according to Avrom Fleishman, and the *Autobiography* presents a deconversion from his father's rationalist doctrine and commmitment to "the ideal of human potentiality" symbolized by Taylor.[19] Mill's turning toward Harriet Taylor as the central figure in his life is not simply a shift of loyalties but an act of self-surrender akin to the convert's yielding of his will to God. Given Mill's great dependence on and identification with his father, his new appreciation of Taylor's significance represented what amounted to a deconversion not only from his father's view of the sources of human happiness but from James Mill's dominating personal presence.

By means of his analogy of a loss of faith and conviction of sin,

Mill suggests indirectly that he had to revise an early idealization verging on worship of his father. On a personal level, the qualities of his father that made him so remote reflect the most disagreeable attributes of the Calvinist God: dominating will, relentless chastisement of any hint of pride, dislike of emotion, and uncompromising adherence to principle. Although he does not discuss the issue of vocation in his autobiography, Mill's crisis was also closely related to uncertainty about a suitable career and to depression at the prospect of a lifetime of working as a bureaucrat in India House—the career that James Mill had chosen for himself and pressed upon his son.[20] As many critics have pointed out, the metaphor of "conviction of sin" and the oedipal implications of the Marmontel passage that so moved him point to Mill's feelings of guilt for his doubts about the adequacy of his father's doctrines and for wishing to escape from his influence. Mill's ambivalence about his father found expression in the form of a new version of deconversion. The interpretation of his crisis as similar to a conviction of sin suggests the sense of betrayal and disloyalty that Mill must have felt with regard to the former center of his allegiance and trust. The metaphor of deconversion expresses figuratively the emotional reality that could not be publically avowed and probably was not consciously recognized.

The torpor leading up to a crisis scene in a conversion narrative is an especially apt form for Mill because of the way it depicted the emotional life. In the works of Augustine, Bunyan, and Carlyle, the crisis of deconversion involved exhaustion and a stifling of the feelings; conversion brought a sudden access of joy overflowing into tears of relief.[21] The central crisis Mill describes in chapter 5 is the one section of the autobiography where his rigorous focus on the logic of ideas is interrupted and he allows himself to express deep emotion. The inadequacy or ineffectiveness of Mill's rendering of his feelings has been much criticized, and some commentators have claimed that this flaw undermines the persuasiveness of his proposed ideal: the integrating of thought and emotion.[22] Regardless of whether Mill's usually abstract and logical style or his occasional sentimental effusions about Taylor seriously harm the autobiography, what is significant for us is that Mill conceived of his narrative's plot in terms of a period of apathy followed by a central crisis that cathartically releases emotion. He sought to demonstrate the inadequacy of the old utilitarian system not simply by explaining its logical limitations—as elsewhere in the book he analyzes philosophical and political theories—but by dramatizing the practical outcome of that system of education in his dull, listless emotional torpor.

Mill and Carlyle adapt the traditional narrative of deconversion and conversion in their autobiographies, describing a central crisis when self-doubts were resolved by commitment to a new vision of the task of the writer and social critic. They interpret their personal transformations as analogous to a loss and recovery of religious faith. For later autobiographers, deconversion becomes a metaphor not only for changes in self-confidence or vocational commitment but for new understandings of matters as various as ethnic or racial identification, political loyalty, and sexual self-understanding and preference (as in shifts to a feminist or gay identity). Deconversion may be used casually, locally, or sporadically, on the one hand, or as the basis for a more comprehensive interpretation of personal transformation. A good example of the variety of uses to which the deconversion metaphor can be put is *The God That Failed*, a collection of six autobiographical essays by ex-communists. Some of the writers, such as Arthur Koestler, frequently compare "blind faith" and then waning confidence in communism to the psychology of religious belief. Koestler's analogy between the Party devotee and the religious believer does not preclude other comparisons, for instance to "the mental world of the drug addict."[23] In Richard Wright's essay, in contrast, the metaphor of religious deconversion does not actively shape his interpretation of his disillusionment with the Party, even though his crisis of doubt and his moral concerns are in many respects similar to those of the autobiographers I have discussed.

Versions of deconversion vary considerably in how consistently, how systematically, and how deeply the metaphor of loss of faith informs and structures the entire account of personal change. Nor is it always the same elements of the Christian paradigm that are appropriated by different writers. An autobiographer may recur to classic tropes of spiritual narratives, structure the stages of his metamorphosis according to a religious model, or present his intellectual doubts or moral critique as similar to the reasons for deconversion. Autobiographers have adapted various elements from narratives of deconversion in order to interpret a radical change of identity and commitment. In chapter 7 I will examine in detail how Sartre uses deconversion as an interpretive framework to present his changing understanding of his work as an author.

A final example of how the loss of faith is used as a metaphor for other forms of identity change is a recent work of sociology that explores the process of "role exit." Helen Rose Fuchs Ebaugh's *Becoming an Ex* describes a wide range of role changes, including those of ex-nuns, divorced people, ex-convicts, ex-alcoholics, ex-doctors, former policemen, mothers without custody of their children, and perhaps the most dramatically altered identity, transsexuals.[24] This sociological study has two autobiographical dimensions. First, Ebaugh's work is based on 185 intensive interviews, and she includes numerous autobiographical quotations that reveal the metaphors with which individuals interpret their loss of a former identity. Second, Ebaugh is herself an ex-nun who wrote an earlier book on nuns leaving their religious orders, and both of her scholarly works reflect on her own experience.[25]

Many of Ebaugh's subjects use the metaphor of lost faith to explain their changes. This is especially so when the role from which a person disengages is central to identity, when this change comes about through disillusionment with an ideal, and when it involves identifying with an entirely new "reference group" than the past one. Ebaugh's insights illuminate the study of the loss of faith in autobiography. For instance, she formulates the concept of an "ex-role": "The process of becoming an ex involves tension between one's past, present, and future. One's previous role identification has to be taken into account and incorporated into a future identity. To be an ex is different from never having been a member of a particular group or role-set. Non-members do not carry with them the 'hangover identity' of a previous role and therefore do not face the challenge of incorporating a previous role identity into a current self-concept."[26] This description applies remarkably well to the way a narrator of a version of deconversion has to establish an identity that takes into account a very specific ex-role.

Ebaugh's theory of the role-exit process is itself a metaphorical version of deconversion, for she proposes four basic stages adapted from her earlier study of nuns leaving the cloister. The chapter titles outline these stages: "First Doubts," "Seeking Alternatives," "The Turning Point," and "Creating the Ex-Role." Ebaugh's understanding of identity transformation is drawn from her insights into ex-nuns (including herself) who have left a religious order. For instance, a turning point is defined as "an event that mobilizes and focuses awareness that old lines of action are complete, have failed, have been disrupted, or are no longer personally satisfying."[27] This symbolically significant event announces publicly that a person has made the decision to change her identity and make final this decision. While a social-scientific conceptualization of the stages of role exit displaces the religious language of a crisis of faith, it is the process of deconversion and conversion that basically shapes her model. For instance, Ebaugh describes a period she calls "the vacuum," when "people felt 'in midair,' 'ungrounded,' 'neither here nor there,' 'nowhere.' It is as though the individual takes one last glance backward to what he or she has been involved with in the past but knows is no longer viable. Yet the person isn't really sure at this point what the future holds. It seems that this last glance backward is necessary before actually taking the leap forward."[28] This anxious, rootless interval between defined identities is reminiscent of Augustine's deathbed period and Carlyle's center of indifference.

Ebaugh's sociological theory of the sequence of stages in the role-exit process views a variety of forms of identity change as analogous to religious deconversion. *Becoming an Ex* reveals how the form of autobiographical narratives may help structure other forms of discourse, such as sociological theory. More specifically, this book suggests another way that the loss of religious commitment may be used as a metaphor for understanding other kinds of identity transformations. I think that a moment of deconversion, and often the explicit language of losing faith, is usually a stage in contemporary psychologies and technologies of identity transformation, such as twelve-step groups, self-help manuals, and counseling strategies.

Most autobiographical versions of deconversion portray a central crisis that changes the narrator dramatically and suddenly. Biographical studies provide evidence that many autobiographers temporally compress what was in fact a much longer period of uncertainty and slow attainment of positive convictions. This has been argued, for example, in the cases of Augustine, Carlyle, Mill, and Edmund Gosse.[29] Newman is unusual in showing a slow progression of stages of doubt marking his journey from Anglicanism to Roman Catholicism. Why have autobiographers shaped their stories to conform to the model of a conversion story with a suddenly resolved crisis?

The deconversion-conversion form, especially the crisis scene, provides an autobiographer with a coherent way of both apprehending and presenting a transition between two very different worldviews, ideological commitments, or ways of life. The form gives a sense of direction and a clear turning point to the narration of events that may have been experienced as unconnected, confusing, or inconclusive. Moreover, a narrative of deconversion and conversion presents a change of identity in a form that is comprehensible and accessible to most readers. One of the primary reasons why deconversion exerts so powerful an influence on the imagination of personal change is that the loss of faith has been described in narratives with a compelling and dramatic form, as increasing doubt and internal conflict come to a sudden crisis and culminate in new belief and commitment. This pattern of tension, climax, and resolution conforms to the basic norms of Western dramatic theory since Aristotle. Conversion narratives with a central crisis have a clear structure that guides readers' expectations, and yet the form is versatile, easily adapted to a wide variety of kinds of personal transformation.

Those aspects of the conversion paradigm related to the loss of faith have been influential, too, because deconversion articulates the issues at stake in many crises of conscience. Deconversion narratives express the fundamental convictions that every individual's beliefs are of momentous import, that they are a matter of choice, and that a person has a moral obligation to believe responsibly. These beliefs are fundamental in Western culture and can be assumed to be shared by readers with a wide variety of religious, antireligious, and other sorts of value commitments. Whereas a story of conversion may not be fully convincing or moving to those who do not hold the author's final beliefs, a story of deconversion can potentially appeal to readers united only by belief in the right and duty of each individual to choose his or her beliefs in a responsible manner. In an age of increasing individualism and religious pluralism, a story of deconversion articulates a widely shared and deeply felt conviction about the importance of "freedom from" any authoritarian or coercive group, even as readers disagree about the best uses of "freedom to"—that is, the postconversion values to which one ought to be committed. In this sense a deconversion narrative has a larger potential audience than a conversion story.

Even when autobiographers do not deal with Christian salvation or damnation, they may well wish to present a moral choice as supremely or ultimately significant. Religious metaphors express a drama of the soul that many autobiographers do not wish to forego in their efforts to define a self. The choice of any positive commitment and the rejection of alternatives may therefore find a natural analogue and a metaphoric vehicle in the form of the Christian conversion narrative. The loss of faith evokes the internal conflict and wrenching pain that may accompany even the most conscientious renunciation or disavowal of former commitments. The experience of losing faith may help express crucial aspects of identity change: self-doubt and despair; emotional lassitude; broken relationships to loved ones; a divisive conflict between ethical principles; shame about losing one's confidence or purpose in life; nostalgia for the sense of belonging to a community; the self-abandonment involved in having to surrender one's will to a new loyalty; and the terrifying sense that one's character is disintegrating.

Using deconversion as a metaphor may help an author to present crucial decisions as broadly significant for many others, even for the fate of humanity. As Mill put it, "Though my dejection, honestly looked at, could not be called other than egotistical, produced by the ruin, as I thought, of my fabric of happiness, yet the destiny of mankind in general was ever in my thoughts, and could not be separated from my own. I felt that the flaw in my life, must be a flaw in life itself" (102). Wishing to give conscientious struggles and development a dramatic form and a significance that is more than merely personal, the autobiographer may adapt the metaphors and crisis-centered plot derived from stories of religious deconversion and conversion.

4

RUSKIN, GOSSE, AND THE AESTHETIC CRITIQUE OF PROTESTANTISM

MANY NEW VERSIONS of deconversion were published during the Victorian era as for the first time in Western culture a public break with Christian beliefs became a live option for many people. Before this the Roman Catholic Church and most Protestant churches did everything they could to suppress direct expressions of atheism. The laws of most European countries prescribed penalties for persons who denied the truth of Christianity. Published expressions of skepticism were confined to a few philosophers, who presented doubts about Christianity in very guarded form, as in Montaigne's *Essays*, Hume's *Dialogues*, and the works of Hobbes and Voltaire. Religious skeptics usually expressed their criticisms indirectly, in coded or guarded ways that protected them from confrontation with the defenders of orthodoxy. Publication of an autobiography confessing one's lack of belief was unthinkable until after the French Revolution, and very difficult well into the nineteenth century. In the nineteenth century, however, controversies arose not simply about the adequacy of particular forms of Christian faith but about the merits and justifiability of faith itself. These public debates in the Anglo-American literary tradition have received extensive scholarly investigation under the various rubrics of "unbelief," "agnosticism," "atheism," and "the Victorian crisis of belief."[1]

This chapter discusses the representation of deconversion in the English autobiographical tradition, concentrating on the depiction of crisis in two key texts. I first discuss some of the issues raised by the larger context of literary works dealing with the loss of faith as a framework for showing the significance of new versions of deconversion by John Ruskin and Edmund Gosse.

Scholars often speak of the Victorian crisis of faith, but there were many different crises, each reflecting a particular constellation of religious doubts and expressed in a distinctive way. The reasons for deconversion included recognition of the incompatibility between the biblical account of the world and the evidence of geology or evolutionary biology, the impact of new forms of biblical scholarship, criticisms of the church's power in British society, and convictions about "the ethics of belief" that precluded treating as a matter of certainty what could not be proved.[2] Deconversions varied greatly as to their origin, their chronology, and their outcome. Some individuals had an intense crisis of weeks or months that permanently changed their lives; other persons pondered their doubts for decades while their daily lives seemed unaffected by religious uncertainties. Some persons who lost faith in Christianity came to hate it, and went on the offensive against it; others felt sorrow and regret for the loss of certainty and solace. Many of the Victorians who lost faith in Christianity still affirmed large portions of Christian morality, and some even tried to practice "the religion and ethics of Jesus," as opposed to doctrinal Christianity. Humanists, agnostics, and atheists presented diverse alternatives to their lost faith, either by devising a new philosophy or by showing which secular values they deemed most worthy of commitment.

Religious doubts are reflected in much of the literature of the Victorian age, including the poetry of Alfred Tennyson, Robert Browning, and Matthew Arnold, novels about the loss of faith, such as Mrs. Humphrey Ward's *Robert Elsmere* and William Hale White's *Mark Rutherford*, and popular essays by such avowed atheists as Thomas Henry Huxley, William Clifford, and Leslie Stephen. Radical journals and organizations were founded by secularists, free thinkers, rationalists, and humanists, who made aggressive efforts to deconvert the English public. Yet the new openness to discussion of religious belief was not unqualified, any more than it is now if one wants to teach in most schools, run for political office, promote one's business interests, or maintain certain personal relationships. There were many reasons for silence about lack of faith and many kinds of evasion. Often skeptics did not want to upset family members. For instance, Charles Darwin was advised by his father to conceal his religious doubts from his wife, for "some women suffered miserably by doubting about the salvation of their husbands, thus making them likewise to suffer."[3] In 1862 John Ruskin promised Mrs. Rose La Touche, a close friend and mother of a girl with whom he was in love, that he would not make any public statements about his loss of belief for ten years.[4] Some doubters did not want to publicize their uncertainties because they shared the widespread conviction that for the mass of English people, morality depended on religious convictions and sanctions.

Writing in 1885, Mrs. Humphrey Ward noted that the English dislike of public confessions made for another sort of resistance to open expressions of doubt: "As a nation we are not fond of direct 'confessions.' All our autobiographical literature, compared to the French or German, has a touch of dryness or reserve. It is in books like *Sartor Resartus*, or *The Nemesis of Faith, Alton Locke*, or *Marius*, rather than in the avowed specimens of self-revelation which the time has produced, that the future student of the nineteenth century will have to look for what is deepest, most intimate, and most real in its personal experience."[5] Mrs. Ward suggests that it is not in autobiography but in fiction that one finds the true spiritual history of the nineteenth century. This comment suggests, and scholarship confirms, that Ward's novel *Robert Elsmere* reflects her own religious doubts and struggle.[6] Many popular Victorian novels dealing with the loss of faith are covertly autobiographical, while many of the age's autobiographies are extremely circumspect about the author's doubts. Thus one of the most intriguing questions about Victorian autobiography is what can be said, what cannot be said, and what must be expressed indirectly by a particular writer. I will explore the tension between open discussion of deconversion and its avoidance in Ruskin's *Praeterita*.

Even though the subject of the loss of faith was often a difficult or suppressed one, there were hundreds of autobiographical narratives that recorded deconversions. It is worth considering both the usual reasons for the loss of faith and the form taken by these accounts as a context for discerning the originality and significance of Ruskin's and Gosse's works. Analyzing 150 documents by "unbelievers," as well as about 200 briefer biographies, Susan Budd compares these accounts to stories of conversion to Christianity and finds marked differences. Deconversions occurred later in life, usually between the ages of thirty and forty, whereas the peak time for conversion is adolescence. In contrast to most Christian conversions, deconversions were an individual process brought on gradually by reading or discussion and rarely occurred suddenly at a large meeting. The loss of faith was often associated with a movement toward more radical politics. In the lives of many agnostics and atheists, "the conversion to unbelief was part of a shift from a religion which was seen as part of established society. For many individuals, secularism was a detour in their movement from religion to left-wing politics."[7]

It is often assumed that the fundamental causes of unbelief were intellectual doubts produced by the theory of evolution and by critical biblical scholarship. Budd argues that more fundamental than these intellectual doubts was moral revulsion against such Christian doctrines as Original Sin, atonement, divine election, and predestination, as well as from Christian practices that were considered to inhibit progressive social reforms. "The weight of feeling behind the attack on Christianity was not that it was untrue but that it was wicked."[8] Relatively few agnostics had read Darwin or the German biblical critic David Strauss before their loss of faith; reading such texts simply confirmed the antagonism they already felt toward the church as an obstacle to social improvement. To separate intellectual and ethical reasons for the loss of faith is in some cases a false distinction, however. Often it was perceiving the unacceptable moral consequences of holding certain beliefs that led to a deconversion. Or a church's attempt to stifle intellectual doubts or criticisms was experienced as a threat to both freedom of thought and personal responsibility. In interpreting the autobiographies of Ruskin and Gosse, I will examine how specific intellectual doubts and ethical criticisms contributed to their deconversions and the interplay between these concerns.

Most of the same issues of conscience that preoccupied Augustine, George Fox, and Newman are also at stake in accounts of the rejection of Christianity: questions of integrity, honesty, and personal responsibility for one's beliefs. Among the reasons for deconversion in the Victorian age a significant new factor emerges that does not inform earlier autobiographies: a wish to affirm certain values in the secular world. A. O. J. Cockshut describes a common complaint about British Protestantism:

Anyone who undertakes a prolonged course of reading in autobiographies of the nineteenth and early twentieth century will emerge dazed with the sensation of listening to a jangling, long-drawn-out and infinitely lugubrious lament. "They told us," it seems to say, "that it was wicked to play on Sundays, that cleanliness was next to godliness, that England was God's chosen race, that foreigners were wicked, that Catholics were idolaters, that the Bible was to be interpreted literally, but that we must on no account take the slightest notice of large parts of it. . . . We can no longer accept this narrow and illogical conglomeration of myths, fallacies and half-truths. We are very desolate and what are we to do? Most terrible of all, we have nothing to love."[9]

"We have nothing to love" mimics Ruskin's words in *Praeterita*, and a similar charge is made by many Victorian writers who stress the beauty of the world and the significance of aesthetic values. The "aesthetic critique" of Christianity affirms a more important place in life for the claims of imagination, the seeking of beauty, and the appreciation and creation of art. Not only in autobiography but in the cultural criticism of Arnold and Pater, in Browning's dramatic monologues by Renaissance painters and Roman Catholic bishops, and in autobiographical fiction by Butler, Lawrence, and Joyce, we can see a common pattern of revulsion against the aesthetic limitations of the middle-class English sensibility (Arnold's "Philistinism"). John Henry Newman makes a similar point when, refering to his youthful hatred of Roman Catholicism, he speaks of it as a "stain upon the imagination." The aesthetic critique of Christianity is central in Ruskin's and Gosse's autobiographies.

Especially fascinating in Victorian versions of deconversion are the ways in which Christian rhetoric and values are appropriated in a writer's attempt to express a new vision of human destiny. The language of Christian culture and community usually imposes itself even when an agnostic or atheist writer expresses confidence that one can live without the consolations of religion, without certainty about human origins or destiny, and without a divine justification for morality. Often the metaphors and structural elements of conversion narratives provide the organizing terms in which a writer envisages movement away from belief in God to agnostic principles and a new understanding of human existence. For instance, the rhetoric of a crisis of faith and the dramatiza-

tion of a climactic scene of agonized choice imitate the traditional spiritual autobiography. Documents of deconversion look
remarkably like stories of conversion, especially when the author
emphasizes the positive convictions attained after losing faith
in Christianity. Ironically, the reasons for deconversion and the
rhetoric used to indict conforming Christians are especially indebted to the character of evangelical Protestantism. Frank Turner
traces affinities between the agnostics' criticisms of religion and
evangelical attacks on Anglicanism as emotionally shallow, intellectually evasive, and ethically weak: "In such books and other
polemics against the complacency of late-eighteenth-century religion the evangelicals had provided a pattern for sharp criticism of
ecclesiastical institutions on the basis of their inadequate moral,
intellectual, and spiritual life. The unbelievers repeatedly echoed
those charges."[10] Doubters presented their lives as more ethically
rigorous and committed to fundamental truth than the lives of
Christian believers, as represented by their own earlier hypocri-
sies and evasions. Ruskin and Gosse, too, in the substance and the
rhetoric of their criticisms of Christianity, imitate the agenda and
language of evangelical Protestantism.

Budd refers to her 350 narratives by unbelievers both as stories
of the loss of faith and as accounts of "conversion to atheism,"
demonstrating once again the inseparability of deconversion and
conversion. Autobiographical stories of deconversion served many
of the same functions in secularist societies as did Christian conversion narratives in churches: "The drama of the spiritual pilgrimage, into or out of faith or sobriety, to be relived again by being
retold in meetings so that the manner of each man's conversion
became general knowledge, was a product of the general cultural
belief in individual responsibility and choice."[11] Whereas many
Christian conversion narratives were recounted at the time of
commitment to a church, most accounts of deconversion, whether
biographical or autobiographical, were published as obituaries in
secularist and rationalist journals. These obituaries were printed
partly to refute the Christian claim that atheists must either repent on their deathbeds or die possessed by terror and remorse. The
atheist's loss of faith in Christianity and commitment to secularism were often presented as a conversion with lasting effects,
using the metaphors and narrative patterns of the most familiar
Western paradigm for individual transformation.

A few agnostics and atheists wanted to break not merely with
the content but also with the form of Christian beliefs. The more

perceptive writers realized that the form and content of belief were deeply related and that the traditional forms of spiritual autobiography reflected habits of mind that needed to be challenged. Some Victorian autobiographers therefore attempted to devise new hermeneutic methods and models to interpret their lives. For example, Harriet Martineau's autobiography (written in 1855, published in 1877) speaks of her change as a revolution rather than a conversion, avoids explicit biblical allusions, and eliminates self-laceration and blame from her treatment of the past. Linda Peterson holds that, in adopting the positivist philosophy of Auguste Comte, Martineau "may well have been the first English autobiographer to substitute a scientific model of self-interpretation for the traditional patterns of biblical hermeneutics."[12] Later autobiographers such as Darwin, Herbert Spencer, Samuel Butler, and Henry Adams approach their lives as if examining a scientific specimen that demonstrates universal laws. The scientific model is probably the most powerful and influential hermeneutic alternative to the Christian paradigm in interpreting personal transformation. In the twentieth century many autobiographers portray the loss of faith in the light of social-scientific theories, especially those derived from Freud and Marx. Accordingly, deconversion may be presented as analogous to recovery from a neurosis or as a rebellion against ratification of social injustice as God's will. We shall see how other versions of deconversion—for example, a feminist's break with patriarchy—seek fresh metaphors and narrative patterns to understand the loss of faith in more adequate terms than the vocabulary and conventions of a supposedly dying religion.

One of the most fascinating issues in interpreting versions of deconversion, then, is whether the author adapts Christian narrative paradigms or searches for an alternative literary form to render the experience of losing faith. I will examine the contrasting ways in which Ruskin and Gosse structure their narratives and the significance of these choices of form in *Praeterita* and *Father and Son*.

John Ruskin's *Praeterita* (published 1885–89) demonstrates both the Victorian era's greater openness to depictions of the loss of faith and some of the evasions and repressions that accompanied most discussions of this topic. The book was written during lucid intervals between attacks of insanity that finally silenced Ruskin completely from 1889 until his death in 1900. Ruskin realized that he needed to avoid disturbing topics and in his Preface says he will speak only "of what it gives me joy to remember . . . and passing in total silence things which I have no pleasure in reviewing."[13] Since the book was also "a dutiful offering at the grave of parents who trained my childhood to all the good it could attain" (1), the memory of the pain his 1858 deconversion gave his parents was a strong incentive to avoid the topic of his loss of faith. Ruskin's unresolved religious speculations after his deconversion and the religious anxieties that surfaced during his fits of "brain fever" were further reasons not to delve deeply into matters of belief and doubt. Yet in spite of conscious and unconscious efforts to avoid the subject, Ruskin's struggle with evangelical thought is a recurring subject throughout *Praeterita*, and his decisive rejection of this system of belief is the climax of the crucial chapter "The Grande Chartreuse," the last coherent one in the autobiography.

Ruskin's mother was a devout and zealous member of the evangelical movement within the Anglican church.[14] From the very outset of the work, Ruskin makes clear the deep influence of his evangelical upbringing and his struggle, both in the past and in the present, to resist this influence. In describing the "dominant calamities" of his childhood, Ruskin states first of all that he had "nothing to love" (35). He saw both his parents and God as powers which left his feelings unmoved—"not that I had any quarrel with Him, or fear of Him; but simply found what people told me was His service, disagreeable; and what people told me was His book, not entertaining" (35). Daily scripture readings with his mother until he was fourteen years old had a tremendous influence on Ruskin, and critics have shown how thoroughly steeped in biblical imagery are all his works, including *Praeterita*.[15] Yet by his very way of characterizing "her unquestioning evangelical faith in the literal truth of the Bible" (117), Ruskin makes clear his distance from rigid fundamentalism. By the time he was a student at Oxford, he could not see any direct application of Scripture's meaning to his own life: "If I had lived in Christ's time, of course I would have gone with Him up to the mountain, or sailed with Him on the Lake of Galilee; but that was quite another thing from going to Beresford chapel, Walworth, or St. Bride's, Fleet Street. . . . I had virtually concluded from my general Bible reading that, never having meant or done any harm that I knew of, I could not be in danger of hell: while I saw also that even the creme de la creme of religious people seemed to be in no hurry to go to heaven" (178–79).

"As zealous, pugnacious, and self-sure a Protestant as you

please" (227), Ruskin for a time shared his parents' intolerance of other religions, particularly their anti-Catholicism. When his family traveled on the Continent, especially in Italy, he began to see his background as ignorant of Christian history, as narrow, complacent, and impoverished. Experiences of Rome's beauty convinced him "how guiltily and meanly dead the Protestant mind was to the whole meaning and end of mediaeval Church splendour" (264). Ruskin traces the stages of his growing toleration for other religions, his deepening interest in Roman Catholic culture and art, and his love of natural, especially Alpine, beauty. The new values that he would serve become clear in several scenes of recognition, such as an overwhelming view of the Alps at Schaffhausen (104) and an encounter with religious painting at the Campo Santo in Pisa (2.6). How far Ruskin had moved from his parents' beliefs is suggested by his response to a painting of St. Ranier in Pisa. Ranier, "playing, evidently with happiest skill, on a kind of zithern-harp," is approached by a maiden who tells him "that his joyful life in that kind was to be ended. And he obeys her, and follows, into a nobler life" (323). That art has displaced religion for Ruskin is indicated by the fact that he pities St. Ranier for his conversion; later he admits he has "no mind whatever to win Heaven at the price of conversion such as St. Ranier's" (356). Aesthetic beauty, as found in both the natural world and artistic creations, was to be the ultimate concern of his life in the years described in *Praeterita*, during which he wrote his principal works of art criticism, *The Stones of Venice* and the five-volume *Modern Painters*. Until about 1860, when he redirected his energies toward social criticism, Ruskin's work may be described as an attempt to say in prose, about art, what the romantic poets had said about nature: that it may become the vehicle for essentially religious experiences. *Praeterita* returns to this central conviction, exploring its autobiographical origins.

In spite of many oblique allusions to the reasons for which he lost his faith, for most of the book Ruskin avoids a probing analysis of this topic. That the subject is still extremely painful to him as he writes is evident in his treatment of his prayers. In 1845, ill while returning from the Continent, he prayed seriously and knew "the consciousness of an answer" and "a thrill of conscious happiness altogether new to me" (346). He mourns the loss of his sense of direct relationship with heaven, without ever explaining how this loss came about: "Little by little, and for little, yet it seemed invincible, causes, it passed away from me. I had scarcely reached home in safety before I had sunk back into the faintness and darkness of the Under-World" (346). Thus ends his discussion of prayer, with Ruskin expressing grief for having lost a sense of constant communion with God but offering no insights into the reasons. The passage contrasts markedly with the joyful exultation of other passages where deconversion frees him to appreciate aesthetic concerns. Ruskin reveals deeply ambivalent feelings about his loss of faith in scattered remarks expressing relief, guilt, nostalgia, and regret.

In some passages in *Praeterita* Ruskin even seems reluctant to admit that he has been through a deconversion. A clear instance of this is in the chapter "The Campo Santo," where he says he found "the entire doctrine of Christianity, painted so that a child could understand it" (320). He defines Christianity as faith in the divinity of Christ: "Christianity is the belief in, and love of, God thus manifested. Anything less than this, the mere acceptance of the sayings of Christ, or assertion of any less than divine power in His Being, may be, for aught I know, enough for virtue, peace, and safety; but they do not make people Christians, or enable them to understand the heart of the simplest believer in the old doctrine" (320). This definition leaves out many evangelical doctrines and attitudes he rejected, including sin, damnation, faith in the Bible's literal truth, and the exclusivist intolerance of other religions and understandings of Christianity. We expect Ruskin to measure his own religious stance by this concise definition of Christianity, but he never does.

Part of Ruskin's reluctance to explore religious issues thoroughly is due, I think, to his unconventional form of Christian faith at the time of writing his autobiography. *Praeterita* is written from a position of partially recovered faith, and it reflects this perspective in its treatment of religious matters, including the deconversion. For seventeen years after his deconversion in 1858, Ruskin was an agnostic, but in 1875 he returned to a personal version of Christianity.[16] His final form of faith was a rather undefined spiritualism, and he wished to avoid both intolerance to other religions and undue claims of certainty about matters of doctrine. Furthermore, during his bouts of madness Ruskin's religious fears of hell and damnation resurfaced.[17] Whereas in fact Ruskin's abhorrence of the ideas of sin, damnation, and hell was a central reason for his deconversion, he largely avoids discussion of this topic in *Praeterita*. Because defining his present religious beliefs was a potentially dangerous task that Ruskin wanted to avoid, matters of faith and doubt receive hesitant and sometimes confusing treatment for most of the book.

In "The Grande Chartreuse" chapter, Ruskin resolves his difficulties in discussing his deconversion by presenting it as a loss of faith only in evangelical doctrine, not in what Ruskin implies is the essential core of Christian faith. Limiting the scope of the faith that is lost in this way allows Ruskin to deal with deconversion from a relatively secure position, without having to define exactly what his present beliefs are. Although this chapter, like so many in *Praeterita*, does wander and digress, its coherence lies in the convergence of the things that eroded Ruskin's faith: "This breaking down of my Puritan faith . . . shall be traced in this chapter to the sorrowful end" (448). However, the chapter also insinuates in several ways that "the sorrowful end" of his deconversion was an extensive and personally damaging loss of all religious faith, not simply a liberation from Puritan dogma.

The title of the chapter is a key to its unity. Almost all the chapter titles in *Praeterita* are the names of places, and each chapter shows an aspect of Ruskin's sensibility through his imaginative response to the places he lives in and visits. Although there is a loose chronology in the book, its basic structure is not provided by the sequence of events or the steady development of Ruskin's identity. Rather, as Elizabeth Helsinger argues, Ruskin reveals his mind and character in his responses to the series of landscape views in each chapter. "The place of the title becomes, in the course of the chapter, first the stimulus and then the emblem for a recurring state of mind. The cumulative effect of these chapters, where places become images for the responses they evoke, is to establish a discontinuous mental geography which takes the place of direct introspective analysis, the guided tour from past to present."[18] In accord with this unusual autobiographical scheme, we can speak of the monastery of the Grande Chartreuse as an emblem of all Ruskin's doubts about Christianity, for it is during his visit to this Carthusian retreat in the French Alps that Ruskin first recognizes the gap between his own beliefs and traditional Christian faith. The chapter's several other accounts of an encounter with some aspect of Christianity all prompt Ruskin to reflect upon his own lack of faith and evoke a state of mind similar to his initial confrontation with a monk at the Grande Chartreuse.

The chapter opens with Ruskin's 1845 poem on Mont Blanc and with his confession of belief in "the power of mountains in sol-

emnizing the thoughts and purifying the hearts of the greatest
nations of antiquity and the greatest teachers of Christian faith"
(440). Ruskin holds that this faith has largely been destroyed in
modern Europe, even among religious persons who spend their
lives in the mountains. He encounters this modern form of in-
sensibility during a visit to the monastery of the Grande Chartreuse, when "a word was said, of significance enough to alter the
courses of religious thought in me, afterwards for ever" (441). A
dull and surly monk who was Ruskin's guide through the monastery speaks the memorable word: "We came to a pause at last in
what I suppose was a type of a modern Carthusian's cell, wherein,
leaning on the window sill, I said something in the style of 'Modern Painters,' about the effect of the scene outside upon religious
minds. Whereupon, with a curl of his lip, 'We do not come here,'
said the monk, 'to look at the mountains.' Under which rebuke
I bent my head silently, thinking however all the same, 'What
then, by all that's stupid, do you come here for at all?' " (442–
43). Why did the monks seek isolation in the mountains, wonders
Ruskin, and how could they not become more interested in plants
and stones, or forgo trying "to draw a bird or a leaf rightly"? The
monk's blindness to the beauty of the landscape leads Ruskin to
speculate about the motivations for various forms of monastic life,
and he next discusses his reactions to other monks and nuns. A
nun who guided him through a convent was cheerful and friendly,
but Ruskin finally concludes that her serene life represents, at
least for himself, a withdrawal from the duty to care for the larger
world: "There was no entering into that rest of hers but by living
on the top of some St. Michael's rock too, which it did not seem to
me I was meant to do" (444). In these encounters with committed
Christian believers, Ruskin presents himself as having to reject
their way of life in order to affirm the two primary concerns that
shaped his vocation: the discernment of beauty and the calling to
reform society.

In this chapter Ruskin sorts out his positive and negative as-
sessments of Roman Catholicism and records the "convictions
[that] prevented me from being ever led into acceptance of Catholic teaching by my reverence for the Catholic art of the great ages"
(447). As much as Ruskin honored Catholicism when it affirmed
his deepest concerns, he could never believe that those values
could only be found within the church. "The only constant form
of pure religion was in useful work, faithful love, and stintless
charity" (447), wherever these were expressed. Obviously strug-

gling to maintain control of his material ("I must not let myself be led aside from my own memories") but often digressing into unrelated fragments, Ruskin keeps returning to his main theme, the "discovery of the falseness of the religious doctrines in which I had been educated" (448).

Several sections of the chapter (13–17) narrate Ruskin's encounters with two very different sorts of Protestant biblical interpretation, both of which seem to him inadequate. The liberal theologian Frederick Maurice interprets Jael's slaying of Sisera as "a merely rhythmic storm of battle-rage" with no contemporary significance. Hearing Maurice's "enlightened" views was "the first time in my life that I had fairly met the lifted head of Earnest and Religious Infidelity—in a man neither vain nor ambitious, but instinctively and innocently trusting his own amiable feelings as the final interpreters of all the possible feelings of men and angels, all the songs of the prophets, and all the ways of God" (452–53). His treatment of this incident shows Ruskin's conviction that the liberal, modernizing impulse represented by Maurice, a nineteenth-century forerunner of demythologization, did not answer his questions about biblical interpretation. Ruskin presents this approach to the Bible as being just as arbitrary and self-interested as was an exegesis of the parable of the Prodigal Son by an evangelical preacher named Molyneux. At a "fashionable seance of Evangelical doctrine" in Belgravia, Molyneux denies that there is a relevant message in the example of the older brother. Ruskin implies that Molyneux's interpretation is tailored to appeal to his affluent congregation, assuring them that God looks with special favor on those who are prodigal with their wealth. Ironically, both of these Protestant clergymen, representing "Maurician free-thinking" and "the Puritan dogmata which forbid thinking at all" (454), are akin in their inability to grasp any significance to the Bible that transcends their own version of Christian faith. Ruskin might have used these incidents to affirm the validity of a typological reading of the Bible or to stress the need for greater scrupulousness in interpretation. It is not clear, however, whether the author of *Praeterita* has more or less faith in the objectivity of the Bible's meaning than the two Protestant preachers; Ruskin simply indicates his growing sense, in the 1850s, of the intellectual shallowness of Protestant biblical hermeneutics.

It was not rejection of the Bible, but close study of it, that led Ruskin to defy one of the strictest practical precepts of Puritan doctrine, the prohibition on Sunday of either useful work or seeking one's pleasure: "In honest Bible reading, I saw that Christ's first article of teaching was to unbind the yoke of the Sabbath, while *as* a Jew, He yet obeyed the Mosaic law concerning it; but that St. Paul had carefully abolished it altogether, and that the rejoicing, in memory of the Resurrection, on the Day of the Sun, the first of the week, was only by misunderstanding, and much wilful obstinacy, confused with the Sabbath of the Jew" (457–58). How very unbiblical, then, was the typically gloomy Protestant Sunday Ruskin had experienced all his life: "the inveterate habit of being unhappy all Sunday did not in any way fulfil the order to call the Sabbath a delight" (458). A turning point for him, and a milestone in the process of deconversion, was his first infringement of this unwritten rule when, in 1858, he made a drawing on a Sunday.

Ruskin's loss of faith in Protestant doctrines was inextricably related to the development of his aesthetic interests. Especially confining to his passion for art was the aesthetic horizon of British Christianity, coupled with its tendency to condemn what it could not understand or appreciate. Ruskin found his "love of toil, and of treasure" satisfied by an exquisitely illustrated fourteenth-century missal. This new appreciation was followed by "the discovery that all beautiful prayers were Catholic,—all wise interpretations of the Bible Catholic;—and every manner of Protestant written services whatsoever either insolently altered corruptions, or washed-out and ground-down rags and debris of the great Catholic collects, litanies, and songs of praise" (457). What is most crucial in this discovery is not the religious truth Ruskin discerned in Catholicism but its beauty. Ruskin saw that if he were to study the greatest music, painting, or architecture, he must move into the cultural world so vehemently condemned by his mother's evangelical outlook and epitomized by Venice and Rome. He was never seriously tempted to become a Roman Catholic, for "I no more believed in the living Pope than I did in the living Khan of Tartary." It was the aesthetic beauty of Catholic tradition, not doctrine or the Catholic Church as a religious community, that drew Ruskin away from the evangelical ethos: "I saw, as clearly as I saw the sky and its stars, that music in Scotland was not to be studied under a Free Church precentor, nor indeed under any disciples of John Knox, but of Signior David; that, similarly, painting in England was not to be admired in the illuminations of Watts' hymns; nor architecture in the design of Mr. Irons' chapel in the Grove" (455).

The climax of "The Grande Chartreuse" and of *Praeterita* as a whole brings to a crisis the irreconcilable clash between Ruskin's original understanding of Christian faith and his deepening commitment to aesthetic beauty. The crisis juxtaposes two experiences in Turin that, in conjunction, led him to reject his evangelical beliefs forever. First he attends a dreary religious service of Waldensians, a tiny sect that usually sequestered itself in the mountains: "Their solitary and clerkless preacher, a somewhat stunted figure in a plain black coat, with a cracked voice, after leading them through the languid forms of prayer which are all that in truth are possible to people whose present life is dull and its terrestrial future unchangeable, put his utmost zeal into a consolatory discourse on the wickedness of the wide world, more especially of the plain of Piedmont and city of Turin, and on the exclusive favour with God, enjoyed by the between nineteen and twenty-four elect members of his congregation" (460). This bitter, self-justifying, and "consolatory" sermon could illustrate the theory of ressentiment, and Ruskin's distaste is as evident as would have been Nietzsche's.

Returning to the "condemned city" of Turin and entering its art gallery, Ruskin finds Paul Veronese's painting "Solomon and the Queen of Sheba": "The gallery windows being open, there came in with the warm air, floating swells and falls of military music, from the courtyard before the palace, which seemed to me more devotional, in their perfect art, tune, and discipline, than anything I remembered of evangelical hymns. And as the perfect colour and sound gradually asserted their power on me, they seemed finally to fasten me in the old article of Jewish faith, that things done delightfully and rightly, were always done by the help and in the Spirit of God" (460–61). This painting is so symbolically significant for Ruskin that in the next chapter he refers to his deconversion as "the Queen of Sheba crash" (462). Ruskin recognized that his deepest loyalty was to "things done delightfully and rightly," whether or not they were approved of by Christian churches or authorities, by preacher, Pope, or Bible-quoting mother. The beauty, mediated by Catholicism's sacramental spirit could be found in the work of a "worldly" painter such as Veronese, whom Ruskin had to defend against his disapproving parents.[19] Although Ruskin says this experience did not represent a sudden conversion but the conclusion of years of thinking and doubting, he concludes the chapter by indicating that this moment marked the decisive rejection of his religious upbringing: "There was no sudden conversion possible to me, either by preacher, picture, or dulcimer. But that day, my evangelical beliefs were put away, to be debated of no more" (461).

Although Ruskin apparently wants to avoid presenting himself as reenacting the traditional sudden conversion, he recreates the classic crisis scene when he claims he abruptly threw off his evangelical beliefs forever. In fact, this scene condenses a movement away from evangelicalism that took decades. Ruskin continued for many years to go to church, to read and cite Scripture, to pray, and even to observe the Sabbath according to Puritan rules.[20] As many scholars have pointed out, there is also much continuity between Ruskin's evangelical background and his secular vocation, especially in terms of such moral values as hard work, self-denial, service to humanity, and struggle against moral evil. Many of his aesthetic interests and presuppositions, such as his interest in allegorical interpretations of art, can be understood as characteristic expressions of his religious sensibility.[21] Like so many Victorians, and like most authors of deconversion narratives, Ruskin was deeply influenced by his religious upbringing long after he consciously rejected it. In "The Grande Chartreuse" chapter, Ruskin presents as a deconversion from evangelical beliefs what was in fact a long-term struggle continuing even into the period when he wrote *Praeterita*. He dramatizes as a completed action in the past what was a central, if partially repressed, aspect of the autobiographical act.

This climactic chapter shows what positive values replaced the ones lost in deconversion. Ruskin affirms his commitments to beauty—in the forms of art, music, and the natural world—and to the forms of service he had confessed as his basic creed: "useful work, faithful love, and stintless charity" (447). Ruskin emphasizes his positive values partly by rearranging his account of the deconversion so that the gallery experience follows the chapel scene, in contrast to his earlier version of these events in his 1877 work *Fors Clavigera*. As George Landow has argued, Ruskin's later version of events stressed his new convictions more than his loss of faith: "When Ruskin inverted the order of events, placing the sermon before his experience in the gallery, he changed the point of his narrative; for whereas *Fors* explains how a painting convinced him that his evangelical religion preached a false doctrine of damnation, *Praeterita* tells how the arts of painting and music taught him how to serve God better than had his earlier belief."[22]

Significantly, *Praeterita* confines the loss of faith to the tenets of Puritan doctrine, while a form of religious belief seems to endure, so that he can still speak of working "by the help and in the Spirit of God" (461). *Fors*, in contrast, had presented the moment of choice in starker terms: "Protestantism or nothing."[23] In *Praeterita*, deconversion is confined to the evangelical understanding of Christian faith, and Ruskin's positive commitments to art and social reform seem essentially religious in spirit and motivation. Ruskin's work is representative of most other Victorian autobiographies in this concern to show that the loss of faith need not result in immorality, nihilism, or despair.

In Ruskin's case this effort is not completely successful, since immediately after the "Grande Chartreuse" chapter *Praeterita* disintegrates into unrelated fragments. Since the next years of his life (the 1860s) were devoted to social criticism and reform, and he believed that his prophetic words had fallen on deaf ears, it is not surprising that Ruskin avoided dealing with the next period of his life, "passing in total silence things which I have no pleasure in reviewing" (1).[24] Taken by itself, in isolation from knowledge of Ruskin's later career, *Praeterita* leaves the strong impression that without the certainties of faith, his life lacked an integrating coherence and confidence. Insinuations to this effect creep into the text, for instance when Ruskin almost superstitiously mentions in passing that after he began to draw on Sundays, "my drawings did not prosper that year, and, in deepest sense, never prospered again" (459).

Just as deconversion is both a subject Ruskin tries to avoid and an insistent topic in *Praeterita*, so the form of this work stands in a complex relationship to traditional Christian conversion narratives. Ruskin might easily have made his autobiography a secular equivalent of a conversion story, tracing the steps of his discovery of his love of art and his vocational commitment. There are suggestions of such a scheme in *Praeterita*, especially several scenes of intense vision such as those at Schaffhausen, Rome, and the Campo Santo at Pisa, and his discovery of his passion for drawing in 1842 at Norwood and Fontainebleau (2:4). Yet the very fact that there are so many of these moments of illumination and that they do not lead to any real change of character, shows Ruskin using these scenes of epiphany in a new way: to show not radical transformation but the continuity of his identity as based on his imaginative capacity. Similarly, the climactic scene in Turin is ambiguously presented both as a decisive choice and as "no sudden conversion" but the conclusion of "courses of thought which had been leading me to such end through many years."

By structuring his work as a series of imaginative responses to external landscapes, Ruskin was trying to avoid certain tendencies of the typical spiritual autobiography, especially the dangers of introspection. As early as 1845 he had scorned Bunyan's *Grace Abounding* as "a particular phase of indigestion, coupled with a good imagination and a bad conscience," and he found it morbid for an author to concentrate obsessively on "the relations of the Deity to his own little self."[25] Like many Victorian autobiographers, Ruskin sought an alternative to traditional crisis autobiography, wishing to avoid a fruitless quest for identity through isolated introspection.[26] The overall structure of *Praeterita*, with its series of illuminative moments that do not produce definitive change, represents an innovation in a traditional genre. Its relationship to previous English spiritual narratives involves both dependence and transformation, in terms of literary form as well as meaning. Ruskin challenges not simply the content of his evangelical beliefs but the way the introspective focus of conventional spiritual autobiography distorts personal life.

Although *Praeterita* is packed with biblical symbolism and typology, in the scenes of illumination Ruskin often finds a secular symbol to crystallize his meaning: a view of the Alps, "a bit of ivy round a thorn stem" that he draws at Norwood (281), or the synesthesis of painting and music in the Turin gallery. Even when he records his appreciation of a work of art with biblical or Roman Catholic meaning, such as the Veronese painting of Solomon and the Queen of Sheba or the illuminated Hours of the Virgin missal, it is not traditional theological meaning that he affirms but the way these objects mediate aesthetic qualities and appeal, for instance, to his "love of toil, and of treasure" (456).

Ruskin asserts as a recent and precious achievement the love of the earth, of its mountains and inhabitants, for their own sakes. Of his view of the Alps at Schaffhausen, he maintains:

A very few years,—within the hundred,—before that, no child could have been born to care for mountains, or for the men who lived among them, in that way. Till Rousseau's time, there had been no "sentimental" love of nature; and till Scott's, no such apprehensive love of "all sorts and conditions of men," not in the soul merely, but in the flesh. St. Bernard of La Fontaine, looking out to Mont

Blanc with his child's eyes, sees above Mont Blanc the Madonna . . .
But for me, the Alps and their people were alike beautiful in their
snow, and their humanity; and I wanted, neither for them nor myself, sight of any thrones in heaven but the rocks, or of any spirits
in heaven but the clouds. (103–4)

Ruskin often juxtaposes a traditional theological view of some
object or landscape with his own this-worldly but deeply appreciative vision of its aesthetic beauty. It is one of Ruskin's chief
literary strategies for dramatizing in powerful symbolic terms the
effect of his deconversion on the way he sees the world. Most
memorably, such an opposition of perspectives structures the
crisis scene's contrast between the Waldensian preacher's negative
verdict on Turin and Ruskin's own experience.

I would summarize *Praeterita*'s significance as a version of deconversion in four ways. First, for all its exceptional qualities,
this work epitomizes many Victorian autobiographies both in its
relative frankness about the subject of deconversion, compared to
earlier works, and in its evasions and repressions of this painful
topic, compared to later treatments of the loss of faith. Deconversion is a recurring subject in the book and the theme of its climactic chapter. Yet the final outcome of Ruskin's religious searching
is not clearly delineated, nor does he record much of the painful
process we can reconstruct from his letters and journals, or even
some of the most significant reasons why he abandoned evangelical beliefs.

Second, the form of the book is a brilliant attempt to describe
deconversion, as well as Ruskin's entire life, in a new way by
patterning his life as a series of responses to a landscape or external setting. Within this scheme, the monastery of the Grande
Chartreuse functions as the initial stimulus for Ruskin's doubts
and as a symbol for all the experiences that forced him to admit
his distance from his original Christian faith. Even as *Praeterita*
involves a striking departure from conventional autobiographical
form, it is influenced by the traditional spiritual autobiography's
scene of crisis, with its portrayal of a moment of illumination
and choice that resolves the author's indecision and indirection.
Ruskin's work is continuous with Christian tradition in that it
presents a crisis, discontinuous in its lack of closure, its failure to
show the outcome of his spiritual searching.

Third, Ruskin presents memorably and powerfully a new reason for the rejection of Christianity, or at least of certain Protestant forms: an aesthetic critique. After Ruskin, the complaint that British Christianity was cold, rigid, unimaginative, and wooden in its forms of worship and its appreciation of the Bible echoes through the autobiographical and fictional works of the nineteenth and twentieth centuries. We will see in chapter 8 that responding to the aesthetic critique of Christianity is a central preoccupation of C. S. Lewis's apology in *Surprised by Joy.*

Finally, Ruskin's presentation of the values that replaced his lost faith is significant. Like Carlyle, Ruskin dramatizes a rejection and replacement of a religious worldview, even as he continues to be deeply influenced by his Puritan upbringing. Ruskin, however, is less concerned than Carlyle to present his new convictions as tantamount to a religious creed or worldview. Although his new aesthetic appreciations reflect spiritual concerns, Ruskin presents them as a this-worldly way of life justifiable in secular terms. He does not authorize the seeking of beauty primarily as a means of apprehending the holy. The values that replaced the faith he lost in deconversion are analogous in certain ways to a religious commitment, but they require neither theological articulation nor institutional commitment. In this he contrasts with earlier versions of deconversion such as the Christian works I examined in chapter 2, which clearly articulate how a new religious faith displaces the lost one. Ruskin differs, too, from Edmund Gosse, whom we shall see presenting his deconversion in comparative isolation from the positive values that replaced his lost faith. Ruskin is a typical Victorian in his concern to show that at least some of the various forms of meaning that Christianity traditionally provided—such as systematic beliefs about reality, ethical motivation and guidance, aesthetic beauty, and participation in a community—may find functional equivalents outside the bounds of institutional Christianity.

It is not surprising that the language and forms of spiritual autobiography have continued to influence even atheists' accounts of deconversion and that ethical concerns very similar to those of Augustine and other Christian writers have shaped most narratives recounting a loss of faith. What might not have been expected is an autobiographer using the conversion pattern to record, not his coming to new beliefs, but simply liberation from Christian belief: a narrative of escape from faith without explanation of the author's final positive convictions. This strategy constitutes a new and intriguing version of the loss of faith.

By the early twentieth century it was possible to conceive of deconversion without reconversion to a new creed or system of belief. A purely secular existence had become a live option when William James wrote *The Varieties of Religious Experience*. James holds that some persons never invest their energies in commitment to anything remotely resembling a religious faith but remain suspended in permanent skepticism:

> Some persons . . . never are, and possibly never under any circumstances could be, converted. Religious ideas cannot become the centre of their spiritual energy. . . . Such inaptitude for religious faith may in some cases be intellectual in its origin. Their religious faculties may be checked in their natural tendency to expand, by beliefs about the world that are inhibitive, the pessimistic and materialistic beliefs, for example, within which so many good souls, who in former times would have freely indulged their religious propensities, find themselves nowadays, as it were, frozen; or the agnostic vetoes upon faith as something weak and shameful, under which so many of us today lie cowering, afraid to use our instincts.[27]

In his discussion of conversion, James includes three instances of what he calls "counter-conversion": the French philosopher Jouffroy, the case of a woman from E. D. Starbuck's research, and a man Tolstoy describes in his *Confessions*. James holds that these experiences of the loss of faith have the same psychological structure as religious conversion: "To find religion is only one out of many ways of reaching unity; and the process of remedying inner incompleteness and reducing inner discord is a general psychological process, which may take place with any sort of mental material, and need not necessarily assume the religious form. . . . In all of these instances we have precisely the same psychological form of event,—a firmness, stability, and equilibrium succeeding a period of storm and stress and inconsistency. In these nonreligious cases the new man may also be born either gradually or suddenly."[28] James suggests, then, that one resolution for the crisis of a divided self is a wholly secular outlook.

Yet James is inconsistent, for he also holds that all conversions must involve a deep and intense commitment to a new set of ideas: "To say that a man is 'converted' means, in these terms, that religious ideas, previously peripheral in his consciousness, now take a central place, and that religious aims form the habitual centre of his energy."[29] James anticipates functional definitions of religion (such as Paul Tillich's conception of "ultimate concern") when he holds that no one can live without a commitment that is, in effect, religious. This would mean that one can never rest in loss of faith. Only the divided self on the verge of either collapse or conversion could be said to lack some conviction which functions as a faith. James's discussion of the loss of faith is ambiguous because while he presents permanent skepticism as a real possibility, he also holds that every human being, even the one who has been through "counterconversion," has some "habitual center of personal energy" that functions like a religious faith to give meaning and purpose. James's treatment of counter-conversion, like the autobiographies of agnostics and Ruskin's *Praeterita*, reminds us that deconversion and conversion may be distinguished but not completely separated in analysis, for they represent differing perspectives on the same human experience of transformed loyalties or altered trust.

It is a rare autobiographer who does not use his story of deconversion to set forth his positive convictions. However, a new and significant version of deconversion is constituted when an autobiographer uses the conversion pattern to place the emphasis squarely on the loss of faith, using the conventions of the conversion narrative but presenting deconversion without reconversion. For Edmund Gosse, writing during the same decade as James, the metaphors and structure of the conversion narrative provide the basic form for his interpretation of the loss of faith. Unlike Ruskin, Gosse does not try to find a new literary form, an alternative to the Christian conversion narrative. Although the reasons for Gosse's deconversion strongly resemble Ruskin's, centering on the aesthetic critique of British evangelical Protestantism, his autobiography is very different in narrative form and instructive in its contrasting treatment of the theme of loss of faith. Although Gosse's *Father and Son* (1907) gives indications of his positive convictions, this work focuses on his loss of religious faith. Deconversion is the climax and culmination of Gosse's spiritual struggles, rather than being the first stage of a process leading to the affirmation of new commitments, whether religious or secular. *Father and Son* is in this sense and in several others an innovative version of deconversion.

Edmund Gosse's deconversion was from the Plymouth Brethren, an extreme sect of Calvinists who gathered "on terms of what may almost be called negation—with no priest, no ritual, no festivals, no ornament of any kind, nothing but the Lord's Supper and the exposition of Holy Scripture drawing these austere spirits into any sort of cohesion."[30] Gosse asserts that this faith is no longer an option for anyone in his audience, describing his book as "a *document*, as a record of educational and religious conditions which, having passed away, will never return" (5). This "diagnosis of a dying Puritanism," of which his father, Philip Gosse, was "perhaps the last surviving type" (237), does not articulate in explicit form the narrator's present convictions. Edmund Gosse's primary interests are in the effect of belief in the creeds of the Brethren on a man as intelligent as was the elder Gosse and in the effect of their religious differences on the relationship between father and son.

Philip Gosse, a zoologist of some distinction, was also a biblical fundamentalist who tried to reconcile science and religion by refuting the new theories of evolution. His "catastrophic" theory of evolution brought only ridicule, for it implied, at least to the popular press, that "God hid the fossils in the rocks in order to tempt geologists into infidelity" (87). One of the reasons for the younger Gosse's deconversion is his perception of the way his father's orthodoxy vitiated his intellectual integrity: "He allowed the turbid volume of superstition to drown the delicate stream of reason. He took one step in the service of truth, and then he drew back in an agony, and accepted the servitude of error" (84). Intellectual doubts based on the best scientific evidence should not be stifled by appeals to religious authority. This conviction the younger Gosse shares with Augustine, whose encounter with Faustus failed to resolve his doubts about discrepancies between Manichee doctrines and astronomical evidence.[31] Gosse presents his father's lack of "that sublime humility which is the crown of genius" as a corrupting influence on Philip's scientific work. A form of agnosticism seems to be requisite for the highest intellectual achievements: "This obstinate persuasion that he alone knew the mind of God, that he alone could interpret the designs of the Creator, what did it result from if not from a congenital lack of that highest modesty which replies 'I do not know' even to the questions which Faith, with menacing finger, insists on having most positively answered?" (96–97). Gosse is troubled not only because his father's scientific work is compromised by his religious views but because he witnesses his father's mental and spiritual anguish, his suffering from the conflict between rigid dogmas and scientific evidence. Gosse's recognition of the self-destructive consequences of stifling intellectual doubts is a primary reason for rejecting his father's brand of Calvinist Christianity.

Gosse's deconversion comes about, as well, because of his moral revulsion from several aspects of his father's faith. He is repelled, first, by his father's well-meaning but tyrannical solicitude about his son's spiritual development. Neither love nor belief can be compelled, asserts the book's epigraph from Schopenhauer: "Der Glaube ist wie die Liebe: Er lässt sich nicht erzwingen." A person in Gosse's position has but two alternatives: "Either he must cease to think for himself; or his individualism must be instantly confirmed, and the necessity of religious independence must be emphasised" (250). Gosse's indictment of his father's bullying depends on a moral value deeply felt by every likely reader: the right to freedom of conscience. The assumption of this right is the most conspicuous of the ways that Gosse's account, like any narrative of deconversion, depends implicitly on positive convictions and ethical standards to explain the loss of faith.

Just as morally repugnant as the elder Gosse's spiritual tyranny is the warped sense of priorities dictated by his "morbid delicacy of conscience" (89). Many incidents in *Father and Son* show how this form of Calvinism fosters a distorted conception of right and wrong, an obsession with minor matters of behavior coupled with insensitivity to actual suffering. Convinced that the slightest sign of levity or simple pleasure might influence others, Philip Gosse determines never to sing another secular song. His egocentric moral perspective cannot accurately assess the weightiness of actions or their actual bearing on other persons. He constantly fears that his most casual actions will precipitate evil: "Act after act became taboo, not because each was sinful in itself, but because it might lead others into sin" (90). Gosse sums up his ethical criticisms at the end of the book:

> Evangelical religion, or any religion in a violent form . . . divides heart from heart. It sets up a vain, chimerical ideal, in the barren pursuit of which all the tender, indulgent affections, all the genial play of life, all the exquisite pleasures and soft resignations of the body, all that enlarges and calms the soul, are exchanged for what is harsh and void and negative. It encourages a stern and ignorant spirit of condemnation; it throws altogether out of gear the healthy movement of the conscience; it invents virtues which are sterile

and cruel; it invents sins which are no sins at all, but which darken the heaven of innocent joy with futile clouds of remorse. (246)

Gosse revolts against the Plymouth Brethren for some of the same reasons Augustine attacks the Manichees: in both cases a warped religious commitment corrupts the moral conscience of the believer so that he cannot accurately discern good and evil, right and wrong.

The passage just cited goes on, however, to suggest a source of Gosse's dissatisfaction not expressed by Christian versions of deconversion: a critique of otherworldliness similar to Ruskin's. "There is something horrible, if we will bring ourselves to face it, in the fanaticism that can do nothing with this pathetic and fugitive existence of ours but treat it as if it were the uncomfortable ante-chamber to a palace which no one has explored and of the plan of which we know absolutely nothing" (246–47). It is the aesthetic and imaginative impoverishment of the Plymouth Brethren as much as their intellectual and moral deficiencies that make this community such poor soil for Gosse's development. When his parents withheld all fiction from their son, they produced the opposite of what they intended: "They desired to make me truthful; the tendency was to make me positive and skeptical" (26). Philip Gosse's narrow version of the faith is a caricature of the Christian tradition; he accepts nothing in the Bible as symbolic, allegorical, or allusive, and has no appreciation for the imaginative riches of Christian poetry, mysticism, and hymnody. Even— and especially—the Book of Revelation becomes in his hands a source of exact predictions to be understood with rigid literalness.

Contrasting with the stultifying practices of the Brethren, Gosse dramatizes several occasions when art awakens his imagination: the first reading of a Dickens novel, "by which I was instantly and gloriously enslaved" (182); his joy on learning to appreciate painting and sculpture—"too beautiful to be so wicked as my Father thought" (199); the discovery of the "miracle" of "the amazing beauty which could exist in the sound of verses" (131), in this case Virgil's; and the boy's dream of the word CARMINE, "a symbol of all that taste and art and wealth could combine to produce" (122). Although *Father and Son* hints at a conversion to the aesthetic life, Gosse's choice of vocation as poet, critic, and man of letters falls outside the scope of this book. The positive values Gosse holds are only implied, primarily by contrast with his religious upbringing. His narrative is not as centrally about the discovery of vocation as are Ruskin's *Praeterita* or the semiautobiographical works of Joyce or Lawrence; little attention is given, for example, to Gosse's first attempts at poetry. The young boy's pleasure in reading *The Tempest* is not developed but is immediately contrasted with the response of a speaker at an evangelical conference, who denounces Shakespeare as "a lost soul now suffering for his sins in hell!" (218).

Father and Son shows the inextricable mixture of religious questions with Gosse's relationship to his father. In Ruskin's autobiography religious questions were also enmeshed with a struggle for autonomy in relation to parental authority, but Ruskin lacked the insight or detachment to explore this complex issue. In contrast, the confusing tangle of religious and familial loyalties constitutes for Gosse, as for later psychologically informed writers, a compelling reason why a system of belief must be rejected. In this way, too, *Father and Son* is a forerunner of things to come. Gosse acknowledges that when he was six his father was "confused . . . in some sense with God," and one of his most vivid early memories is his amazed discovery that his father "was not, as I had supposed, omniscient" (33). It takes years for Gosse to understand and accept the full implications of this discovery. For him, as for a host of later apostates, the recognition that Christianity is intertwined with some other form of authority—parental, racial, political, or sexual—leads to both rebellion against a fallible secular authority and repudiation of religious faith.

Unlike many others who lost their faith, however, Gosse distinguishes between the variety of Christianity he rejects and a reinterpreted standard of true Christianity. It has not always been appreciated that Gosse's rebellion against a narrow version of Christianity depends on intellectual, moral, and aesthetic criteria of an authentic Christianity that he does not undermine. Some critics have taken Gosse's portrayal of his father's faith as a wholesale rejection of Christianity, failing to discern the Christian basis of the standard by which the autobiographer judges and criticizes. For instance, one of his main criticisms of his father's beliefs is that he dwelled "so much on the possible anger of the Lord, rather than on his pity and love" (121).

Gosse does not simply denounce most of the Brethren's religious practices; more often, he presents them as authentic forms of piety and devotion for those with more faith than himself. For instance he asserts that "there is no greater proof of complete religious sincerity than fervour in private prayer" (174). His own prayers were perfunctory, reflecting a feeling of spiritual deadness. His description of his own deficiencies reveals insight and understanding of the possible loss of self in fervent prayer: "There never was a moment in which my heart truly responded, with native ardour, to the words which flowed so readily, in such a stream of unction, from my anointed lips. I cannot recall anything but an intellectual surrender; there was never joy in the act of resignation, never the mystic's rapture at feeling his phantom self, his own threadbare soul, suffused, thrilled through, robed again in glory by a fire which burns up everything personal and individual about him" (158). With regard to the practice of prayer, Gosse's deconversion reflects not a wholesale rejection of the practices of the Brethren but the verdict of his conscience that he cannot personally continue praying without hypocrisy.

Similarly, Gosse never denies that some persons actually experience what his father means by conversion: "There must be a new birth and being, a fresh creation in God. This crisis he was accustomed to regard as manifesting itself in a sudden and definite upheaval. There might have been prolonged practical piety, deep and true contrition for sin, but these, although the natural and suitable prologue to conversion, were not conversion itself. . . . The very root of human nature had to be changed, and, in the majority of cases, this change was sudden, patent, palpable" (139–40). The Brethren believed that conversion depended on an adult's voluntary acceptance of the way of salvation, and they usually baptized a convert soon after such an experience. Philip Gosse persuades his congregation that his son's conversion took place unperceived when he was a child and that therefore the ten-year-old boy should be baptized and accepted into communion. Edmund goes through the motions of the baptismal service without either genuine contrition for sin or awareness of grace. Gosse's public baptism, "the central event of my whole childhood" (145), is from his own point of view not only a hollow pretense but, in retrospect, an occasion of spiritual pride: "I was puffed out with a sense of my own holiness" (150). Here the autobiographer's criticisms are directed not against the practices or convictions of the Brethren but against his father's wishful thinking and manipulations, and against Gosse's own pride, using the ages-old Christian vocabulary of sin. What is attacked is a failure to live up to the demands and ideals of authentic Christian faith, not those demands, ideals, or faith itself.

Other criteria of true Christianity are used to convict the Brethren of what amounts to unorthodoxy. Like Ruskin, Gosse asserts that the view that the Lord's Day must be used exclusively for worship is "based much more on a Jewish than upon a Christian law" (186). The unbearable narrowness and rigidity of his adolescent years seem to him a "bondage to the Law and the Prophets" (161). When Gosse begins to read and understand the Scriptures from his own point of view, he realizes that his father's understanding of the faith is extraordinarily limited in scope, leaving out not only the mystics, artists, and musicians of the church, but Catholics, Unitarians, and even the Church of England. "I began to perceive, without animosity, the strange narrowness of my Father's system, which seemed to take into consideration only a selected circle of persons, a group of disciples peculiarly illuminated, and to have no message whatever for the wider Christian community" (227). Gosse justifies his deconversion by appealing to a wider, more imaginative, tolerant, and liberal form of Christianity, one epitomized by an emphasis on God's love rather than his jealousy and wrath.[32]

Gosse uses a striking variety of metaphors to interpret his life before deconversion, especially images of cages, traps, and prisons. He describes himself as a boy as being a prisoner, passive observer, or spectator of adventures from which he is excluded. Prominent, too, are biological metaphors involving frustrated or precarious organic growth, as in the image of his soul as a flower on a ledge which "offered no lodgment, no hope of salvation, to any rootlet which should stray beyond its inexorable limits" (19). His stunted imaginative growth is compared to "a plant on which a pot has been placed, with the effect that the centre is crushed and arrested, while shoots are straggling up to the light on all sides" (205). The use of scientific allusion in *Father and Son*, writes Peterson, "provides a means of resisting his father's language system." Gosse does not simply substitute a scientific system of interpretation for biblical typology, however. "Biological metaphor is not elevated to the status of system. It never becomes fully 'scientific.' "[33] All Gosse's metaphors are local rather than part of a comprehensive hermeneutical method. This flexible use of many kinds of metaphor without recourse to a single system of self-interpretation is characteristic of Gosse's interest in the variety of ways the human and natural worlds may be construed.

Gosse does not try to escape biblical analogies altogether; rather, he uses his knowledge of Scripture to counter his father's typological reading of events. Three times he refers to the story of Naaman and Elisha in the fifth chapter of II Kings, characterizing instances of prudent conformity to his father's demands as "bowing in the House of Rimmon" (80, 229, 244). When his father refuses an uncle's offer to establish the son in a banking position, Gosse uses this same biblical chapter to describe his disappointed hope for material prosperity: "I felt very much like Gehazi, and I would fain have followed after the banker if I had dared to do so, into the night. I would have excused to him the ardour of my Elisha, and I would have reminded him of the sons of the prophets—'Give me, I pray thee,' I would have said, 'a talent of silver and two changes of garments' " (209). Since the elder Gosse dominates by interpreting all of his son's experience in terms of biblical patterns, Edmund's best defense is to propose alternative readings, substituting a different biblical reference as the most appropriate metaphor for the immediate situation. In casting himself in the role of idolater or sinner, he shows his continued reliance on the biblical worldview even as he breaks with some of its demands.

Gosse does not use biblical typology only to undermine the validity of Christian values.[34] Gosse quotes a letter in which his father justifies his oversolicitous paternal style through a comparison with Job, who suspected that his sons might have sinned, and was driven to God in intercession. The father queries: "Was not his suspicion much like mine, grounded on the same reasons and productive of the same results?" (240). Edmund proposes a better analogy: "What youth of eighteen would willingly be compared with the sons of Job? And indeed, for my part, I felt much more like that justly exasperated character, Elihu the Buzite, of the kindred of Ram" (241). The apt comparison with Elihu, who rebukes Job for his self-righteousness and presumptuousness before God's mystery, places the father and son in a far different light from Philip's chosen text. "Elihu was angry at Job because he justified himself rather than God" (Job 32:2). Gosse uses biblical allusions to legitimate his anger and to interpret the theological and moral errors of his father and of his childhood faith. In doing this he often relies on essentially biblical values, such as the criticism of self-righteousness and certainty.

As a narrative frame for his story of deconversion, Gosse employs many of the elements and patterns of the traditional conversion narrative. The climactic scenes of the book—the dedication of the child at his mother's deathbed, the public baptism, the final crisis of insight and emotion near a garden—all echo incidents in the Bible and in earlier autobiographies. Yet these scenes subvert the traditional meanings. Referring to his mother's dedication of the six-year-old boy, Gosse stresses the oppressive duties he had to assume: "What a weight, intolerable as the burden of Atlas, to lay on the shoulders of a little fragile child!" (62). The public baptism is a sham because the boy goes through the motions mechanically. And what finally comes to Gosse at "the highest moment of my religious life, the apex of my striving after holiness" (231), as he fervently prays for Lord Jesus to "come now," is the realization that his faith has dissolved. " 'The Lord has not come, the Lord will never come,' I muttered, and in my heart the artificial edifice of extravagant faith began to totter and crumble" (232). These scenes of failed epiphany present deconversion using the motifs and conventions of traditional spiritual autobiography. By this time it had become possible for an author to treat the loss of faith in a comic manner, as when Gosse presents himself deliberately committing idolatry by substituting "O Chair" for the customary recipient of his prayers.[35]

Linda Peterson sees the originality of *Father and Son* in its use of parody, which she defines as "the repetition of formal generic patterns with a displacement of meaning."[36] So defined, parody need not entail satire, mockery, or destructive intent. Rather, it involves emptying a form of its traditional content. "Words, phrases, and sentences create episodes that are simulacra; they use the language of genuine spiritual experience to expose a feigned or hollow experience that the language tends to (or tries to) disguise."[37] In this sense we may say that Gosse parodies the traditional conversion narrative by using its form to recount an experience of deconversion. Parody in its common usage is not the best term to describe this strategy, however, in that it denotes a ridiculous or feeble imitation. Ironically, Gosse's scenes of failed epiphany are genuine spiritual experiences, in which the boy's deepest convictions are clarified, his conscience asserts its judgment, and his divided self begins to cohere. There is a wry tone and a humorous aspect to Gosse's handling of these incidents, but he conveys, too, an unmistakable sense that the rubrics of conversion are not simply empty forms. The elements of the traditional conversion narrative retain much of their power to render profound personal metamorphosis. In describing his deconversion as analogous to a conversion, casting his story of the loss of faith in the mold of a traditional Christian narrative, Gosse conveys not an attitude of irreverence or ridicule but rather one of genuine spiritual searching as he tests his experience against the expectations associated with the traditional form.

Biographical evidence indicates that neither Gosse's break with his father nor his deconversion was as decisive as he portrays them in *Father and Son*. The last sentence of that work says that at the age of twenty "the young man's conscience threw off once for all the yoke of his 'dedication,' and, as respectfully as he could, without parade or remonstrance, he took a human being's privilege to fashion his inner life for himself" (250). In fact, Gosse's theological beliefs continued to evolve, and he even taught Sunday School for a number of years.[38] Gosse's ambivalence about his father and about the religion of his childhood went on for some time, and these two unresolved conflicts are the source of much of *Father and Son*'s compelling power.

The presentation of loss of faith as a conversion gives *Father and Son* fascinating ambiguity and makes it a highly original and distinctive version of deconversion. Gosse discerned that, although his father's Puritan beliefs were no longer compelling, the ways Christians organized their experience were still highly influential even among those who had lost their faith. Gosse was at once critical of the traditional form of Christian autobiography and appreciative of its continuing power and persuasiveness. He shows that all the elements of conversion—both the experience itself and the literary form that renders it—are conventions that may be imitated without conviction or commitment. Reputed conversions such as the boy's baptismal experience may be feigned, and adaptations of the conversion narrative such as *Father and Son* may displace the form's traditional meaning by focusing the central scene of crisis on the loss of faith.

Unlike many agnostics, however, Gosse does not simply reject conversion as a wholly delusory experience while retaining the narrative form traditionally associated with it. The son accepts his father's criterion for a genuine conversion as he exposes his own conformity to expectation as a false pretense, an empty sham. Gosse does not devise an alternative narrative structure to the traditional form of conversion, as does Ruskin; rather he uses the conversion paradigm to interpret his own experience of losing faith. The Christian metaphors and narrative pattern are for him not dispensable conventions; they retain their value as one—not the exclusive—form by which experience may be apprehended, interpreted, and presented. Gosse's ironic use of the conversion narrative's conventions to interpret his deconversion expresses unresolved beliefs, mixed feelings, and a divided conscience about the merits of participation in a Christian community. It is this complex and unfinished assessment of Christianity, along with Gosse's emotional ambivalence toward his father, that gives *Father and Son* its appeal and its insights. Deeply indebted to the tradition of spiritual autobiography, Gosse's version of deconversion is a distinctive account of the loss of faith. It highlights the aesthetic and imaginative needs contributing to the loss of faith and presents deconversion as leading not to a clearly specified set of new beliefs but to freedom, openness, and a more responsible conscience.

5

CHRISTIANITY AND "THE WHITE MAN'S RELIGION"

THE FIRST AUTOBIOGRAPHIES by African Americans and Native Americans display a number of similarities. Both slave narratives and Indian autobiographies have strong roots in oral forms of narrative, are greatly influenced by the demands of white editors, publishers, and readers, and usually portray the author as representative of a broader community based on race or tribe. This chapter explores another parallel between these two forms of autobiography, which are often discussed in isolation. While there is great diversity within "multicultural autobiography," a common rhetorical strategy in these works involves the attempt to deconvert readers from a particular religious belief.[1] Both black and Indian autobiographers show the reader the difference between Christianity and "the white man's religion," which is the religious justification of white superiority. Recognition of the difference between these two systems of belief has not always come easily for white people, since there are deep-rooted and tenacious links between certain Christian attitudes and the belief in white superiority. Encouraging this form of deconversion—the loss of faith in the identity between Christianity and the white man's religion—is a central goal of autobiographies by persons of color. This has been so whether the author is a Christian, is committed to some other religious tradition, or is reassessing an ambivalent relationship to Christianity. I will compare several early autobiographies whose rhetorical strategy depends on the distinction between Christianity and the white man's religion, focusing on the works of Frederick Douglass and Charles Eastman. I then discuss two modern works by non-Christian writers that devise new versions of this same strategy: *The Autobiography of Malcolm X* and *Lame Deer: Seeker of Visions.*

The distinctive origins of African American autobiography are the slave narratives published between 1760 and 1865. The large majority of these works were written primarily to provide evidence of the terrible inhumanity of slavery and to demand immediate freedom for all slaves. Nearly all of the slave narratives are by Christians and appeal directly to Christian values the authors assume to be shared by their readers. Especially in the concluding chapter of such works, the author asks how slavery can be perpetuated or tolerated by professed Christians. For example, Henry Bibb closes his narrative by asking the reader to decide "whether a man can be a Bible Christian, and yet hold his Christian brethren as property, so that they may be sold at any time in market, as sheep or oxen, to pay his debts. . . . I believe slave holding to be a sin against God and man under all circumstances."[2]

At the same time that they appeal to Christian beliefs to condemn slavery, early black autobiographers attack the use of Christianity to uphold the slave system. William Wells Brown, like many early African American writers, points out how slaveholders approve of the religion of the slaves because it makes them more docile and obedient: "The religious teaching consists in teaching the slave that he must never strike a white man; that God made him for a slave; and that, when whipped, he must not find fault,— for the Bible says, 'He that knoweth his master's will, and doeth it not, shall be beaten with many stripes!' And slaveholders find such religion very profitable to them."[3] From the very start black autobiography has involved a mixed assessment of Christianity, invoking the norms of this religion as an ideal yet criticizing the constant and widespread failure of Christians to practice what they preach. Harriet Jacobs shows how the slaveholders' approved preachers tailored the Christian message so that its basic content was for slaves to obey their masters. She dramatizes how slaves saw through this obvious ploy and in one instance "went home, highly amused." The slaves had a much more profound understanding of Christianity than their masters. Jacobs inverts her audience's understanding of missionary work, asking that the gospel of true Christianity be brought to American slaveholders: "I am glad that missionaries go out to the dark corners of the earth; but I ask them not to overlook the dark corners at home. Talk to American slaveholders as you talk to savages in Africa. Tell *them* it was wrong to traffic in men. . . . Tell them they are answerable to God for sealing up the Fountain of Life from souls that are thirsting for it."[4] Jacobs is greatly surprised when her master, Dr. Flint, who incessantly demands that she become his mistress, joins the Episcopalian Church. But Flint's character becomes even worse after he joins the church: "I had supposed that religion had a purifying effect on the character of man, but the worst persecutions I endured from him were after he was a communicant."[5]

Bibb, Brown, and Jacobs all adopt rhetorical strategies devised by the most influential of slave narratives, *The Narrative of Frederick Douglass* (1845). Douglass's master, Thomas Auld, became "more cruel and hateful" after his religious conversion, for "he found religious sanction and support for his slaveholding cruelty."[6] To justify whipping a slave woman, Auld quotes the much-cited passage in Luke 12: "He that knoweth his master's will, and doeth it not, shall be beaten with many stripes" (68). Douglass depicts white Christians breaking up a slave Sunday School, the drastic distortion of the gospel in preaching to the slaves, and the use of Christian holidays as "safety-valves." The masters' encouragement of drinking at Christmas was intended "to disgust their slaves with freedom, by plunging them into the lowest depths of dissipation" (85). Douglass portrays a stark contrast between William Freeland, his master who was neither religious nor especially cruel, and Edward Covey, a famous "nigger-breaker" hired to destroy Douglass's will and self-respect, who was a "professor of religion—a pious soul—a member and a class-leader in the Methodist Church" (70). Douglass asserts that "the religion of the south is a mere covering for the most horrid crimes" (86) and that of all masters, "religious slaveholders are the worst" (87).

In his Appendix, Douglass makes explicit the crucial distinction that shapes the narrative strategies of so many autobiographies by members of American minority groups. "What I have said respecting and against religion, I mean strictly to apply to the *slaveholding religion* of this land, and with no possible reference to Christianity proper; for, between the Christianity of this land and the Christianity of Christ, I recognize the widest possible difference" (120). Although Douglass begins by saying he is not an opponent of all religion, he immediately makes clear how broadly his accusation extends: "I love the pure, peaceable, and impartial Christianity of Christ: I therefore hate the corrupt, slaveholding, women-whipping, cradle-plundering, partial and hypocritical Christianity of this land. Indeed, I can see no reason, but the most deceitful one, for calling the religion of this land Christianity. I look upon it as the climax of all misnomers, the boldest of all frauds, and the grossest of all libels" (120). The accusation of hypocrisy extends not simply to the religion of the South but to the "overwhelming mass of professed Christians in America," for northern Christians, by their failure to oppose slavery, commit the same moral sin. By "the religion of this land," Douglass means nothing less sweeping than "that which is revealed in the words, deeds, and actions, of those bodies, north and south, calling themselves Christian churches, and yet in union with slaveholders" (123–24). The religion of the South is, "by communion and fellowship, the religion of the north."

The central aim of Douglass's *Narrative* is not to destroy the religious faith of his audience but to contribute to the abolitionist cause. To do this, Douglass appeals to white Christians to put in practice what they profess to believe, to live up to their ideals, to love their neighbor as Christ taught. Douglass's work stands in the tradition of the American jeremiad, prophetically criticizing a departure from an ethical norm.[7] In one sense, then, Douglass's narrative is a call for conversion, for genuine commitment to the ideals of Christianity (as well as to American democratic ideals). However, the theme of deconversion is also an essential element of the prophetic tradition, implicit in the demand for repentance, the denunciation of idolatry, and the call to turn away from a false god. In its focus on the reader's need to reject "the white man's religion," Douglass's *Narrative* represents a paradigmatic version of deconversion that shapes the agenda and rhetoric of many later autobiographers. Douglass challenged two of the most pervasive and firmly entrenched beliefs of nineteenth-century America: the belief that Christianity sanctioned slaveholding and the belief that white persons were inherently superior to blacks. In the *Narrative*, and in his even more pointed *My Bondage and My Freedom* (1855), Douglass tried to confront his audience with testimony that would undermine these convictions. Douglass saw that before white readers could recognize the full humanity of black persons they would have to lose faith in the religious basis for their claim to innate superiority and for the institution of slavery.

Douglass criticizes "the Christianity of this land," and he also appeals to Christian beliefs such as love of neighbor to condemn slavery. He closes the *Narrative*'s account of the horrors of slavery by quoting the Lord's warning in Jeremiah: "Shall I not visit for these things?" (124). Yet although Douglass invokes Christian values, we begin to wonder how he can maintain his own faith in Christianity after what he has seen of it in practice. The *Narrative* hints at Douglass's own deconversion without stating explicitly that he lost his religious faith. Douglass could hardly have risked alienating his audience by pronouncing Christianity itself to be immoral. He saw some positive resources for social justice in Christianity, and he realized that his best hope for ending slavery lay in enlisting the efforts of the church. Yet one senses from the tone of the *Narrative* Douglass's skepticism about the religion whose practice by both blacks and whites had helped to perpetuate the slave system. Douglass's *Narrative* is a paradigm for many later autobiographers not only in the deliberate attempt to deconvert the reader from "the white man's religion" but also in the veiled, indirect ways that the writer's own doubts about Christianity must be expressed, given the circumstances of a minority writer in America.

Douglass's doubts about Christianity are more strongly suggested in *My Bondage and My Freedom*. For example, in his description of his fight with Covey, Douglass presents himself as "feeling that I had no friend on earth, and doubting if I had one in heaven" (144).[8] While hiding in the woods, Douglass finds he cannot pray: "But how could I pray? Covey could pray—Capt. Auld could pray—I would fain pray; but doubts (arising partly from my own neglect of the means of grace, and partly from the sham religion which everywhere prevailed, cast in my mind a doubt upon all religion, and led me to the conviction that prayers were unavailing and delusive) prevented my embracing the opportunity, as a religious one" (145). Only when he is liberated from religious scruples about opposing his master does Douglass resolve to defend himself: "My religious views on the subject of resisting my master, had suffered a serious shock, by the savage persecution to which I had been subjected, and my hands were no longer tied by my religion" (148). Ironically, Douglass's "resurrection from the dark and pestiferous tomb of slavery," described with the metaphors of Christian conversion narratives, comes about when he begins to rely not on the Lord's protection but on his own spirit of "manly independence" (152).

In *My Bondage* Douglass often uses metaphors of Satan and the devil to portray himself. Douglass preaches hatred, opposes order and authority, and admits his pride, ambition, and selfish motives. William Andrews asserts that "the rebellious shadow comes to the fore in Douglass only when all his gods and fathers fail and he must become his own self-authorizing presence in a world bereft of legitimate structure or sanction."[9] Andrews interprets this pattern in terms of Douglass's use of the Prometheus myth and his exploitation of the trickster figure's savior-satan duality. We can also interpret Douglass's presentation of himself as a "devil" as a form of "signifying" on Christian metaphors. Signifying (or "signifyin' "), as Henry Louis Gates has argued, is a distinctive African American system of rhetoric and interpretation.[10] It involves ironic repetition of terms in white discourse to question and critique their meaning. For example, Gates shows how the monkey, a racist image of the black, is reinterpreted within African American literature so that the monkey becomes a symbol of verbal fluency and of the power to escape determination by white discourse. By appropriating "devilish" negative terms of Christian discourse, reversing their meaning, and applying them to himself, Douglass is signifying on Christian rhetoric. This pattern reveals Douglass's complex and ambivalent relationship to Christianity. He is dependent upon it for many of his primary metaphors and moral values, yet he is simultaneously ironic and critical as he shows this religion's ambiguous role in the experience of African Americans. The effect of such signifying upon conventional Christian metaphors is unsettling to many Christian readers, forcing them to examine more critically the central terms of their religious discourse and the ways these terms are used.

Other differences between *My Freedom and My Bondage* and the 1845 *Narrative* also suggest Douglass's increasing alienation not only from the slaveholding religion of the southern United States but from Christianity itself.[11] In New Bedford, Douglass, though "lukewarm and in a backslidden state" (214), mistakenly believed it was his duty to join the Methodist Church: "I was not then aware of the powerful influence of that religious body in favor of the enslavement of my race, nor did I see how the northern churches could be responsible for the conduct of southern churches; neither did I fully understand how it could be my duty to remain separate from the church, because bad men were connected with it" (214). Douglass left the Methodist Church because he saw it "sanctioning the christianity" of slaveholders. Later Douglass left the New Bedford Zion Methodists, an all-black congregation, because "I found that it consented to the same spirit which held my brethren in chains" (215).

When describing his twenty-one months in Great Britain, Douglass emphasizes his efforts to arouse the churches there to the cause of abolition, culminating in several dramatic debates. Unfortunately, the Christian churches were often on the wrong side of the issue. For example, the Free Church of Scotland had taken money from slave dealers to build churches. Given the opportunity to repent, this church refused to send the money back to America: "The Free Church held on to the blood-stained money, and continued to justify itself in its position—and of course to apologize for slavery—and does so till this day. She lost a glorious opportunity for giving her voice, her vote, and her example to the cause of humanity; and to-day she is staggering under the curse of the enslaved, whose blood is in her skirts" (235). Another controversy concerned the "Evangelical Alliance," an ecumenical movement of Christians from around the world. Douglass saw the participation of some American divines in this movement as an attempt "to weave a world-wide garment with which to clothe evangelical slave-holders" (236). In his account of these events, Douglass and other abolitionists appealed to the conscience of the nation, since "the question of slavery is too large a question to be finally disposed of, even by the Evangelical Alliance" (236). Douglass emphasizes the Christian churches' weakness or active opposition to the movement for abolition.

When he wrote *My Bondage and My Freedom*, Douglass continued to appeal to Christianity as he denounced slavery. However, I contend that Douglass's criticisms of Christianity go much deeper and suggest a further stage in his own deconversion. His portrayal of how Christian beliefs "tied his hands" and kept him in bondage, the positive consequences of his beginning to rely on his own efforts rather than trust in God's providence, the unsettling effect of his signifying on Christian symbols, and his inability to find a force for opposing slavery within any institutionalized form of Christianity, all suggest Douglass's growing skepticism about the value and truth of Christianity. Douglass implies that a pure essence of Christianity cannot be disentangled from the white man's religion.[12]

Because of Douglass's relationship to his audience—his overriding need to win them to the cause of abolition—his own deconversion is only hinted at or implied. The contexts in which most African and Native Americans wrote during the nineteenth century were in some respects similar to Douglass's circumstances. Certain topics and ideas were welcome to white editors, publishers, and audiences, while explicit rejection of Christianity was unacceptable before the twentieth century. Thus the process of an autobiographer's deconversion usually appears in a disguised or covert way and with considerable ambiguity because of the author's wish to appeal to the audience's Christian values. Both in its attempt to deconvert the reader from the white man's religion and in its oblique suggestion of the author's loss of faith in Christianity itself, then, Douglass's *Narrative* is a key work for understanding many nineteenth-century autobiographies.

The first autobiographies written by American Indians are by Christians.[13] William Apes and George Copway were Christian converts whose written works resemble the spiritual memoirs and confessional literature of Puritan New England. Each writer makes conversion the climax of his work, and Apes concludes with his activities preaching the gospel. Both conversion and writing an autobiography represent the author's attainment of equality with whites, demonstrating his spiritual struggles, achievement of literacy, and expression of a coherent sense of selfhood. Like the slave narratives, the first autobiographies by Indians criticize injustices to the author's people and assert their full humanity and equality. Although Apes and Copway tied their own identities to the measures of white civilization, these writers did not reject their Indian identity, as modern interpreters often hold.[14] While they chose to adopt many aspects of the dominant culture, Apes and Copway distinguished their faith in Christianity from belief in the inherent superiority of the white man.

In 1829 Apes initiated a tradition in Indian autobiographical texts of graphically depicting white cruelty and injustice. Apes holds white influence responsible for causing the vices that Indians sometimes display—specifically "their passionate fondness for spiritous liquors, and the foolish notion they hold in common with many professing Christians, of gaining reputation and esteem by their prowess in war."[15] Using personal narrative and a long Appendix (as long as the main text), Apes inaugurates the mixture of personal history and political criticism that characterizes much Native American writing. While Apes's work is a conversion narrative, it is highly significant that his acceptance of Christianity does not mean the rejection of his Indian identity, as his white readers would have automatically assumed. Instead, Apes uses Christian beliefs and norms to criticize the dominant

culture's abuse and subordination of Indians and to attack the ideology that justifies these practices.[16]

George Copway's work (1847) originates another tradition in
Native American writing, the sympathetic and nostalgic depiction of his people's way of life before contact with white culture.
He describes in detail Ojibway customs and traditions, stressing
the essential humanity of his people and the value of their tribal
way of life.[17] While Apes and Copway are—by their very choos-
ing to write an autobiography—clearly committed to many of the
values of white civilization, they affirm the value of Indian culture
and point out the deficiencies of white culture. Apes and Copway
demonstrate two permanent preoccupations of the genre of Indian
autobiography: the author's reconciliation of Indian identity with
certain values of white culture and the appeal to white audiences
to appreciate Indian ways. In seeking these goals, Apes and Copway distinguish between the ideal of Christianity they embrace
and the arrogant assumption that equates Christianity with belief
in the superiority of white people.

The same basic strategy can be seen some seventy years later in
Charles Eastman's *From the Deep Woods to Civilization* (1916).
Eastman saw the traditional way of life of the Sioux people as
doomed to extinction and portrayed himself as a role model of
successful adaptation to the mainstream of American life. He
went to Dartmouth, received his medical degree from Boston University in 1890, and returned as a physician to the Pine Ridge
Agency just months before the traumatic events of the Wounded
Knee Massacre. Later he moved to Minnesota and worked in a
variety of organizations including the Y.M.C.A. and Indian reform movements. Eastman was firmly committed to Christianity
and to "civilization" and saw these as deeply connected. Yet he
distinguished sharply between "civiliation as preached and practiced," as he titles one chapter. Like many other Native American
writers, he presents Christianity as consistent with traditional
Indian spirituality: "The Christ ideal might be radical, visionary, even impractical, as judged in the light of my later experiences; it still seemed to me logical, and in line with most of my
Indian training."[18] He shows similarities between certain Native
American virtues and the Christian virtues and records the conviction of an anonymous Indian elder that "Jesus was an Indian"
(143) because of his opposition to materialism and love of peace.
As preached, then, Christianity is consistent with the fulfilment
of Indian spirituality. But through painful experience Eastman

learned that Christianity and white ideals of civilization are sel-
dom practiced: "I had not seen half of the savagery of civilization!" (139).

Eastman's message to Indians asserts the legitimacy of the
Christian ideal in spite of the white man's failure to practice it:
"My effort was to make the Indian feel that Christianity is not
at fault for the white man's sins, but rather the lack of it, and I
freely admitted that this nation is not Christian, but declared that
the Christians in it are trying to make it so" (149–50). In relation to white readers, Eastman uses the distinction between ideal
and actuality in a very different way: to prod them to practice
true Christianity. For instance, Eastman describes his encounters
with traditional Indians who challenged his Christian beliefs and
rebuked him for advocating white standards of civilization. By
including long quotations from Indians who reject white ways,
Eastman makes clear to white readers their failures, as well as his
own ambivalence about his role as an advocate of assimilation.
At the same time he clearly points out the better course white
Christians ought to take in their future relations with Indians.

In his final chapter, "The Soul of the White Man," Eastman
employs a rhetorical strategy similar to that used by Douglass in
the Appendix to his *Narrative*, pointing out the hypocrisy of the
white man's failure to practice the religion he is so eager to spread:
"They are anxious to pass on their religion to all races of man,
but keep very little of it themselves" (193). The central principle
of white civilization, and what in actuality functions as the white
man's religion, is not Christian love but economic self-interest:
"When I reduce civilization to its lowest terms, it becomes a system of life based upon trade" (194). Eastman views Western history
as the "licenced murder and the plundering of weaker and less
developed peoples" (194). Nonetheless, he still advocates civilization for Native Americans, because "our former simple life is gone
forever" and because "the white man's religion is not responsible
for his mistakes" (195).[19] Eastman's appeal to white people to practice what they preach, as well as his advocacy of Christianity and
civilization to Native Americans, depends on his hope that the
permanent value of these ideals can be separated from the historical record of their use to justify the conquest and destruction of
Native American peoples and cultures. Yet, as in the case of Douglass and so many other multicultural autobiographers, what Eastman shows about the effects of Christianity seems to undermine
his own case and suggests a certain skepticism and doubt.

Eastman, too, makes central to his autobiography an attempt to force white readers to reconsider and reject habitual attitudes and beliefs about their religious and cultural superiority to Indians. He tries to encourage the reader's deconversion from this false ideal as the necessary condition for moving away from hypocrisy toward "the spirit of Christianity, of universal brotherhood" (190).

Autobiographies by African and Native Americans continue to criticize the racism of American culture and to contrast it with Christian ideals. In this they resemble many American social reformers, from the Puritans through Emerson and Melville to Reinhold Niebuhr and Martin Luther King, Jr., who have criticized their supposedly Christian culture in the name of true or authentic Christianity. What might not have been expected, however, is the adoption of this rhetorical strategy even in works by authors who reject Christianity. Autobiographers who view Christianity as inappropriate, misguided, or outright destructive still appeal to the reader to see the difference between this religion properly understood and quasi-religious justifications for white privilege. In numerous recent works by non-Christian writers, the essential goal remains the same as for Douglass and Eastman: to get a largely white audience to see the difference between authentic Christianity and the self-aggrandizing rationales whites have used to justify their power and their exploitation of other races. At the same time, autobiographers who are not Christian devise interesting new rhetorical strategies to achieve this goal. Both continuity and innovation may be seen in the ways *The Autobiography of Malcolm X* and *Lame Deer: Seeker of Visions* critique the white man's religion.

During Malcolm's twelve years as a member of the Nation of Islam (the "Black Muslims"), he delivered countless stinging attacks on Christianity as responsible for the plight of African Americans. He urged blacks to abandon Christianity and embrace his own religion. This message is proclaimed through most of his autobiography. After he converted to Islam, Malcolm maintained a similar position, contrasting Christianity with his new faith: "America needs to understand Islam, because this is the one religion that erases from its society the race problem."[20] During most of his life, and in most of the passages in the autobiography that discuss religion, Malcolm completely rejected Christianity as being inherently racist. He lamented that African Americans did not follow him into orthodox Islam, blaming it on the fact that they "are too indelibly soaked in Christianity's double standard of oppression" (364). Christianity *is* the white man's religion, according to Malcolm X, and he called for massive deconversion. To the end of his life, Malcolm insisted that Christian beliefs helped hold black people in oppressive conditions in America. For example, in a passage used at the end of Spike Lee's 1989 movie *Do the Right Thing*, Malcolm rejects the Christian justification of non-violence: "I believe it's a crime for anyone who is being brutalized to continue to accept that brutality without doing something to defend himself. If that's how 'Christian' philosophy is interpreted, if that's what Gandhian philosophy teaches, well, then, I will call them criminal philosophies" (366–67).

Malcolm X maintained that Christianity was indelibly tainted by its association with racism: "The Christian church became infected with racism when it entered white Europe. The Christian church returned to Africa under the banner of the Cross—conquering, killing, exploiting, pillaging, raping, bullying, beating—and teaching white supremacy. . . . The black man needs to reflect that he has been America's most fervent Christian—and where has it gotten him? In fact, in the white man's hands, in the white man's interpretation . . . where has Christianity brought this *world?*" (368–69). He believed that "very close at hand is the *end* of Christianity," citing Protestant "death-of-God" theology that referred to this as the "post-Christian era" (369). Statements such as these assert what is probably the most negative view of Christianity in African American autobiography, the claim that Christian faith in America is so deeply stained with racism that it should be rejected by anyone, black or white, for moral reasons.

In the last few months of his life, however, Malcolm introduced hints of a new message into his speeches, and his autobiography reveals these evolving ideas. Malcolm realized that it was more realistic and effective to appeal to ideals already held by most Americans than to convert them to Islam. He therefore began to appeal to what I have elsewhere called "public virtues," those virtues affirmed to be normative for persons from any community, rather than only for the members of a particular group or community.[21] In addition, he invoked the moral norms of a form of Christianity that could be distinguished from white racist beliefs and practices. Malcolm recognized that Christianity and Islam share certain beliefs and values, and he began to ask Christians not to abandon their religion but to live up to their professed ideals. At times Malcolm called not for deconversion from Christianity but for repentance and atonement:

I believe that God now is giving the world's so-called "Christian" white society its last opportunity to repent and atone for the crimes of exploiting and enslaving the world's non-white peoples. It is exactly as when God gave Pharaoh a chance to repent. But Pharaoh persisted in his refusal to give justice to those whom he oppressed. And, we know, God finally destroyed Pharaoh.

Is white America really sorry for her crimes against the black people? Does white America have the capacity to repent—and to atone? Does the capacity to repent, to atone, exist in a majority, in one-half, in even one-third of American white society? (370)

Malcolm was skeptical that the will to atone existed in white America. Moreover, the very meaning of atonement was not obvious: "How *can* white society atone for enslaving, for raping, for unmanning, for otherwise brutalizing *millions* of human beings, for centuries? What atonement would the God of Justice demand?" (370). Nonetheless, Malcolm told white persons that what they could do concretely to help African Americans was to fight against racism in their own communities, including churches. His hopes lay in the slim chance that a large number of white Americans would recognize the threats that racism posed to their society.

Malcolm was not sanguine about the likelihood of a radical transformation of attitude and action. For he saw racist attitudes not simply as a matter of conscious belief but as involving unconscious attitudes: "Here in America, the seeds of racism are so deeply rooted in the white people collectively, their belief that they are 'superior' in some way is so deeply rooted, that these things are in the national white subconscious" (363). And racism is not only a matter of individual beliefs but a much more insidious and pervasive matter of social conditioning: "The white man is *not* inherently evil, but America's racist society influences him to act evilly. The society has produced and nourishes a psychology which brings out the lowest, most base part of human beings" (371). If such deeply ingrained attitudes were to be changed, white persons would have to go through a form of deconversion, losing faith in the religious justification of white superiority.

Because Malcolm X was assassinated before he could see the final text of his autobiography, it is impossible to say whether he would have completely approved of Alex Haley's editing of their tape-recorded conversations. It seems fair to conclude, however, that the ambivalence Malcolm felt about Christianity was an essential element shaping his account of his life. On the one hand, far more than most multicultural writers before him, he rejected this faith as hopelessly racist, and by showing its complicity with historical injustices he hoped to encourage widespread deconversions, especially among African Americans. Yet in the last year of his life, assessing more realistically the most probable strategies for achieving his primary goal of racial justice in America, Malcolm adopted tentatively a more constructive message to Christians. Like Frederick Douglass, he appealed to his white audience to recognize and reform racist habits and ideas. He not only continued to condemn the hypocritical religiosity of white Christians but called on them truly to live according to Christian ideals of brotherhood and equality.

Lame Deer: Seeker of Visions is similarly concerned to use the autobiographer's personal story to help his people. Lame Deer was a *wicasa wican*, a Lakota holy man, born in 1903. His autobiography, an "as-told-to" collaboration written with Richard Erdoes, was published in 1972. The narrative is organized topically by chapters, focusing on the central rituals and symbols of the Lakota religious tradition. For instance, particular chapters interpret vision quests, animals, the sweat bath, the ghost dance, the sun dance, the sacred pipe, and the yuwipi ceremony. Lame Deer is not primarily interested in reforming Christianity but rather in describing and winning respect for his own religious tradition. Yet like many other Native American writers since the nineteenth century, Lame Deer seeks this goal by challenging the assumption that only Christianity has value or validity as an understanding of the sacred.

One of his basic strategies is to compare Lakota symbols and rituals with similar Christian practices. The yuwipi ceremony involves the use of 405 tiny rocks found on anthills. These rocks are put in gourds used in the yuwipi rites, in which a medicine man is tied up, released, and delivers messages regarding questions such as the location of lost objects. The yuwipi ritual probably seems incomprehensible to most white readers. To explain the ritual, Lame Deer discusses the broader significance of rocks as sacred symbols in Indian religion, directly addressing the white reader: "To white people this kind of talk seems strange. They have short memories. I have heard that in all the prehistoric caves the world over one finds painted pebbles used in religious rites. Your Bible is full of stories of sacred rocks set up in high places. Think of the Rock of Ages, of St. Peter, whose name means rock. Think of Stonehenge. White people have forgotten this and have lost the power which is in the rocks."[22] Lame Deer wants his white readers to realize that this seemingly bizarre ritual has a commonality with Christian symbolism.

When Lame Deer discusses the sun dance, he recognizes that many readers will condemn as "barbaric" or "savage torture" the four-day ordeal, which involves intense suffering from hunger and thirst, sleeplessness, and piercing of the flesh. So he appeals to Christianity's chief symbol of redemptive suffering, the crucifixion: "Some white men shudder when I tell them these things. Yet the idea of enduring pain so that others may live should not strike you as strange. Do you not in your churches pray to one who is 'pierced,' nailed to a cross for the sake of his people? No Indian ever called a white man uncivilized for his beliefs or forbade him to worship as he pleased" (208–9). For the Lakota, the ordeal of voluntarily endured suffering is not limited to the originating event of a religion's founding figure but is an opportunity and extremely difficult challenge that any believer may seek: "The difference between the white man and us is this: You believe in the redeeming powers of suffering, if this suffering was done by somebody else, far away, two thousand years ago. We believe that it is up to every one of us to help each other, even through the pain of our bodies. . . . Insight does not come cheaply, and we want no angel or saint to gain it for us and give it to us secondhand" (209). The ideal of vicarious suffering emerges clearly in this passage. Again the Christian reader should discern a deeply spiritual experience in what first appeared as only a savage rite.

Lame Deer was a member of the Native American Church for five years, during which time he took peyote. Although when he narrated his autobiography he no longer went to their meetings or took peyote, he presents a sympathetic portrait of "the peyote way" as a form of vision quest. The search for visions, according to Lame Deer, lies at the heart not only of Indian religions but of all religious experience: "At the core of all Indian beliefs are visions gotten in various ways. The Christian and Jewish religion, the great religions of the East, are based on the same thing, only white people have forgotten this" (217). Lame Deer does not deny the significance of differences among religions. However, to help his reader understand Lakota religion and view it sympathetically, he presents the unfamiliar in terms of what the reader presumably knows. Furthermore, Lame Deer directly confronts and challenges the assumption of many readers that only Christianity has any religious value or truth. He must undermine that rigid standard before the non-Indian reader can discern and rightly appreciate the holiness of Native American traditions.

Unlike Malcolm X, Lame Deer does not criticize Christianity at great length, or deny its legitimacy as a religious faith. Yet his challenge to Christians is not peripheral to his main purpose of explaining and affirming Lakota spirituality. He, too, makes the crucial distinction between an original ideal or essence of Christianity and what in fact functions as white society's supreme value: "The trouble is not with Christianity, with religion, but with what you have made out of it. You have turned it upside down. You have made the religion of the protest leader and hippie Jesus into the religion of missionaries, army padres, Bureau of Indian Affairs officials. These are two altogether different religions, my friend" (216). Lame Deer suggests that Christianity has become simply a convenient justification for the established powers.

It is not racism that Lame Deer primarily criticizes as the white man's religion but materialism and exploitation of nature. He asserts that in actuality what functions for whites as the basic determiner of value is money. His first encounter with a white person demonstrated this, when he witnessed a man trying to buy his grandmother's beaded moccasins (24). Lame Deer asserts that white people finally assess everything in the world simply in terms of its economic value, how many "green frog skins" it costs: "The green frog skin—that's what I call a dollar bill. In our attitude toward it lies the biggest difference between Indians and whites. . . . For the white man each blade of grass or spring of water has a price tag on it" (42–43). For instance, only animals that have immediate monetary value are protected on the prairie, so prairie dogs, badgers, foxes, coyotes, and birds of prey are endangered. Lame Deer makes an ironic point out of the threats to the bald eagle, the symbol of the United States: "The big birds of prey used to feed on prairie dogs, too. So you hardly see an eagle these days. The bald eagle is your symbol. You see him on your money, but your money is killing him. When a people start killing off their own symbols they are in a bad way" (44). This little parable suggests the self-destructiveness of white society's economic approach to all reality. The green frog-skin perspective threatens the natural world on which human life depends, including the very symbols with which Americans give meaning to life.

According to Lame Deer, Indians do not accept the frog-skin version of reality but have a fundamentally different understanding of the world. Consequently, they are rejected and despised by whites:

"Because we refuse to step out of our reality into this frog-skin illusion, we are called dumb, lazy, improvident, immature, other-worldly" (44). Lame Deer offers the example of a well-educated Indian who returns to the reservation to open a cafeteria and gas station. His business fails because he will not refuse the many Indians who cannot pay for what they need. It was this Indian's sense of tribal solidarity that brought about failure in the business world. "The whole damn tribe is one big family; that's our kind of reality" (45). Indians fail in the American economy because they have a fundamentally different—a religious—understanding of reality:

> I made up a new proverb: "Indians chase the vision, white men chase the dollar." We are lousy raw material from which to form a capitalist. We could do it easily, but then we would stop being Indians. . . . We make lousy farmers, too, because deep down within us lingers a feeling that land, water, air, the earth and what lies beneath its surface cannot be owned as someone's private property. That belongs to everybody, and if man wants to survive, he had better come around to this Indian point of view, the sooner the better, because there isn't much time left to think it over. (46)

As the last sentence in this quotation reveals, Lame Deer not only describes his understanding of reality but directly challenges the white version. He criticizes both the ecological destructiveness and social injustice of the white man's worldview and its spiritual poverty. The white man's religion is the green frog-skin view of the world, the valuing of everything in terms of its monetary worth. The dominant culture is therefore blind to crucial dimensions of reality: our dependence on the natural world, the interdependence of human beings, the sources of healing and good humor, and the presence of Wakan Tanka—the Great Spirit, the source of sacred power—in the world.

In the final paragraphs of his autobiography, Lame Deer suggests that the Indian's sense of reality, as symbolized by "our most sacred possession" (250), the pipe, may help save the world from destruction at the hands of the white man: "We must try to use the pipe for mankind, which is on the road to self-destruction. We must try to save the white man from himself. This can be done only if all of us, Indians and non-Indians alike, can again see ourselves as part of this earth, not as an enemy from the outside who tries to impose its will on it" (265–66). Lame Deer suggests that what might save the world from destruction is white society's deconversion from the frog-skin version of reality, as well as learning from Native Americans how to apprehend the world in new ways. Seeking these goals, he, too, makes central to his autobiography a critique of the white man's religion.

As we have seen, the white man's religion as differentiated from true Christianity means different things to various writers. Douglass criticizes the "slaveholding religion of this land," and Malcolm X asserts that America nourishes a deep-rooted racist psychology. Eastman speaks of the "licenced murder and plundering of weaker and less developed peoples," while Lame Deer satirically challenges the green frog-skin view of reality. Yet according to each autobiographer, what in fact operates as the highest value in white society inevitably becomes confused with Christian belief. Therefore each writer makes central to his work an attack on the ways Christianity has become entangled with ideas about white culture's inherent superiority or right to dominate other peoples. Each autobiographer acknowledges, in his own way, that it will not be easy to dislodge white readers from their deep-seated belief in their own superiority. In effect, they all hold that what is required is a form of deconversion, a loss of faith in a belief that functions to give meaning, orientation, and reassurance to individuals and to sanction and shape the organization of an entire society.

Native American and African American writers have attempted by various strategies to precipitate such a deconversion by showing white readers the historical consequences of Christian beliefs, presenting the autobiographer's own experiences as an epitome of the lives of people of color. The subtitle of William Apes's collection of autobiographical accounts of five Christian Indians reveals this purpose clearly: "An Indian's Looking-Glass for the White Man."[23] Before the white reader can be recalled to the ideals of authentic Christianity, he must see himself as others do. Self-serving ideals and hypocritical practices must be challenged if Christianity is to be other than a convenient rationalization for privilege and power. In this way, a central task of multicultural autobiography is the prophetic denunciation of idolatry: the form of idolatry that identifies the meaning of Christianity with all that these writers mean by "the white man's religion." Even among those writers most critical of Christianity, such as Malcolm X, most autobiographers have recognized that far more effective than

simply rejecting Christianity is the rhetorical strategy of appealing to the ideals of true Christianity at the same time one criticizes the identification of this faith with the white man's religion. In this way an essentially religious concern—the criticism
of idolatry—continues to shape multicultural autobiography even
in its overtly secular forms.

It would be misleading, however, to see African American and
Native American writers as entirely dominated by their rhetorical
situation in relation to white readers. While there is no question
that, like all writers, black and Indian autobiographers have had to
adapt their stories to their audiences and that the American racial
situation has forced accommodations and silences, it is also true
that people of color have found creative ways to narrate their lives
with integrity—"to tell a free story," as William Andrews puts it.
Distinguishing between Christianity and the white man's religion
is an important act not only in relation to the white reader but
also for the autobiographer's own project of assessing the values
that have shaped his existence and define his present religious
commitments. For many multicultural writers who are Christian,
a crucial issue in the writing of autobiography is how to reconcile this religious commitment with loyalty to one's race, tribe, or
people.

People of color in the United States experienced Christianity
as the religion of the race that enslaved them or violently took
away their land. Furthermore, the early missionaries demanded
not merely adherence to a set of beliefs or doctrinal formulas
but total cultural assimilation. In practice conversion and conquest were inextricably linked, as James Axtell has shown for
the treatment of Indians in colonial America.[24] The conditions
for acceptance into Christianity included the adoption of many
white-defined measures of civilization regarding dress, diet, mode
of dwelling, work, marriage and child-rearing practices, and language. It is not surprising that multicultural writers have been
concerned to demonstrate that the adoption of Christianity does
not necessarily mean the abandonment of ethnic identity. For
this reason the distinction between the white man's religion and
Christianity has been essential not only to educate a white audience but also to show other Indians or African Americans that
Christianity may be affirmed without endorsing cultural genocide
or self-hatred. The delineation of a form of Christianity not linked
to racism shows the possiblility of an act of creative adaptation, of
selective grafting of elements, of synthesis and integration of the

dominant culture of Europe with the distinctive perspective of a minority culture.

The autobiographer's effort to discriminate between Christianity and the white man's religion represents not only a critique of ideology but an act of religious imagination, of identity formation, and of cultural creativity. Scholars of the religions of Native Americans and African Americans have analyzed how these groups have adapted Christianity to their unique situations. For instance, the Native American Church, the ghost dance, the "slave religion" of the American South, and African American spirituals and preaching all involve an ongoing synthesis of elements of the dominant culture's Christianity with distinctively black or Indian traditions. The act of writing an autobiography represents an analogous form of religious creativity. Minority autobiographers work in a literary form that had no exact counterpart in an oral culture that subordinated individual self-expression to the needs of the group. They often employ the themes, conventions, and narrative strategies of the Christian literary tradition, specifically the rhetoric and topics of the conversion narrative, confession, and missionary record. Yet in numerous ways autobiographers assert their racial identity, modifying conventions to tell a story that could only be told in just this way by a person of color.

The term *minority autobiography* is for this reason less accurate than *multicultural autobiography* to describe the personal narratives of people of color. Such autobiographies are inherently multicultural because they reflect an integration of distinct cultures. Writing an autobiography represents the possibility of converting bicultural identity from a source of tragic conflict or self-division into an opportunity for reassessment and creative synthesis of the cultures that shaped the writer. The self-consciously Christian writer such as Eastman, one who rejects Christianity such as Malcolm X or Lame Deer, and a writer with a marked ambivalence and mixed assessment of Christianity such as Frederick Douglass, all undertake in their different ways a critical evaluation and integration of values from both the dominant white culture and their own racial community.

What is most striking about multicultural autobiography is the commonality of the central goal of seeking the reader's deconversion from the white man's religion, regardless of the autobiographer's own relationship to Christianity. In autobiographies by both Native Americans and African Americans for more than 150 years, in writers with vastly differing religious beliefs and political agendas, the fundamental question addressed to white readers is whether they understand—in practice, in the effect on the lives of people of color in the United States—the full implications of the difference between Christianity and the white man's religion.

6

HYPOCRISY AND THE

ETHICS OF DISBELIEF

LOSING ONE'S FAITH may raise various kinds of ethical issues. Past commitments and vows may have to be broken, bonds with loved ones ruptured, and a person may have to defend a negative decision without much confidence in having a better alternative. At whatever point one articulates one's doubts, one may appear to have been dissembling or hiding one's ideas, raising questions about one's truthfulness in both the past and the present. A particular dilemma for conscience arises when a person who has lost religious faith is called to assent publicly to a creed or confessional statement. During the Victorian era a major public controversy, often called the "ethics of belief" debate, concerned the conflict between the demand for assent to the creeds of the Church of England and the commitment to intellectual honesty and integrity.[1] While the terms and topics of this debate have changed, the essential moral issue of honesty in the expression of belief continues to shape twentieth-century discussions of religious belief.[2] The debate about the ethics of belief is not confined to forms of philosophical and theological discourse. Newman's *Apologia* is the paradigmatic example of an autobiography scrupulously examining the morality of expressing doubt and assent about particular Christian doctrines. In autobiographies the logical and epistemological status of a particular belief is not usually analyzed with the detail and rigor of more abstract discourse. However, autobiography's narrative form is especially suited for exploring the ethical dilemma arising when a person has begun to doubt a belief and must decide when and how to inform others, especially those who are part of the rejected religious community.

The doubter who is a member of a religious community falls easily into a position of hypocrisy or false pretense. As the *Oxford English Dictionary* makes clear, hypocrisy originally meant acting a part on the stage. The primary contemporary meaning of hypocrisy is "assuming a false appearance of virtue or goodness, with dissimulation of real character or inclination, especially in respect of religious life or belief." The criticism of hypocrisy arises from the demands of religious faith itself. Hypocrisy is one of the worst sins excoriated in the Bible by Old Testament prophets, Jesus, and Paul. The founder of the Christian autobiographical tradition, Augustine, is also notably adamant about the danger of false outward pretenses of piety, a possibility even when a Christian confesses sins. To feel that one is deceiving others about one's religious beliefs may be equally painful for a person who has lost faith in God. By continuing within the religious community, the doubter may feel that he or she is playing a part, pretending, acting as though in possession of a belief or conviction not there. Such a person may experience troubling uncertainty about how far to comply with the public forms of assent required by a faith community.

What I will call "the ethics of disbelief" means the moral considerations that guide what an individual can believe in good conscience and the scruples that guide how one informs other people of beliefs and doubts. In this chapter, I compare two autobiographies that, in dramatizing a deconversion from Roman Catholicism, highlight the author's search for a morally acceptable resolution to a predicament of religious hypocrisy. Mary McCarthy's *Memories of a Catholic Girlhood* and Anthony Kenny's *A Path from Rome* each shows how growing disbelief placed the author in a position of hypocrisy and how an implicit ethics of disbelief guided the author's exit from the church. McCarthy's work is intriguing in its exploration of an adolescent's developing conscience, and Kenny's autobiography is a particularly significant interpretation of deconversion as a crisis of vocation.

The introductory section of *Memories of a Catholic Girlhood*, "To the Reader," sets forth some of McCarthy's ambivalent feelings about her Catholic upbringing. On the positive side, her mother, who converted to Catholicism at the time of her marriage, gave her children the feeling that it was a "special treat" and a privilege to be a Catholic, that "our religion was a present to us from God."[3] In particular, the aesthetic heritage of Catholicism nurtured Mary's passionate love of beauty. Yet if the faith she learned from her mother and certain priests and nuns was "on the whole, a religion of beauty and goodness, however imperfectly realized" (21), another strain of Catholicism she encountered was "a sour, baneful doctrine in which old hates and rancors had been stewing for generations, with ignorance proudly stirring the pot" (21). McCarthy confronts this narrowness of spirit more among the laity, specifically in some of her own relatives, than among priests and nuns. It is primarily because she discerns pernicious moral consequences of Catholic belief that McCarthy assesses her former faith negatively:

> From what I have seen, I am driven to the conclusion that religion is only good for good people, and I do not mean this as a paradox, but simply as an observable fact. Only good people can afford to be religious. For the others, it is too great a temptation—a temptation to the deadly sins of pride and anger, chiefly, but one might also add sloth. . . . The Catholic religion, I believe, is the most dangerous of all, morally, . . . because, with its claim to be the only true religion, it fosters that sense of privilege I spoke of earlier—the notion that not everyone is lucky enough to be a Catholic. (23)

In addition to uncomfortable encounters with the smugly pious, McCarthy's Catholic upbringing frequently produces situations of disturbing moral ambiguity. From the very start, McCarthy's activities in the church place her in a position of hypocrisy. Her first moral crisis occurs when, on the morning of her first communion, she inadvertently takes a drink of water. After a struggle with her conscience, she does not confess this act, and takes communion in what she believes is a state of mortal sin. The resulting state of "outward holiness and inward horror" is a formative experience that influences not only her later encounters with Catholic Church authorities but her conception of all her moral dilemmas: "Every subsequent moral crisis of my life, moreover, has had precisely the pattern of this struggle over the first Communion; I have battled, usually without avail, against a temptation to do something which only I knew was bad, being swept on by a need to preserve outward appearances and to live up to other people's expectations of me" (20–21). Although McCarthy says that she usually sacrificed her scruples to the need to preserve others' good opinion of her, these situations of hypocrisy are still crucially formative events in her moral development. Even when she fails to live up to her ideals of integrity or honesty, she internalizes the standards that, when violated, produce guilt or shame.[4] Through painful experiences of moral failure, she develops a hatred of hypocrisy that decisively shapes her interpretation of her deconversion.

The crisis that precipitates McCarthy's deconversion is recounted in the story "C'est le Premier Pas Qui Coûte." In this story Mary is a twelve-year-old student at a convent school run by the Ladies of the Sacred Heart. As a new girl at the school, Mary unsuccessfully attempts to gain social recognition. Failing to win fame by goodness, she determines to "do it by badness." The nuns criticize not only "skepticism, deism, and the dread spirit of atheism" but any sign of "the sin of doubt, that curse of fine intellects" (104). Mary decides to "lose-my-faith" before she really comprehends what this means, beyond the fact that the nuns warn the girls against succumbing to this temptation. McCarthy's deconversion is initiated not by deep inward struggles but by an adolescent quest for notoriety. Yet when she tells Madame MacIllvra, the Madame Superior, about her loss of faith, Mary's awkward situation, at first presented very comically, develops into a serious probing of the ethics of disbelief. McCarthy's situation of hypocrisy is as foolish in its origin as Augustine's vandalism of the pears and as significant in its eventual consequences for the autobiographer's self-understanding.

Mary meets with the Jesuit chaplain, Father Dennis. Not wanting to back down and be exposed as a liar, she searches for arguments to explain her claim to have lost faith. Disdaining prayer ("A prayer for atheistic arguments . . . would only bring out the stern side of God"), she thinks about her uncertainties, remembering earlier doubts about miracles, the resurrection of the body, and the divinity of Christ. The priest dismisses her "scholastic questions" and asserts that the Catholic Church has answers for them. But when he cannot or will not explain these answers, Mary suspects that something is being hidden from her. When Father Dennis finally appeals to her to have faith, Mary realizes that she lacks the essential quality that he insists will resolve her uncertainties: "He was not answering my arguments; in fact, he was looking down at me with a grave, troubled expression, as if he, too, were suddenly conscious of a gulf between us, a gulf that could not be bridged by words. The awesome thought struck me that perhaps I *had* lost my faith. Could it have slipped away without my knowing it?" (118). In response to Mary's doubts about the existence of God, the priest recites the five a posteriori proofs of God's existence. Mary's precocious mind discovers a flaw noted by many atheists: "Why can't the universe be self-sufficient if God can? Why can't something in matter be the uncaused cause?" (121). At this, Father Dennis reproaches her for blindness and reading "atheistic filth," adjures her to pray for faith, and abruptly terminates their interview.

The twelve-year-old feels that the entire convent has been so upset by the scandal of her public deconversion that she must recover her faith. Try as she may to produce the feeling of faith, Mary has to recognize her lack of belief. However, out of a sense of public duty she enacts a simulated conversion. "I had a sense of obligation to others and not to my own soul or to God, which was a proof in itself that I had lost God, for our chief obligation in life was supposed to be to please Him" (122). Rather surprisingly, Mary does not feel ashamed of her hypocrisy in this situation. Instead, she blames a second priest who also tries to overcome her doubts by appealing to faith and who Mary feels is forcing her into deception. "By failing to convert me and treating my case so lightly—calling me Thomasina, for instance, in a would-be funny reference to doubting Thomas—he was driving me straight into fraud" (123). And so, after pretending to have a dream, Mary acts out the role of a lost soul reclaimed by God's grace. Although she finds these events extremely disturbing, young Mary feels no guilt or shame, and McCarthy as narrator expresses no regrets about the "simulated conversion" that ends the tense situation. She places the blame for her act of hypocrisy squarely on the shoulders of the church's representatives. This incident is the crisis, the decisive turning point that marks her break from Catholicism.

A striking image concludes McCarthy's version of deconversion: "My own chief sensation was one of detached surprise at how far I had come from my old mainstays, as once, when learning to swim, I had been doing the dead-man's float and looked back, raising my doused head, to see my water wings drifting, far behind me, on the lake's surface" (123). This incident seems a metaphor for McCarthy's lifelong quest for independence and her wish to be free of whatever "mainstays" tether her. The "water wings" she looks back on may represent both her lost faith and her old identity as a good Catholic girl. The passage evokes the strange sensation of self-recognition and self-estrangement that sometimes happens when one looks back on oneself in the past. This final image in the story is a fitting symbol both of autobiography's act of retrospection and of the event of deconversion. Significantly, it is the moment when McCarthy fully acknowledges her deconversion that first elicits the autobiographer's double consciousness of the self's continuing identity and its transformation.

The intriguing title of the story, "C'est le Premier Pas Qui Coûte," suggests connections with the theme of role-playing in the rest of McCarthy's autobiography. Acting a part is not simply a vice always to be condemned. Here the first step for Mary is acting as if she has lost her faith. While role-playing is often experienced as a false position that McCarthy tries to escape, role-playing situations also allow her to envision new possibilities for herself and to experiment with other ways of acting and feeling. Given the convent's "clockwork obedience to authority" (102), this first tentative deviation from prescribed norms of belief allows her to imagine alternatives and raise critical questions. It is the first step that "counts," or "costs," in the sense that it is the hardest or most painful step but sets one's later course. Her role-playing prepares Mary for the actual deconversion that follows later, when she fully adopts as part of her self-understanding the identity of a person who has lost faith.

McCarthy's deconversion is extremely significant not only in its effect on her religious convictions but also in the formation of her identity. For the first time she realizes that she can impress other people by being an intellectual, a non-conformist, and an iconoclast. In the ethos of the convent, doubt is viewed as the "curse of fine intellects" (104). In this story Mary begins to see herself as a person with an independent, critical mind who does not accept the pronouncements of any authority, even though by her outward submission she cannot yet put this new self-conception fully into practice. The way she loses her faith shapes McCarthy's view of several later crises. Again and again, she finds herself in a false position that produces deep feelings of shame because her own role-playing helped to bring about a situation of hypocrisy. It is usually by violating an expectation or rejecting pressures to conform that she believes she can maintain her integrity, although she does not always announce this immediately and publicly. A struggle with her scruples about being a hypocrite marks most of McCarthy's autobiographical stories, and the plot often involves a search for an honorable way of acting or speaking that will resolve the discrepancy between her public image and her private beliefs—or, more often, disbelief. While religious deconversion is the subject of only one story in *Memories*, this incident influences

the way McCarthy interprets the ethical significance of other crucial transitions in her life.

Like the other autobiographers examined in this book, Mc-
Carthy bears the stamp of her faith long after she renounces it. Her
Catholic education shapes the intense scrupulosity that marks her
character both as a girl and, in the italicized comments between
the stories in *Memories*, as narrating autobiographer. She does
not leave Catholicism completely behind with childhood but discloses several ways in which it permanently affected her character.
The strong streak of rebelliousness in her nature is partly attributable to identification with lost causes in Catholic history: "To
care for the quarrels of the past, to identify oneself passionately
with a cause that became, politically speaking, a losing cause with
the birth of the modern world, is to experience a kind of straining
against reality, a rebellious nonconformity that, again, is rare in
America" (25). The "spiritual atmosphere of the convent" (92) plays
an important role in attracting McCarthy to the idea of eventual
purification after much sin: "It might well turn out that the worst
girl in the school, whose pretty, haughty face wore rouge and a
calm, closed look that advertised even to us younger ones some
secret knowledge of men, was in the dark of her heart another
Mary of Egypt, the strumpet saint in our midst" (92). McCarthy's
rebelliousness, which leads to conflicts with Catholic authority
figures, is itself fostered by what she calls the "dark-horse doctrine
of salvation" (93). When, in the story "The Blackguard," a teacher
compares her to Lord Byron as "brilliant but unsound," Mary "had
never felt so flattered" (94). Her conception of the holy sinner
plays a role not only in McCarthy's youthful rebellions but in the
confessional stance of chastened repentance that characterizes so
much of her autobiographical writing.

McCarthy's criticisms of the Catholic Church and its representatives depend partly on the tradition's own standards. The priests
who fail to reckon with her religious doubts blunder not simply
in terms of intellectual acumen but in relation to any conception
of pastoral care. A similar sort of priestly error as was evident in
her deconversion occurs when McCarthy goes to confession after
taking to heart a sermon on unchastity. She had been looking up
details of human anatomy in a medical dictionary and discussing
them with friends. The priest sees no significance in this trivial
action: " 'Is that *all?*' His voice sounded positively indignant. 'Yes,
Father.' 'You mean to tell me that this is your only sin of impurity?' 'Yes.' Before I knew it, he had pronounced absolution, and

the door of the confessional grate was shut almost with a bang, as though I had been imposing on his valuable time. This experience mystified and annoyed me; all through his sermon he had been dwelling on the terrible offense given to God by an impure *thought*" (100–101). If the main effect of this encounter on the young girl was to awaken her curiosity about which sins might be more interesting, the autobiographer looking back discerns the priest's failure to understand and respond to children in a way appropriate to their level of spiritual and moral development. If purity and impurity have any relevence to a girl of this age, Mary's confessor fails utterly to make this clear to her. McCarthy does not criticize the ideal of purity but rather the priest's careless dismissal of what he cannot categorize in terms of a list of sins formulated as physical acts. Although the priest's pastoral practices are inadequate by the church's own standards, McCarthy judges primarily by a common standard of human decency. When the ecclesiastical representatives dismiss Mary's doubts or attribute her ideas to her having read forbidden atheist literature, they show a disrespect for Mary's mind and integrity. Their reaction to her disbelief contrasts unfavorably with Mary's grandfather Preston, who never questioned her sincerity by treating her doubts simply as a "dodge for getting out of Mass." "That a person, even a child, was acting from conscientious motives seemed to him natural and fitting. His fair-mindedness rested on this assumption" (125).

While McCarthy's moral standards are influenced by her Catholic background, she decisively rejects theological beliefs. Her atheistic conclusions are summed up in the final paragraph of "To the Reader," when she rejects Pascal's wager as "too prudential." She finds the idea of a God who would reward her for striking such a bargain to be morally repugnant: "For myself, I prefer not to play it so safe, and I shall never send for a priest or recite an Act of Contrition in my last moments. I do not mind if I lose my soul for all eternity. If the kind of God exists Who would damn me for not working out a deal with Him, then that is unfortunate. I should not care to spend eternity in the company of such a person" (27). In distinguishing between disinterested trust in God and merely prudential concern, McCarthy implicitly formulates a definition of true faith with which many Christians would agree. However, I think McCarthy would reject not only Pascal's wager but any deity who would save or damn human beings according to their theological beliefs. No form of theistic faith is a viable possibility for her, and she is "more than doubtful" that God exists.

Her continuing disbelief is determined by her conscience, by ethical principles that reflect both her Catholic background and her efforts to define her own moral standards. The story of McCarthy's loss of faith represents a twelve-year-old's first inchoate attempt to work out the principles of an ethics of disbelief that would reconcile personal convictions with pressure for public avowal. Even though her "simulated conversion" means that she does not successfully put her ethics of disbelief into practice, the significance of this story is not the immediate success or failure of her actions but the incident's long-term effects on her moral development. McCarthy's position of hypocrisy forced her to think for the first time about the ethics of disbelief. This reflection initiated her mind and her conscience into making more independent and critical judgments and precipitated a deconversion that permanently altered her conception of herself.

One of the primary forms of deconversion narrative is the story of a person for whom a crisis of faith is also a crisis of vocation. The "ethics of belief" controversy in nineteenth-century Britain originally arose in terms of the question of whether a clergyman had to accept the Thirty-nine Articles of the Church of England. Newman's Tract 90 suggested that the Articles could be interpreted in a Catholic manner, and strident arguments ensued as to the validity of such an understanding, whether one had to explain publicly how one understood the Articles, and whether assent could be "general" or required adherence to each particular article. The debate widened to more general questions about the moral justification of any religious belief, and the integrity, sincerity, and candor of all believers.[5] The dilemma of an individual forced into hypocrisy because of a vocational commitment continues to arise, and can provide the narrative structure of a compelling version of deconversion.

A crisis of faith is particularly acute and lends itself to extended autobiographical interpretation when it requires dramatic changes such as rejecting vows of chastity and obedience, leaving a supportive religious community, and finding meaningful and gainful work. In recent decades there have been many such stories, especially by former nuns who have left the convent or the Catholic Church.[6] Yet for most ex-priests and ex-nuns, abandoning their vows is neither precipitated by, nor does it lead to, loss of faith in God. One recent sociological study reports that, for most ex-nuns, leaving the convent did not mean dissatisfaction with their church, but a vocational crisis: "Less than 3% left the church after exiting religious life. The exit process, therefore, and the establishment of an ex identity, involved change in their role as nun, not as Catholic."[7]

An exceptional and unusually powerful account of a vocational crisis that does derive from a deconversion is Anthony Kenny's *A Path from Rome*. This work explores the ethics of disbelief with exceptional clarity and detail and places the analysis of logical and epistemological difficulties within a larger drama of character development. I know of no other work besides Newman's *Apologia* that, in rendering a personal stuggle with highly theoretical ideas, shows how "the whole man moves; paper logic is but the record of it."[8]

Anthony Kenny was born in 1931 and grew up in Liverpool. When he was twelve he decided to be a priest, largely because he admired an uncle who was a priest. The first half of *A Path from Rome* describes Kenny's education in Junior Seminary and then in Rome at the Gregorian University and the Venerable English College. In retrospect Kenny sees that the sheltered life of a seminarian kept him from realizing the disparity between the needs of his own character and the life of a priest. The training for the priesthood provided by the seminary was a misleading preparation for a parish priest's actual way of life. This was so, first, in the very different character of a life of celibacy as seen "from within the walls of a community of fellow-celibates, and from the point of view of a solitary bachelor in a parish of families."[9] Because seminary discipline prescribes both the daily details and the long-range goals of the student's life, one is unlikely to raise fundamental questions. And a seminarian's isolation from secular influences deprives him of the experiences and self-knowledge necessary for a fully informed commitment to the priesthood.

Much of Kenny's mature philosophical work concerns problems of freedom and necessity. An intriguing dimension of *A Path from Rome* is Kenny's analysis of the interplay between elements of choice and the cultural influences that shaped his life. For Kenny, understanding how a particular social environment structured and oriented his actions is not incompatible with discerning degrees of agency, any more than providence conflicts with human freedom for Augustine.

The first philosophical doubts to worry Kenny arise when he examines metaphysical theories the Catholic Church uses to support certain theological doctrines. The proofs for the existence of God seem to him flimsy, and the metaphysics intended to uphold the doctrine of transubstantiation call into question all human knowledge of the world: "For all I could tell, my type-writer might be Benjamin Disraeli transubstantiated; since all I could see were mere accidents, and I lacked any metaphysical eye to see through to the real substance" (72). For a young seminarist in Rome in 1952, to doubt any Catholic dogma is a temptation to deny the faith itself: "The implausibility of the philosophy did strain the student's faith in the dogmas themselves: if they needed support from such ramshackle philosophy, how sound could they be in themselves? This thought, when it presented itself, was of course perceived as a temptation: a temptation to one of the worst sins, doubting the Faith" (72). For the first time, Kenny questions whether his vocation to the priesthood might be a serious mis-take: "I began to realize what misery could lie in a life devoted to the spread of doctrines in which one only half-believed" (73). Giving up Catholicism itself is not yet an issue, only whether he should place himself in the position of defending dogmas he does not fully believe. On his first visit to Oxford during a vacation, the future Master of Balliol College "thought ruefully how agree-able, in those congenial suroundings, would be a life of scholarship untied to a set of dogmas" (74).

For several years Kenny puts aside his doubts while he turns from the study of philosophy to theology. He is emotionally com-mitted to the service of the church, full of "romantic feelings of devout affection" as he performs his first Masses. Yet "the emo-tional investment provided no more adequate a basis for life of fidelity to the priestly ideal than infatuation does for a lasting marriage" (111). From his present vantage point, his dissertation's arguments for the validity of religious commitment look like "a licence to wallow in make-believe."

Kenny's doubts resurface when he goes to Oxford from 1957 to 1959 to study the implications of new forms of linguistic analysis for understanding religious language. As Kenny immerses himself in the analytic philosophy of G. E. Moore and Bertrand Russell, the Vienna circle of logical positivists, and the later work of Witt-genstein, his faith begins to erode. He becomes convinced that Christian beliefs can be justified only if God's existence can be proved: "Faith will not do instead of proof; for faith is believing something on the word of God; and one cannot take God's word for it that He exists" (147). Logically, belief in God's existence is prior to belief in revelation, and Kenny is not convinced by the proofs of

God's existence. At the same time recurring doubts about transubstantiation undermine his confidence in the Catholic sacramental system.

Underlying all these difficulties is a fundamental issue that he can no longer avoid facing: the ethical validity of a faith that dismisses all doubts. Doubt about any one doctrine calls in question the Catholic Church's basic conception of the virtue of faith. If one has this virtue, one does not pick and choose among articles of belief but believes every defined dogma. Kenny, however, cannot give irrevocable assent to many of the "preambles of faith" on which faith rests, including historical assertions about the early church and its authority. He is therefore increasingly troubled by the church's ideal of faith as irrevocable and by its condemnation of every doubt as a sin. "For a Catholic, a doubt about any doctrine is, in a manner, a doubt about every doctrine" (148). Rather surprisingly, Kenny does not discuss the considerable debate within the Roman Catholic Church since Vatican II as to the limits of infallibility in the church's teaching and as to the proper role of dissent.

Certain matters of Catholic ethics trouble Kenny when he becomes a parish priest. The practice of taking stipends for saying a Mass begins to seem obnoxious to him. The arguments for the wrongness of contraception are not compelling. On these issues of Catholic discipline, unlike his intellectual doubts, it would be others who would pay the price if Kenny's teaching of church doctrine was wrong. As a curate in Liverpool, he thinks more and more about laicization, even as he throws himself into forms of social work whose basic goodness does not depend on the truth of Catholic doctrinal claims.

Yet the moral concern that most grips his conscience leads to conflict with the ecclesiastical hierarchy. Although during his seven years at the Gregorian University only one hour had been dedicated to the ethics of warfare, Kenny sees the question of nuclear disarmament as a crucial issue for the Catholic Church. He becomes actively involved in the 1962 campaign to abolish nuclear weapons, convinced that not simply the use but also the possession of nuclear arms is immoral in terms of the Catholic Church's own tradition of ethical reflection on the conduct of warfare. He writes essays to persuade other Catholics that the Christian just-war tradition and secular morality alike proscribe the policy of nuclear deterrence. *A Path from Rome* reproduces numerous letters and essays by Kenny and others concerned with this issue. From Kenny's point of view most Catholic writers leave their readers far too acquiescent about the justification of Britain's deterrent policy. In contrast, Kenny advocates unilateral nuclear disarmament as a moral imperative required by the Christian just-war tradition.

Another issue emerges in these documents: a pattern of subtle censorship whereby the church hierarchy tries to prevent Kenny from expressing his views in Catholic publications. His archbishop cautions him that since "only the simplest statements can be grasped by the average reader" (187), Kenny should not write articles that disturb Catholics by arguing that Britain's nuclear deterrence policies are immoral. Eventually Kenny is forbidden to publish in a Catholic lay publication. Kenny's outspoken honesty about his convictions contrasts strikingly with the equivocation and evasiveness of Catholicism's official spokesmen. And his forthright attempt to educate the average Catholic reader puts in a very bad light the official bureaucracy's pessimism about the laity's ethical capacities. Although Kenny does not directly attack the church for dishonesty, cowardice, or hypocrisy in regard to this issue, he dramatizes how a conflict between his conscience and the pressures brought to bear by Catholic authorities led to another situation involving the ethics of belief and contributed to his decision to leave the priesthood. In discussing the morality of nuclear deterrence, Kenny again found himself caught between his own scruples and views he was supposed to advocate publicly as a representative of the Roman Catholic Church.

In 1963 his increasing doubts about church doctrines and the controversy about nuclear weapons finally compel Kenny to seek laicization. For someone whose entire life had been dedicated to his church, this was not an easy step, and Kenny describes the painful emotions accompanying the public act of disavowal. Adopting the rhetoric of conversion, he describes the difficulty of taking the final step: "I found the leap of disbelief as hard to take as others have found the leap of faith: to walk out of the institution around which my own life and that of all those closest to me had centered for so many years" (189). Examining his motives scrupulously, he ponders T. S. Eliot's lines from *Murder in the Cathedral:* "The last temptation is the greatest treason / To do the right deed for the wrong reason." Finally he decides that "it was a worse treason to postpone the right deed for fear that one was doing it for the wrong reason" (191). For by this time he feels himself to be living the double life of a hypocrite, having to represent and advocate things he privately doubts. "Faith began to seem to be a sacrifice of integrity rather than a virtue" (196). After conversations with other priests, friends, and his archbishop, Kenny petitions the pope to be released from the priesthood. When he marries three years later, he is automatically excommunicated from the Catholic Church.

Of the stages in his deconversion, almost all of Kenny's narration explains the decision to seek laicization; very little is said of his further steps in rejecting any church commitment and any form of theism. The epilogue briefly describes Kenny's life after the priesthood, which centers on his family and his career as Oxford don and philosopher. Summarizing the essential meaning of his deconversion, he presents it as a matter of leaving a situation of hypocrisy: "Having failed as a saint, the best I could do was to gather courage to cease to be a hypocrite" (205). The plot of his autobiography is supposedly "a story of failure": "I have told how I pursued an ideal, failed to achieve it, and grew disillusioned with the ideal itself" (205). In spite of this disclaimer, Kenny's story could only be construed as a failure in the eyes of those committed to the conception of faith he rejects, which certainly does not mean all Christians. A Path from Rome is actually an apologia for his own conduct and a vindication of new ideals discovered in the course of his gradual exit from the church.

This autobiography demonstrates, in particular, the meaning of a central moral virtue that Kenny contrasts with the Catholic virtue of faith. In the last paragraph of the book, Kenny explains the theme of lectures he published as Faith and Reason: "I described the virtue of rationality—the virtue of right belief, standing between the opposed vices of credulity (which believes too much) and scepticism (which believes too little)" (210). If "the virtue of right belief" is defined in an Aristotelian manner as a mean between extremes, different individuals will have to learn to compensate in different ways for the bias of their character and cultural background. For Anthony Kenny, learning to practice right belief means moving away from the uncritical faith of his early years, which he would now interpret as a form of the vice of credulity. Learning the meaning of the virtue of right belief means, too, formulating an ethics of disbelief that will justify and guide the expression of questions and doubts.

Unlike most ex-priests and ex-nuns, Kenny is not a practicing Catholic, and he cannot imagine himself ever making this sacrifice of integrity: "However much the pendulum of faith and disbelief may swing within my mind, I can never again imagine accepting the infallible authority of the Catholic Church and the full panoply of Catholic teaching" (207). The reforms within the Roman Catholic Church since the Vatican II Council do not make acceptance of the church's authority any more palatable for him, for developments of doctrine raise the basic question of whether other—or any—beliefs or practices should be accepted as dogma. Things now regarded as certain, essential, or infallible may prove with hindsight to have been mistakes. "If the Church has been as wrong in the past on so many topics as forward-looking clergy believe, then her claims to impose belief and obedience on others are, in the form in which they have traditionally been made, mere impudence" (207). Here one wishes Kenny had discussed Catholic ideas about the development of doctrine, though perhaps he sees these as evasive. One wonders, too, how Kenny views the many practicing Roman Catholics, including feminist nuns and priests committed to liberation theology, who in good conscience feel free to disagree with current church teaching.

The virtue of right belief does not mean that Kenny rejects all aspects of Catholic tradition. As well as his continuing appreciation for the life of religious communities and for the intellectual and aesthetic riches of Christian tradition, Kenny affirms many aspects of the Catholic Church's moral teachings. He would still argue, I think, that the just-war tradition provides sound arguments against the use or possession of nuclear weapons, even though he can no longer take comfort in "the thought of a divine Judge standing beside the righteous who have disarmed themselves before the Russian threat" (182). He asserts against "the liberal agnosticism of the world in which I live" (207) that Catholicism is fundamentally right in opposing abortion, even though it is fundamentally wrong in opposing contraception. There is much in Catholic practice and thought that Kenny still affirms, and his autobiography includes not only judicious criticism but appreciation for the life of worship, service, learning, and companionship that he knew as a priest.

The virtue of right belief as Kenny interprets it requires that he be not an atheist but a certain kind of agnostic. He must be a "restless" agnostic who continues to search for whatever knowledge is possible on matters of ultimate concern:

> I do not know whether there is a God or not. Some philosophers
> believe that it is impossible for anyone to know whether there is a

God or not: they claim that agnosticism about the existence of God is something built into the human condition rightly understood. I do not find their arguments convincing, any more than I find the arguments for theism or for atheism convincing. The agnosticism which I profess is, in philosophical terms, a contingent and not a necessary agnosticism: the agnosticism of a man who says "I do not know whether there is a God, but perhaps it can be known; I have no proof that it cannot be known." Contingent agnosticism of this kind is bound to be a restless agnosticism: on a topic so important one is bound to prefer knowledge to uncertainty. (208)

Kenny continues to attend church services (usually Anglican), though he does not receive communion or recite any creed. His philosophical writings often concern natural theology and the relationship between reason and religious beliefs. Although he concludes that logically there cannot be a God with all the traditional attributes asserted by Christians, he rather surprisingly concludes one of his books with a defense of agnostic prayer. Although the image of an agnostic praying to a God whose existence he doubts may seem comic, this action is "no more unreasonable than the act of a man adrift in the ocean, trapped in a cave, or stranded on a mountainside, who cries for help though he may never be heard or fires a signal which may never be seen" (210).

A Path from Rome ends, then, with Kenny explaining how his present convictions and uncertainties differ from those of theists and atheists. His conclusions are decisively influenced by his having been caught for so long in a situation of hypocrisy, and by his efforts to practice "the virtue of rationality—the virtue of right belief." In Kenny's life, learning the meaning of this virtue involved developing an ethics of disbelief to correct the vice of credulity, to authorize his expression of doubts, to justify his leaving a position of hypocrisy as a priest, and to guide his future avowals and disavowals in a more conscientious and responsible way.

7

SARTRE'S
AMBIGUOUS ATHEISM
"A Cruel and
Long-range Affair"

SARTRE'S TREATMENT OF his loss of faith in Christianity shows
that theistic belief was never a real possibility for him. He portrays himself as simply turning away in indifference from ancient
beliefs that are irrelevent to most people in the twentieth century. *The Words* resembles the works I discussed in chapter 3, in
which deconversion from religious faith provides a metaphor for
a different kind of personal transformation. Sartre's focus is not
on institutionalized religion, orthodox doctrines, or a traditional
community of faith but on his loss of faith in a secular alternative to religion. He uses the form of the conversion narrative to
interpret his commitment to what I shall call "the myth of literature." Sartre's originality is that although he does not directly describe the process of deconversion from this myth, he constantly
reminds us that he has lost faith in it. He frequently points out
analogies between his youthful commitment to a literary vocation
and a religious conversion, but always from an ironic, detached,
and disillusioned perspective. Sartre's atheism is deeply ambiguous, for in spite of his criticisms of theistic beliefs and the rhetoric
of conversion, both the values and the language of Christianity

decisively mold his perspective on his childhood. Similarly, his devastating criticisms of his faith in the redemptive power of literature do not disguise his continued commitment to aspects of this myth. *The Words* is a fascinating and paradoxical version of deconversion, not least because of the ironies involved in using autobiographical "words" to criticize the bad faith that motivated his boyhood commitment to the words of literature.

Sartre grew up in a nominally Christian home but was indifferent to religion and had lost his faith by the age of twelve. He was officially raised as a Catholic by his mother and grandmother, but the influence of his anticlerical grandfather was stronger. Sartre intuited the hollowness of his family's professed beliefs. He presents Christianity in the Schweitzer family, as in most members of the French bourgeoisie, as an empty formality: "My family had been affected by the slow movement of dechristianization that started among the Voltairian upper bourgeoisie and took a century to spread to all levels of society. Without that general weakening of faith, Louise Guillemin, a Catholic young lady from the provinces, would have made a show of greater reluctance to marry a Lutheran. Of course, our whole family believed in God, as a matter of discretion."[1] Christianity was "the common heritage," the normal condition, a comfortable and tolerant identity that demanded little. "In our circle, in my family, faith was merely a high-sounding name for sweet French freedom" (99). Belief in God was not an active force in this society, but the heritage of Christianity survived as an opportunity for social occasions or aesthetic appreciation. Sartre's mother and grandmother believed "in God long enough to enjoy a toccata" (27). Seeing that religion made no real difference in the lives of his relatives, Sartre could simply reject it as irrelevent. "At bottom, the whole business bored me. I was led to disbelief not by the conflict of dogmas, but by my grandparents' indifference" (100–101).

In contrast to these descriptions of a gradual fading of interest in religion, Sartre provides one brief scene in *The Words* dramatizing the young boy's decision to reject God: "Only once did I have the feeling that He existed. I had been playing with matches and burned a small rug. I was in the process of covering up my crime when suddenly God saw me. I felt His gaze inside my head and on my hands. I whirled about in the bathroom, horribly visible, a live target. Indignation saved me. I flew into a rage against so crude an indiscretion, I blasphemed, I muttered like my grandfather: 'God damn it, God damn it, God damn it.' He never looked at me again"

(102). The incident echoes the theme of "the look" in Sartre's philosophy: the idea that consciousness of another person's judgment can corrupt one's integrity. God appears in this scene as a violator of the human conscience, a spying, accusing authority who subjects the individual to an arbitrary standard. Sartre concludes that religious faith never had a chance: "Failing to take root in my heart, He vegetated in me for a while, then He died" (102).

The place of Christianity in Sartre's life was taken by a surrogate religious faith: the myth of literature. Sartre makes this secular alternative to religious faith the focus of *The Words*, exploring in great depth how he became committed to a literary vocation. The myth of literature involves a number of related components, such as the romantic conception of the writer as a man set apart from others and accountable only to his own genius. Literature's value was tied to the nineteenth-century bourgeois ideal of individuality and to belief in progress—"progress, that long, steep path which leads to me" (34). Sartre presents his desire to live by and for words as bound up with his relationship to his family, especially his grandfather, and as a commitment to an essentially bourgeois conception of order, hierarchy, and value. The virtues of the writer—hard, solitary work that would lead to fame and prosperity—were the virtues of the middle class during a particular historical epoch. The myth of literature was essentially optimistic, patriotic, and, for the aspiring would-be genius, self-congratulatory: "We young gentlemen . . . discovered to our satisfaction that our individual progress went hand in hand with that of the nation" (235).

As we shall see, Sartre recognized that a fundamental aspect of his character was the desire to break free from belief in any supposedly authoritative value outside the self. Hence *The Words* might alternatively be said to portray a deconversion from the myth of the family, or French nationalist ideology, or the modern doctrine of progress in history, or teleological conceptions of either the individual person or human history—from any belief, in fact, that denies the freedom and responsibility of the individual to choose the nature of his or her existence.[2] In my view, the central myth that Sartre attacks in *The Words* is indicated by the title of this work: the faith that the ordering of words in literature is the most important human endeavor. It is the origin and development of his belief in the supreme value of "words" that Sartre's autobiography simultaneously dramatizes and denounces. In this regard, *The Words* has much in common with Sartre's massive (2,800 page) work on Flaubert, *L'Idiot de la famille*, which explores the great novelist's commitment to "art for art's sake" in the form of literary authorship.

Sartre presents his commitment to literature using numerous explicitly religious metaphors: "I had found my religion: nothing seemed to me more important than a book. I regarded the library as a temple" (59). Reading and rereading stories with his mother becomes a ritual that imparts the sense of a fixed and eternal order: "I was at Mass: I witnessed the eternal recurrence of names and events" (48). Sartre's grandfather, a teacher of foreign languages, functions as the chief priest of this religion, "the minister of the cult" (62). Charles Schweitzer is a patriarch who "so resembled God the Father that he was often taken for Him" (22). Schweitzer, "minister manqué, faithful to his father's will, had retained the Divine and invested it with Culture" (178). Sartre says that through his entire life he struggled to overcome his boyhood idolization of his grandfather and his values.

The two parts of *The Words*, "Reading" and "Writing," demonstrate how literature functions for Sartre to give meaning to a boring life and to "justify" his existence, which as an orphan he felt to be precarious, unsubstantial, and unnecessary. Sartre dramatizes how as a boy he turns to literature to escape these feelings of worthlessness. In one such moment of ennui he thinks: "I'm a fly, I've always been one. This time I've touched bottom. The only thing left for me to do is to pick up *The Adventures of Captain Corcoran*" (247). Suddenly life recovers its meaning as the boy feels called to heroic achievement: "It's this thrilling instant that my glory chooses for returning to its abode; at that moment, Mankind awakes with a start and calls me to the rescue and the Holy Ghost whispers its staggering words in my ear: 'You would not seek me if you had not found me'" (248). Reading provides young Sartre with an imaginary existence possessing the meaning, excitement, and justification he feels are lacking in his life.

Sartre's emerging sense of identity as a writer was first based on being a hero: "I palmed off on the writer the sacred powers of the hero" (167). Later he "transformed the writer-knight into a writer-martyr" who sacrificed his own life for others: "I regarded works of art for a long time as metaphysical events, the birth of which affected the universe. I dug up that fierce religion and made it mine in order to gild my dull vocation. . . . I confused literature with prayer, I made a human sacrifice of it. My brothers, I decided, were quite simply asking me to devote my pen to their redemption. They suffered from an insufficiency of being which, were it not for the intercession of the Saints, would have doomed them permanently to destruction" (179). At the heart of the myth of literature lie the central Christian promises: martyrdom, salvation, and immortality. Sartre believes that he is like a priest, "offering myself up as an expiatory victim" (180); he imagines the Holy Ghost looking over his shoulder as he writes, appeased by the would-be author's patience and suffering. Instead of eternal life, the literary artist was to be rewarded for his self-denial with earthly immortality. "Removed from Catholicism, the sacred was deposited in belles-lettres and the penman appeared, an *ersatz* of the Christian that I was unable to be: his sole concern was salvation; the only purpose of his sojourn here below was that he merit posthumous bliss by enduring ordeals in worthy fashion" (249).

Sartre shows a variety of ways in which the myth of literature takes on dimensions of religious faith, including the ritualized, ceremonial aspects of reading and writing, the provision of an ascetic code of behavior, an ideal of altruism, a concept of destiny much like predestination, and an idealistic view of language as the supreme reality: "To name the thing was both to create it and take it. Without this fundamental illusion I would never have written" (60). As writer, Sartre acts out most of the roles the church has offered: priest, saint, savior, member of the predestined Elect, martyr, and mystic. Although the Christian God is dead for Sartre, the Holy Ghost of Literature usurps his place in the young boy's life: "The Other One remained, the Invisible One, the Holy Ghost, the one who guaranteed my mandate and who ran my life with his great anonymous and sacred powers. . . . For a long time, to write was to ask Death and my masked Religion to preserve my life from chance. I was of the Church. As a militant, I wanted to save myself by works; as a mystic, I attempted to reveal the silence of being by a thwarted rustling of words and, what was most important, I confused things with their names: that amounts to believing" (251). By using these numerous and varied Christian metaphors, then, Sartre presents his adoption of the vocation of a writer as a faith commitment. "I thought I was devoting myself to literature, whereas I was actually taking Holy Orders" (250).

The originality and interest of Sartre's work for this study of deconversion lies especially in the peculiar way he presents his faith in the myth of literature. Sartre does not explain how he came to reject his literary ambitions as a form of "bad faith." Nor does he dramatize his later conversion to a political conception of the writer's vocation, which provides the normative perspective from which he condemns his misplaced beliefs. Yet *The Words* depends, in an indirect way, on this second conversion, as Philippe Lejeune asserts: "The authentic sequel to *Les Mots* would be, on the level of analysis, the story of what made the writing of *Les Mots* possible, that is to say, of the *conversion*. *Les Mots*, as a matter of fact, is related to religious autobiographies of conversion. Backward conversion here, that goes without saying. But it doesn't matter. The new convert examines his past mistakes in light of the truths he has conquered."[3]

Although neither deconversion from the myth of literature nor conversion to new beliefs is the explicit subject matter of *The Words*, both experiences are constantly implied and assumed by the narrator's perspective on the past. The reader is continually reminded that the author of *The Words* completely rejects his former view of literature. The narrator's perspective is not merely detached; it is harshly acerbic, criticizing his former illusions in a bitter tone only occasionally relieved by a more wry humor. For instance, the book *Michael Strogoff*, which inflamed Sartre's desire to be a romantic hero, gave him false notions of destiny: "For me that book was poison: was it true that certain individuals were chosen?" (131). Again and again we are reminded of the illusory nature of the beliefs the boy accepts: "Filthy twaddle: I gulped it down without quite understanding it; I still believed it at the age of twenty" (179). Sartre discloses the underlying motivations and psychological needs expressed in the boy's budding desire to be an author. Young "Poulou" was searching for a way to justify his existence, seeking the acclaim of others, and avoiding the reality of his own humdrum life and certain mortality. "This hocus-pocus succeeded: I buried death in the shroud of glory" (195). The narrator is disdainful, sarcastic, and cynical—almost unrelentingly negative about his childhood: "I loathe my childhood and whatever has survived of it" (164). Sartre's primary interest is debunking his illusions as a naive youth and mercilessly criticizing their sources in the family and culture that shaped him.

The reader glimpses only fleeting hints of how and when the actual process of deconversion took place—for instance, in a passing reference to "the lucid blindness from which I suffered for thirty years" (250). (Even the dating is ambiguous: thirty years from his first years, when Sartre began to appropriate the myth of literature, or from when the autobiography ends, when Sartre was eleven?) At the end of *The Words* Sartre states that "for the last ten years or so I've been a man who's been waking up, cured of a long, bitter-sweet madness" (253). (Does this statement refer backwards from the mid-1950s, when Sartre did most of the writing of the autobiography, or from 1964, when *Les Mots* was published?) We can date his deconversion from the myth of literature very roughly as occurring during the late 1940s and early 1950s, when Sartre's political consciousness gradually awakened and he asserted the need for a writer to be engaged in larger issues than his own career.[4] Sartre's political commitments evolved over a number of stages from the outbreak of World War II through his commitment to Marxism in the early 1950s. Perhaps it is partly because his deconversion from the myth of literature was a drawn-out process that took place haltingly in relation to these transformations of political conviction that Sartre avoided the difficult task of dramatizing it. Perhaps he did not want to define his present beliefs in a way that would suggest a permanence and finality insulated from further historical events. In any case, while there are scattered references to his evolving understanding of literature in shorter pieces such as *What Is Literature?* Sartre did not include those years in his principal autobiographical work, which ends in 1916, when Sartre was eleven.

The Words reflects, but does not record, this prolonged midlife crisis and reconception of the proper goals of writing. What is most striking about the book as a version of deconversion is its deliberate avoidance of any positive assertions of the author's later views. In this respect, *The Words* is similar to Gosse's *Father and Son.* But whereas Gosse dramatizes the actual process of deconversion, Sartre only describes his conversion to a faith that he later came to see as a dangerous illusion. Without actually knowing how it came about, we are continually reminded of the author's deconversion, as he debunks the ideological bias and self-serving implications of the myth on which his life was based. Deconversion is reflected in narrative point of view but not the plot—in Sartre's tone and sensibility, not his represented experience as protagonist.

In the last few pages of *The Words* Sartre suggests that deconversion—the rejection of all forms of faith—shapes his view of his whole life. "The retrospective illusion has been smashed to bits; martyrdom, salvation, and immortality are falling to pieces; the edifice is going to rack and ruin; I collared the Holy Ghost in the cellar and threw him out; atheism is a cruel and long-range affair: I think I've carried it through" (253). Sartre indicates here that he views his life as a systematic effort to destroy the various faiths that in turn captured his loyalty. Thus deconversion is presented as a dominant plot of his life's story and a project that continues to orient his activity as autobiographer.[5] (The other primary narrative pattern Sartre uses repeatedly in *The Words* is recovery from a mental illness, which takes the form of the psychological case history.)[6] Just as the myth of literature is presented as the equivalent of a form of faith, so atheism is a metaphor for Sartre's attempts to debunk this secular faith. Atheism is not a fixed position but "a cruel and long-range affair": a process and project of deconversion.

Both forms of Sartre's atheism—his rejections of Christian faith and of the myth of literature—are ambiguous in their incompleteness. Throughout his life Sartre's thought reflects his involvement with religious issues.[7] Early in *The Words*, Sartre comments humorously on the contrast between the polite indifference to religion characteristic of his social milieu and the passionate convictions of the professed atheist:

> An atheist was a "character," a wildman whom one did not invite to dinner lest he "lash out," a fanatic encumbered with taboos who refused the right to kneel in church, to weep sweetly there, to give his daughters a religious wedding, who took it upon himself to prove the truth of his doctrine by the purity of his morals, who hounded himself and his happiness to the point of depriving himself of the means of dying comforted, a God-obsessed crank who saw His absence everywhere and who could not open his mouth without uttering His name, in short, a gentleman who had religious convictions. The believer had none. (98)

This passage does not simply caricature a comic figure; it defines Sartre's character as atheist and as autobiographer. Just like the declared disbeliever who is a "God-obsessed crank," Sartre displays his fascination with what he professes to hate. This is true on two levels. In spite of his lack of faith in God, *The Words* is permeated with such Christian themes and symbols as the nature of salvation, providence, the Incarnation, and expiatory suffering. Secondly, in spite of Sartre's professed disbelief in his substitute for religious faith, that is, in the myth of literature, *The Words* demonstrates his continuing faith in the writer's power to give meaning to existence.

Sartre's ironic use of the form of the conversion narrative is the perfect vehicle for expressing these complex ambivalences. Believing in the capacity for conversion, for total transformation of character, suits Sartre's deepest desires to escape his own past: "A few years ago, someone pointed out to me that the characters in my plays and novels make their decisions abruptly and in a state of crisis, that, for example, in *The Flies*, a moment is enough for Orestes to effect his conversion. Of course! Because I create them in my own image; not as I am, no doubt, but as I wanted to be" (238). The language of conversion was used by Sartre throughout his life, for example in a famous remark in *Being and Nothingness:* "These considerations do not exclude the possibility of an ethics of deliverance and salvation. But this can be achieved only after a radical conversion which we cannot discuss here."[8] Sartre saw a radical conversion of consciousness as crucial to authenticity and escaping from bad faith.

However, it is not conversion but deconversion, "the noble mandate to be unfaithful to everything" (242), that best expresses Sartre's character. He devalues everything about his past and stresses its discontinuity with his present identity. The theme of treachery and betrayal, a central one in his other works, applies to his own psychology: "I became a traitor and have remained one" (238). To criticize his past actions is not difficult for Sartre, for to do so implies that he has advanced, developed, overcome old errors. "I'm always ready to criticize myself, provided I'm not forced to. In 1936 and 1945, the individual who bears my name was treated badly: does that concern me? . . . I heap abuse on myself: I behaved conceitedly, I acted selfishly, I'm heartless; it's a joyful massacre; I revel in my lucidity; to recognize my misbehavior with such good grace is to prove to myself that I couldn't act that way now" (240). One can always believe that one will do better tomorrow. Sartre shows the inescapability of "the chronological hierarchy, the only one that leaves me a chance to do better tomorrow" (241), and thus provides confidence about the future. This passage also suggests why his fundamental commitment to human freedom is expressed in the distinctive form of a narrative that implies his deconversion. Sartre is always casting off from the past; choice and change are more often symbolized by decisive rejection of old ideas or commitments than by new undertakings. "Sartre's method of moving forward was to move violently against his earlier self. . . . Sartre could never quite afford to let his self-hatred catch up with him, but he gave it carte blanche to play against his past."[9]

Although at the end of *The Words* Sartre questions the validity of faith in progress and seems unable to decide whether he still maintains that faith, he never doubts that moving away from old commitments brings freedom. He provides a telling image of this basic tendency in his character:

> In 1948, in Utrecht, Professor Van Lennep showed me some tests in which slides are used. My attention was riveted by a certain card: it showed a horse galloping, a man walking, an eagle flying, and a motor-boat shooting forward. You were asked to tell which picture gave you the greatest feeling of speed. I said: "It's the motor-boat." . . . At the age of ten, I had the impression that my prow was cleaving the present and yanking me out of it; since then, I have been running, I'm still running. For me, speed is measured not so much by the distance covered in a given time as by the power of uprooting. (231–32)

The power to uproot or wrench oneself away from the past is for Sartre the crucial index of an individual's freedom. Thus there are particular reasons involving his temperament and fundamental outlook that make the theme of deconversion highly appropriate for expressing Sartre's interpretation of his life.

The Words does not explain which new values replaced Sartre's lost faith in the myth of literature. His work is "one of the comparatively rare instances of an autobiography that inverts this [conversion] pattern, moving as it does from the discovery of belief to the eventual loss of conviction *without* at the same time affirming an alternative vision of the truth."[10] As we have seen earlier in this book, however, especially in the case of Edmund Gosse, it is virtually impossible for an autobiographer not to reveal his present values as he criticizes a religious faith. Furthermore, one never leaves the past behind completely, and the idea of a complete rejection of earlier beliefs is usually too simple to account for those beliefs' continued influence. As Sartre says of his faith in "the chronological hierarchy," for instance, "more recently acquired knowledge undermines my old certainties without quite destroying them" (241). Let us look more closely at these ambiguities, examining first the continuity between his early beliefs and his view of literature at the time when he composes his autobiography.

In the last few pages of *The Words*, Sartre reveals the long-term influence of the myth of literature even on his present aims in writing. He notes the irony that he continues to write despite his theoretical rejection of writing as a way to save or justify oneself. "I've given up the office but not the frock: I still write. What else can I do?" (253). Writing is not just a bad habit but an essential need that has become part of his character: "That old, crumbling structure, my imposture, is also my character: one gets rid of a neurosis, one doesn't get cured of one's self" (254). Some of his earliest motivation for writing persists, for "all of the child's traits are still to be found in the quinquagenarian" (254). Sartre shows that his early attitude to literature was not simply a neurosis from which he could recover but a much deeper commitment that shaped his essential project in life. He describes his life's work as an attempt to see his atheism through to the end, that is, to demolish all total systems of belief and commitment. Nonetheless, Sartre all but confesses that his continued effort to realize this goal in the form of writing expresses what amounts to a religious faith.

One form of continuity between Sartre's pre- and postdeconversion attitudes toward writing is his scrupulous conscience. Sartre's assertion that, because of the early death of his father, he has "no superego" is obviously false. Much of his writing, including *The Words* itself, is vitally concerned to denounce as immoral various forms of self-righteousness in both others and himself. In this sense Sartre reveals a typically Protestant preoccupation with the "sins" of complacency and pride. According to one scholar, "Protestant as well as Catholic services include the words: 'If we say we have no sin, we deceive ourselves and the truth is not in us,' and his denunciations of bourgeois hypocrisy and self-satisfaction have a quality which recalls the diatribes which Protestant thinkers from Calvin to Kierkegaard have hurled against the morally complacent."[11] Sartre's attitude to his own writing reveals unrelentingly harsh self-criticism: "My commandments were sewn into my skin; if I go a day without writing, the scar burns me; if I write too easily, it also burns me" (164). He discerns that his compulsive need to write reflects the long-term influence of Charles Schweitzer and wonders "whether I have not consumed so many days and nights, covered so many pages with ink, thrown on the market so many books that nobody wanted, solely in the mad hope of pleasing my grandfather" (163). Although Sartre tries to break the grip of his earlier beliefs about literature, his present compulsions and scruples about writing indicate that the myth of literature has permanently affected his conscience and his character as a writer.

Sartre's tone at the end of his work is enigmatic: Is he bitterly disillusioned or bemused at his inability to break free from the past? Is his continuing adherence to the myth of literature painful to admit, or is he largely playing a role, assuming a part?[12] In any case, he is highly conscious of the irony that it is through writing that he frees himself from the idolatry of the written word, through cleverly deploring the effect of words upon him that he effects his liberation, and through a skillful rhetorical performance that he overcomes his mystification by the myth of literature. *The Words* both perpetuates and critizes his obsession with and idolatry of words. Sartre's deconversion is not complete, then, and this plot is an only partially adequate narrative strategy for interpreting his life.

Although Sartre discerns continuity with his earliest motivation, his changed view of literature does make a crucial difference in the reasons why he continues to write. Another ambiguity in *The Words* is that in spite of Sartre's apparent determination to withhold his present convictions, he cannot help revealing the standards by which he judges the myth of literature to be pernicious. At the conclusion of *The Words*, Sartre examines the validity of his motivation for writing after his deconversion from the myth of literature, and in doing this he reveals obliquely some of his present convictions. Perhaps, he reflects, he is still hoping for a kind of literary immortality, still secretly waiting for the writer's reward of future glory: "I sometimes wonder whether I'm not playing winner loses and not trying hard to stamp out my one-time hopes so that everything will be restored to me a hundredfold" (254). By acknowledging and criticizing this as a possible motivation, Sartre shows the distance he has come from his earlier days as a writer. If literature cannot claim the sort of ultimacy it once had for him, there are still valid reasons for writing: "Culture doesn't save anything or anyone, it doesn't justify. But it's a product of man: he projects himself into it, he recognizes himself in it; that critical mirror alone offers him his image" (254). This passage suggests that while writing cannot provide sufficient meaning to provide the sole purpose of a life, it may still play an essential role as a "critical mirror" in which a writer—and readers—may move closer to self-knowledge. Although this hope is considerably more modest than some of Sartre's claims about politically committed literature, it is a distinctly different ideal from the aesthetic pleasure of belles lettres or simply an artist's personal glory. It is no coincidence that in 1964, the year *Les Mots* was published, Sartre declined the Nobel Prize for Literature partly because of his "unwillingness to be 'consecrated' or taken over by European humanism and the middle classes, that is, his desire to remain a radicalized figure."[13] Sartre's idealism about the social and political role of literature was not purged but continued to shape his writing in *The Words*.

Sartre's grandfather announced the boy's destiny to be a writer as if he were "Moses dictating the new law" (158). What is objectionable about the myth of literature to Sartre is not only its understanding of the writer's role but the fact that this identity was imposed on him and that he accepted it passively: "I fled; external forces shaped my flight and made me" (248). Sartre sees all religious faiths as based on an abdication of personal responsibility, on accepting alien values and refusing to freely choose one's own values. In this sense, as he once put it, a person's experience of "the sacred is the mark of his alienation."[14] When Sartre allowed himself to be defined as a writer, it was tantamount to a religious conversion, a flight from the task of authentic self-creation: "A tremendous collective power had entered me. Lodged in my heart, it lay in wait. It was the Faith of others. All that was needed was to rename its customary object and to modify it superficially. Faith recognized the object beneath its disguises, which fooled me, and then sprang at it, squeezing it in its claws" (250). Although Sartre criticizes the conception of the writer-as-genius that is part of the myth of literature, there is nothing intrinsically wrong with writing per se. It is just that this identity—or better, this project—should be freely chosen, not accepted in a blind act of faith. Sartre had to go through a deconversion before he could devote himself to writing as a mature, self-critical commitment. By devising a narrative structure that both records a misplaced conversion and reflects a deconversion, Sartre demonstrates the wrong kind of commitment not simply to writing but to any vocation or project.

Traditional Christian accounts of conversion experiences usually express the writer's sense of the invasion of personality and the overwhelming of the self by an outside authority. Sartre opposed this aspect of conversion, in spite of his acceptance of other elements associated with conversion, such as the ideal of a radical redirection of one's life through one's own efforts. This ambivalence about conversion may explain why Sartre does not dramatize his turn toward the values that replaced the myth of literature. It would be impossible for Sartre to write—without the considerable irony we see in *The Words*—the usual kind of conversion story, even one recording his coming to his present political convictions. Instead, he used the narrative form of a conversion story as rendered from the perspective of a deconverted nonbeliever to express his beliefs in individual freedom and responsibility.

A striking aspect of the ending of The Words is Sartre's continued adherence to the myth of self-creation. As Charmé argues, a pervasive theme in Sartre's work is the way biographical and autobiographical writing may use the terms of sacred myth to express a person's struggle for self-definition.[15] This belief in the possibility of self-creation is deeply enmeshed with the myth of literature that Sartre rejects in The Words. Sartre criticizes the extreme individualism of the view that a person can save himself and transcend his society simply by putting words on paper, pointing out that a writer is always a product of his or her environment. Yet in spite of his rejection of this aspect of the myth of literature, Sartre implicitly continues to believe in the possibility of self-creation, and, indeed, believes that this process is the most essential task of his life. His belief in the imperative of self-creation functions like a sacred myth for Sartre.[16] The Words perpetuates this myth, dramatizing Sartre's continuing efforts to break free of past determinations through the writing process, especially by means of the autobiographical act. Sartre's reflections at the end of The Words show that he can only partially liberate himself from his former faith in literature as an effective means of self-transformation and as a strategy for creating a new version of the self. His deconversion from early illusions about literature is incomplete so long as he still believes in the possibility of self-creation through writing.

In the last paragraph of the book, Sartre discloses the ambiguity of his atheism. He shows both his character's continuity before and after his loss of faith in the myth of literature, as well as the difference that deconversion makes to his understanding of the proper motivation for writing: "What I like about my madness is that it has protected me from the very beginning against the charms of the 'elite': never have I thought that I was the happy possessor of a 'talent'; my sole concern has been to save myself— nothing in my hands, nothing up my sleeve—by work and faith. As a result, my pure choice did not raise me above anyone. Without equipment, without tools, I set all of me to work in order to save all of me. If I relegate impossible Salvation to the proproom, what remains? A whole man, composed of all men and as good as all of them and no better than any" (255). This passage reveals Sartre's undiminished commitment to hard work as a means of giving one's life meaning (and probably reflects the long-term influence of certain Protestant virtues). Faith is his constant concern when he rejects religion for writing, and even now, as he denounces his former faith in writing because of new commitments. The final paragraph demonstrates his continuing ambivalence about the idea of salvation, which is both "relegated" as "impossible" "to the proproom" and yet asserted to be his "sole concern."

Sartre struggles, too, to denounce elitism in every form, and to assert the fundamental equality of all humans. His "madness"—his commitment to a literary vocation—protected him from one form of elitism because he believed that he must earn any success the hard way rather than simply displaying a natural talent. This is one of the few aspects of his early years that Sartre defends: his belief that talent does not elevate him above others. When in his forties he began to criticize the traditional conception of literary success, he came to see his early ambitions as involving a more subtle kind of elitism. In rejecting the myth of literature, what Sartre most wishes to affirm are the values of equality and solidarity with others, epitomized in his consciousness that he is "as good as all of them and no better than any." Sartre distinguishes his new sense of solidarity with others from his solitary and isolated existence as a bourgeois intellectual. Yet ironically he expresses his solidarity primarily though the solitary activity of writing.

Thus the ending of *The Words* epitomizes the ambiguities involved in Sartre's use of deconversion to interpret his life. Sartre's reflections reveal his consciousness that the pattern is too simple, for the values he rejected in the past insistently make their presence felt—for instance in his continuing need to write despite the theoretical assertion that such writing will not save anyone or justify a writer's existence. Both of his forms of atheism are ambiguous, for his loss of faith both in Christianity and in the myth of literature is belied by the persistence of the beliefs and forms of language whose legitimacy he denies.

In addition, Sartre's work shows the impossibility of separating his story of deconversion from the beliefs and values to which he turned. The past is judged as false according to a standard that is reflected in a narrator's perspective on his former life. Aspects of Sartre's later beliefs are revealed in spite of his attempt to maintain the pose of a sarcastic, iconoclastic critic of all affirmations.

Sartre makes deconversion a matter of the narrator's perspective rather than the protagonist's experience—of the autobiographer's point of view rather than his subject matter—to express his understanding of freedom and authenticity. As he presents the story of his conversion to the myth of literature, dramatizing his self-deceiving commitment but not the process of disillusionment, Sartre implies his reasons for deconversion from that secular faith. While he does not articulate his present views in depth, *The Words* reveals both the continuity of Sartre's lifelong commitment to words as his primary work and destiny and the difference his deconversion from the myth of literature makes to his view of writing.

8

APOSTASY AND APOLOGY
IN CHRISTIAN
AUTOBIOGRAPHY

WE HAVE EXAMINED variations, revisions, and innovations in both the content and the form of deconversion narratives as autobiographers have interpreted their experiences of transformed loyalties. All the autobiographers discussed so far have looked back on a lost faith from very different religious perspectives. What happens when autobiographers interpret deconversion after returning to the original religious faith they abandoned? New issues arise and new narrative strategies are called for when writers perceive their deconversion as the act of apostasy, or rebellion against God.

C. S. Lewis, Dorothy Day, Langdon Gilkey, and Edwin Muir all went through a deconversion that they later reversed by returning to Christian faith. These writers were swayed by a modern critique of religion or by distinctively modern attitudes to Christianity as an obsolete and discredited ideology. In writing an autobiography, each writer dramatizes the ordeal of conscience that led first to alienation from Christian faith and then to a recovery of faith. From the perspective of recovered faith, each views a deconversion experience as apostasy, rebellion against God. Each autobiographer offers an appology for Christian beliefs that focuses on the experience of apostasy, defending the faith from the criticisms that once seemed decisive.

The term *apostasy* originally implied a normative claim about the truth and authority of the beliefs denied. It therefore has a different sense from the neutral modern word *deconversion,* although both words denote a loss of religious faith. *Apostasy* is a strongly judgmental word implying condemnation, like *schismatic* or *heretic.* The original meaning of apostasy denoted a public renunciation of faith and was reserved for those who abandoned Christianity for another exclusive and institutionalized religion. In the early centuries apostasy came to be applied especially to false prophets and teachers, those heretics on the ambiguous margins of the Church.[1] As in Judaism, widespread apostasy was predicted at the impending apocalyptic end of the world. Apostasy was a term used by a Christian to speak of another person who publicly renounced Christianity. In this chapter reference to apostasy within autobiography assumes the perspective of one who has recovered his or her faith. In keeping with the history of this term, and to distinguish it as one form of deconversion, reference to an autobiographer's apostasy implies the vantage point of religious commitment to a faith once rejected.

An apology is not an excuse or expression of regret but a vindication or justification of a course of action or set of beliefs—or, as in Cardinal Newman's *Apologia Pro Vita Sua,* of an entire life as founded upon deliberate belief. Christian autobiography is apologetic theology in the first-person mode.[2] The most compelling modern apologies, I think, take the form of autobiographies that recognize the insights of modern critiques of religion and reinterpret Christian faith in their light but do so without compromising the core of Christian tradition. In autobiography this is not achieved by correlating theories and doctrines or by means of a systematic interpretation and explanation of all the articles of Christian belief, central tasks in other modes of Christian apologetic. The autobiographer's method is to show the existential consequences of different systems of belief. Apologetic theology in the first-person mode analyzes and demonstrates the practical implications of disparate beliefs in the writer's life.

In the autobiographical works of Day, Lewis, Gilkey, and Muir, an experience of deconversion decisively shapes the interpretation of reconversion and the presentation of the nature of Christian faith. In these compelling modern Christian autobiographies the reasons for a loss of faith are not simply condemned or dismissed. Rather, the entire autobiography is structured by the writer's attempt to respond to the genuine insights of a modern critique of religion.[3] Each writer explains why the arguments against Christianity that were once so convincing are no longer persuasive. The experience of apostasy, then, is of crucial importance in the writer's apologetic efforts to interpret the meaning and significance of Christian faith to an age and audience in which disbelief and skepticism about religion are widespread. The interpretation of apostasy from the perspective of recovered faith is the organizing principle of these apologies for Christianity.

These works are in this sense Augustinian, for the *Confessions* is not only a story of conversion (and of deconversion from Manicheism) but a profound meditation on the reasons why Augustine fell away from his youthful training in Christianity. Like modern apologies, too, Augustine's work refutes a challenger and rival of orthodox Christian faith, contrasting the Christian understanding of God and of the material world with the Manichaean faith that had led him away from the church.

Like Augustine, Christian autobiographers through the ages have dramatized an early falling away from faith as apostasy even when it did not involve public denunciation of Christianity. A preeminent example of a Christian autobiographer who views a youthful loss of faith as apostasy is Tolstoy, whose *Confession* records the dissolution of his Orthodox Christian beliefs when he was eighteen. Tolstoy interprets his waning faith in terms of the influence of his social class, which isolated religion from the rest of life: "My break with faith occurred in me as it did and still does among people of our social and cultural type. . . . The teachings of faith are left to some other realm, separated from life and independent of it."[4] His presentation of his return to Christian faith some three decades later reflects the same contrast between the corrupting influence of the educated and affluent classes and the inspiring example of the Russian peasants. After an exhaustive and disillusioning survey of human wisdom, Tolstoy adheres to the life and faith of his idealized Russian peasant. Rejecting the decadent "parasites" and "spoiled children" among whom he had lived and worked for most of his life, Tolstoy finds the answer to his agonized search for ultimate truth in the faith of simple, uneducated working people. Their basic virtues and faith contrast with all the elements of the Orthodox Church Tolstoy opposed: "the sacraments, church services, fasts, bowing before relics and icons" (77).

Tolstoy does not attempt to refute specific ideologies or critiques of Christian faith, and in this he differs from the twentieth-century autobiographers to be discussed. However, he is intensely concerned to demonstrate the folly of the secular outlook that he adopted (as well as the errors of Orthodox believers). Tolstoy's apology for his version of Christian faith takes the form of showing the ultimate meaninglessness and the destructive consequences of the values he held during his time of apostasy. Tolstoy's "faith" as an apostate was in "knowledge, poetry, and the evolution of life," and as an artist he was one of its "priests" (19). He castigates the vanity of modern intellectuals and artists who believe that their activities will somehow benefit others and thus justify their lives. "In order to avoid the obvious question—'What do I know and what can I teach?'—the theory explained that it is not necessary to know anything and that the artist and the poet teach unconsciously" (19). Believing this self-congratulatory theory resulted in "a pathological pride and the insane conviction that it was my mission to teach people without knowing what I was teaching them" (20). Tolstoy tries to demolish another modern article of faith, confidence in evolutionary progress, by describing the shattering effects of witnessing an execution and of seeing his brother's agonizing death. He dramatizes his recognition of the futility of all his literary ambitions: "Very well, you will be more famous than Gogol, Pushkin, Shakespeare, Molière, more famous than all the writers in the world—so what?" (27). Tolstoy suggests that all human achievements and joys—family, wealth, literary achievement, fame—are illusory and empty without faith in God. Every secular value claims preeminence, and should be seen as potentially idolatrous from the point of view of Christian faith.

Tolstoy's and Augustine's works demonstrate that a harsh and bitter condemnation of the secular world and of one's own past may struggle with a Christian autobiographer's desire to discern God's providence and grace in all things. This conflict is rarely resolved completely; Augustine and his successors deeply regret that they did not find God sooner, even as they try to discern some good in the past life they so completely reject. Christians who have once abandoned their faith may become compelling autobiographers if they can exercise both empathy and judgment toward that mysterious and alien individual, the apostate self. Persons who have changed so radically as to have experienced a total reversal of orientation toward their deepest commitment—twice— lack an obvious coherence of self and temporal continuity in their lives. They may therefore seek to order their conceptions of identity and personal history through an act of the imagination. Such a Christian autobiographer, subjecting both past and present acts and beliefs to the assessment of conscience, will probably discern continuities between the period of apostasy and the present life. Yet each may well puzzle over the mystery and otherness of that former self, asking "How *could* I once have believed that, and rejected God for so long?"

In the first of the three parts of *The Long Loneliness*, "Searching," Dorothy Day describes how her education, work as a journalist, and involvement in socialist organizations destroyed her youthful faith. She made a deliberate choice to stifle religious yearnings, viewing Christianity according to Marxist doctrine: "I felt at the time that religion would only impede my work. I wanted to have nothing to do with the religion of those whom I saw all about me. I felt that I must turn from it as from a drug. I felt it indeed to be an opiate of the people and not a very attractive one, so I hardened my heart. It was a conscious and deliberate process."[5] The church's only function seemed to her to be that of comforting the victims of social evils, and since Day believed in the necessity of basic structural changes in social organization, "the word charity became something to gag over" (87). Her desire to struggle actively for justice came to "conflict with religion, which preached peace and meekness and joy" (41). To Day it appeared that only those committed to a socialist society were capable of self-sacrifice and energetic resistance to evil. So she abandoned her Christianity as an impediment to progressive social change. Day also rebelled against the conflict between the spirit and the flesh engendered by her Protestant background. She quotes from letters written when she was fifteen, which hold that it is wrong to "think so much about human love. All those feelings and cravings that come to us are sexual desires. . . . It is sensual and God is spiritual" (34). Like most Anglo-Saxons, wrote Day, her sexual mores made her "more intense, more sensual, more conscious of the flesh which we continually denied. . . . To me the world meant the flesh and the lure of the flesh, the pride of life one felt when in love. This conflict was to go on for years" (35). Day rejected Christianity for many years because she felt that it denigrated the goodness of the world and of human love. These two reasons for Day's apostasy, her commitment to social justice and her rejection of what she saw as a world-denying Puritanism, set the terms for her Christian apology in the second and third parts of *The Long Loneliness*.

In the second part of her autobiography, entitled "Natural Happiness," Day explains how the experiences of love and having a baby brought her to God. Speaking of her love for her common-law husband, Forster Batterham, she affirms that "his ardent love of creation brought me to the Creator of all things" (134). She was moved not by a world-denying flight from reality but by a wish to affirm the natural world's ultimate ground and source. Thus, Day emphasizes the continuity of concerns motivating first her deconversion and later her conversion to Roman Catholicism. Wrestling with her earlier belief that religion is the opiate of the people, she reasoned that "I am praying because I am happy, not because I am unhappy. I did not turn to God in unhappiness, in grief, in despair—to get consolation, to get something from Him" (133). The crucial chapter "Love Overflows" strongly accentuates Day's primary motive of gratitude to God for the good things of creation: "Forster had made the physical world come alive for me and had awakened in my heart a flood of gratitude. The final object of this love and gratitude was God. No human creature could receive or contain so vast a flood of love and joy as I often felt after the birth of my child. With this came the need to worship, to adore" (139). Insisting on her overwhelming desire to affirm "a whole love," she rejects that interpretation of her conversion that typified her own earlier view of Christianity: "It was not because I was tired of sex, satiated, disillusioned, that I turned to God. Radical friends used to insinuate this. It was because through a whole love, both physical and spiritual, I came to know God" (140).

Many Christian autobiographies simply ignore the skeptic's doubts about the validity of conversion; critical perspectives are dismissed as reflecting a lack of faith. Day's apology, however, shows her understanding of some of the psychological repressions that can be involved in Christian belief and practice. And her lyrical evocation of the period of her life on Staten Island with Forster, the baby, the ocean, and the sensual delights of the seashore demonstrates that Day's understanding of Christian faith discerns common grace at work in the natural world, in contrast to the life-denying version of Christianity she always rejected.

Day became a Roman Catholic in 1927, but for the next five years her conscience was troubled by her apparent defection from the political struggle for justice: "I was just as much against capitalism and imperialism as ever, and here I was going over to the opposition, because of course the Church was lined up with property, with the wealthy, with the state, with capitalism, with all the forces of reaction. This I had been taught to think and this I still think to a great extent" (149). The third section of *The Long Loneliness*, "Love Is the Measure," is primarily the story of the organization that Day founded with Peter Maurin, the Catholic Worker

Movement. Her interpretation of this movement's significance is strongly influenced by her period of apostasy. Her communist background determined the choice of the name for the movement's newspaper, *The Catholic Worker*, which echoes *The Daily Worker* (175). She presents her personal vocation and the Catholic Worker Movement as Christian responses to the injustices that had originally motivated her commitment to a socialist program and principles. The newspaper, the soup kitchens, "houses of hospitality," protests against the inequities and suffering in a capitalist economy, pacifist activities, and attempts to create and enlarge communities of cooperation on every level—all these activities demonstrate concretely that Christian faith need not lead to passivity or acquiescence in an unjust social system. Day reveals, as well, the spiritual searching and the trust in God that guided and sustained the involvement of the Catholic Worker Movement in so many political issues. Thus she makes clear that the life of the Christian is more than moral action, essential as such action is. Day strongly suggests that without such a religious faith, efforts to change society will either expire in frustration or lead to bitter cynicism and violence.

Unlike many Christian responses to the Marxist critique, Day acknowledges the truth of the charge that the church has often legitimated oppression by tacit consent if not open advocacy. Day's attitude toward official Christianity was one of decided ambivalence—or, more positively stated, of loyal opposition and prophetic internal challenge: "I loved the Church for Christ made visible. Not for itself, because it was so often a scandal to me. Romano Guardini said the Church is the Cross on which Christ was crucified; one could not separate Christ from His Cross, and one must live in a state of permanent dissatisfaction with the Church" (149–50). Her testimony provides compelling autobiographical evidence that socialist ideals and the Christian faith may be not only compatible but mutually supportive.

The Long Loneliness, then, is a sustained effort to respond to the two criticisms of Christian faith that led Dorothy Day to abandon her religion. Her apology defends Christianity in terms of the same values that explained and justified her apostasy: her wish to affirm the goodness of the natural world and her commitment to social justice.

C. S. Lewis describes the reasons for his apostasy in an early chapter of *Surprised by Joy*, ironically entitled "I Broaden My Mind."

While he later found philosophical reasons to justify his lack of faith, Lewis experienced elusive feelings during his thirteenth year that for many years predisposed him to agnosticism. "It is perhaps just these early experiences which are so fugitive and, to an adult, so grotesque, that give the mind its earliest bias, its habitual sense of what is or is not plausible."[6] Lewis describes the influence of a school matron whose "passion for the Occult" and "spiritual lust" for the preternatural "loosened the whole framework, blunted all the sharp edges, of my belief" (60). He recreates his childish difficulties with prayer when a "false conscience" set an impossible standard of "realization" for each act of prayer. Reading the classics led him to doubt the grounds for Christianity's claim to be the one true religion. And a certain fatalism and pessimism inclined him to accept a sort of "Argument from Undesign" in the universe's slipshod organization. These factors were not logically connected, but they all worked against Christianity. "And so, little by little, with fluctuations which I cannot now trace, I became an apostate, dropping my faith with no sense of loss but with the greatest relief" (66). Moral criticism of Puritanism did not figure in his rejection of Christianity, as it did for so many English apostates and for Dorothy Day. Having a "pagan" sensibility in his attitude to the flesh and the world, he was not struggling to break free of irrational guilt: "This is why I often find myself at such cross-purposes with the modern world: I have been a converted Pagan living among apostate Puritans" (69).

Lewis describes his book as "not a general autobiography" but "the story of my conversion" (vii). The early parts of his life are explored only so that his spiritual crisis may be understood in the context of his long-term development: "In the earlier chapters the net has to be spread pretty wide in order that, when the explicitly spiritual crisis arrives, the reader may understand what sort of person my childhood and adolescence had made me" (vii–viii). Among the things that his net takes in, Lewis is most interested in an elusive feeling he calls "joy," which is quite distinct from mundane pleasures. Joy is "an unsatisfied desire which is more desireable than any other satisfaction" (17–18). Unlike pleasure, joy is never in our power, and unlike happiness, joy involves an element of grief or unsatisfied longing. Much of *Surprised by Joy* details Lewis's frustrations in trying to produce this experience by his own efforts. When joy does come to him, it is usually as an element of imaginative encounters, as in his discovery of "Northernness" in Norse mythology, or his childhood desire to "possess Autumn," inspired by reading Beatrix Potter's *Squirrel Nutkin* (16). Lewis's experiences of joy in connection with "Northernness" taught him to appreciate something that had been totally lacking in his prior knowledge of Christianity—the disinterested adoration that is the essence of worship: "If the Northernness seemed then a bigger thing than my religion, that may partly have been because my attitude toward it contained elements which my religion ought to have contained and did not. . . . There was in it something very like adoration, some kind of quite disinterested self-abandonment to an object which securely claimed this by simply being the object it was. . . . Sometimes I can almost think that I was sent back to the false gods there to acquire some capacity for worship against the day when the true God should recall me to Himself" (76–77).

Lewis's intense search for joy thus stands in the sharpest contrast with his bored disaffection with Christianity. We may attribute his apostasy to the total failure of Christianity as he had known it to satisfy one of the deepest parts of his nature, his imagination. The reasons for Lewis's loss of faith are similar to the aesthetic critique of Protestantism in the autobiographies of Gosse and Ruskin, discussed in chapter 4. The story of "a life in which, plainly, imagination of one sort or another played the dominant part" (82), *Surprised by Joy* responds to criticisms of Christianity that Lewis associates with the romantic movement, which takes imaginative experience as its highest value. Some romantics, such as Wordsworth, from whom *Surprised by Joy* takes its title, maintained a positive connection with Christianity, reinterpreting the natural world and human experience with its symbols. Other advocates of the imagination turned away in disgust from a religion seen as dismally stale and dull, as Edmund Gosse rejected the form of Calvinism he knew as a child.

Lewis identifies himself early on as a romantic (5, 7), interprets his experiences of nature as romantic (152, 155), and undergoes a phase of rebellion against "all that sort of romanticism which had hitherto been the chief concern of my life" (201). He describes his frustrations in recapturing joy as "the Wordsworthian predicament, lamenting that 'a glory' had passed away" (166). When Lewis devotes so much of his autobiography to classifying different kinds of imaginative experience and recording his development in these terms, he demonstrates his concern to reconcile Christianity and the romantic vision of human life. During his time of apostasy Lewis saw nothing in common between Chris-

tian faith and the search for joy. His presentation of his early
life emphasizes the aesthetic and imaginative poverty of a certain sort of routinized Christianity and shows how during his
apostate period he searched for joy in literature, music, and the
natural world.

Lewis's description of his conversion is interpreted largely in
terms drawn from his analysis of joy. His return to faith is a progression from materialistic realism through idealist metaphysics
to a vague theism, and finally to orthodox Christianity. In the
course of these shifts, Lewis slowly reconciles the imaginative
and intellectual sides of his nature. At the beginning of this evolution of belief, "the two hemispheres of my mind were in the
sharpest contrast. On the one side a many-islanded sea of poetry
and myth; on the other a glib and shallow 'rationalism'" (170).
Lewis carefully documents his intellectual development before
his final conversion to Christianity, about which he says surprisingly little. He realized that joy is only possible when one ceases
making one's own experience an object of desire and attends dis-
interestedly to whatever outside the self arouses desire. Since the
"enjoyment and the contemplation of our inner activities are incompatible" (218), joy vanishes when we begin to contemplate this
feeling rather than what evokes it. He linked his new clarity about
joy as "a road right out of the self" with his idealistic philosophy,
holding that our yearning for unity with a greater reality gives us
"a root in the Absolute" (221). Then he realized that one cannot
worship an ideal or a Hegelian Absolute. Finally, "in the Trinity
Term of 1929 I gave in, and admitted that God was God, and knelt
and prayed: perhaps, that night, the most dejected and reluctant
convert in all England" (228).

In the final chapter Lewis presents Christianity, rather too
briefly, as the only religion able to satisfy the claims of both imagination and intellect: "If ever a myth had become fact, had been
incarnated, it would be just like this. . . . Here and here only in
all time the myth must have become fact; the Word, flesh; God,
Man. This is not 'a religion,' nor 'a philosophy.' It is the summing
up and actuality of them all" (236). The Christian story resembles
myth as well as history and it appeals to the moral sense; "the
intellect and the conscience, as well as the orgy and the ritual,
must be our guide" (235). Although complex theological questions
are skirted at the end of the book, it is important to recognize the
focus of Lewis's purpose in his autobiography. He is not writing
systematic theology but an apology that centers on the place of

imaginative experience in personal development. His basic argument, I think, is that Christianity does nurture the imagination, at the same time that it locates the proper place of imagination in the larger context of human existence. Lewis also suggests that the unsatisfied longing in his search for joy was finally a yearning for God.

Lewis comes to understand that true worship requires the kind of self-abandonment and awe that he had previously associated only with aesthetic experience or communion with nature. In spite of his concluding disclaimer that "the subject has lost nearly all interest to me since I became a Christian" and that joy is "valuable only as a pointer to something other and outer" (238), his conversion story takes the life of the imagination as the hermeneutic lens for understanding both his own life and the nature of Christian faith. He asserts that while imaginative experience is "not necessarily and by its own nature" a step toward the religious life, "God can cause it to be such a beginning" (167n). Lewis figures the relation of the imagination to the spiritual life as a "reflected image" of a superior reality: "I think that all things, in their way, reflect heavenly truth, the imagination not least. 'Reflect' is the important word. This lower life of the imagination is not a beginning of, nor a step toward, the higher life of the spirit, merely an image. In me, at any rate, it contained no element either of belief or of ethics; however far pursued, it would never have made me either wiser or better. But it still had, at however many removes, the shape of the reality it reflected" (167).

Thus Lewis interprets his deconversion from Christianity in terms of a search for joy outside that tradition and presents his reconversion in the light of his new understanding of how the life of the imagination is properly understood within the Christian life: as a potential aspect of all experience and an essential ingredient in the act of worship. Lewis's first-person apology interprets both his apostasy and his return to God in terms of an essential value in his literary and cultural context, the imagination. As do the other Christian autobiographers examined in this chapter, Lewis appeals to values and concerns that have often been used to criticize Christianity to explain both what motivated his apostasy and why his renewed faith does not dismiss or deny those values. He shows how Christianity integrates the imaginative life into its conception of human existence more adequately than do other outlooks. In particular, Lewis demonstrates that making the meaning and purpose of one's life consist solely in the pursuit of imaginative joy leads finally to an egocentric life that is blind to the real sources of joy, which lie outside the self.

Langdon Gilkey's *Shantung Compound* does not cover the author's entire life but focuses on a crucially formative period, the three years he spent in a Japanese internment camp in China during the Second World War. During this period Gilkey moved from an optimistic liberal theology to a "crisis in belief," when he lost interest and confidence in Christianity, and finally to a "realistic" theology based upon the insights of Paul Tillich and Reinhold Niebuhr. *Shantung Compound* uses insights gained from an experience of apostasy to explain the author's renewed and reinterpreted Christian faith.

Gilkey's "crisis in belief" arises when he perceives the deep-rooted self-interest that makes his fellow internees unwilling to cooperate, share material resources, or make a sacrifice for others.[7] This recognition threatens the shallow optimism of theological liberalism and naturalistic humanism alike. Gilkey had already begun to question his "collegiate idealism, resting uneasily on a naturalistic base" (72) during the years of Hitler's rise to power, when he saw that the ideals of peace and justice conflicted. Although he had been deeply interested in the work of Reinhold Niebuhr, Gilkey's faith before his internment "was not so much the result of any personal religious experience as it was the intellectual conviction that only in terms of the Christian view of things could I make sense out of the social history in which we live and the ethical decisions we humans have to make" (73). His "theological jargon" and "secondhand concepts" at first seem hopelessly out of place in the camp at Weihsien, when so much practical work needs to be done. "It was not that I thought religion wrong. I simply thought it irrelevant" (73).

Perhaps it exaggerates Gilkey's alienation from Christianity to speak of his apostasy, for he never actively opposes this religion or embraces atheism. His rejection of Christianity, like that of many modern apostates, is less dramatic than this, and simply relegates faith to a matter of individual preference. His loss of faith appears in retrospect as a gradual adoption of the "secular" outlook that religion is "merely a matter of personal taste" without any essential "value for the common life of mankind. . . . I was a man convinced that while religion might help those who liked it, it was a waste of time for others. Certainly 'the others' now included myself" (74). Thinking that religion makes no practical difference to the pressing daily concerns of Shantung Compound, Gilkey abandons Christian faith, not with any grand gesture, but, as is true for most twentieth-century apostates, gradually and casually, through a loss of interest and the press of alternative commitments. "I went back to the confident humanism so characteristic of the liberal academic circles in America I had recently quitted" (75).

Gilkey does not use the term *conversion* in speaking of his renewed appreciation of the truths of the Christian theological tradition. His religious development involves correlating his personal experiences in the internment camp with the theological works of Reinhold Niebuhr and Paul Tillich. Yet *Shantung Compound* is as much a conversion narrative as Augustine's or Lewis's; it is a compelling story of how a person comes to both a deeper faith in God and a more adequate theological position. Gilkey realizes that his recently adopted humanism, as much as the theological liberalism of the early twentieth century, has a naive and unrealistic confidence in both human rationality and human goodness. His work on a housing committee and in the kitchen shows him the extreme difficulty—the virtual incapacity—human beings experience in being generous or even fair when they are not completely secure about their future. This insight is expressed in the book's epigraph, a phrase from Brecht's *Threepenny Opera:* "For even saintly folk will act like sinners / Unless they have their customary dinners."

At the same time that Gilkey comes to see the great difficulties humans have in being just, he realizes why the very survival of human community depends on the moral capacity of its members. As the various nationalities and age groups, dormitories and units of labor quarrel over space, food, and "perks," the threat of violence looms ever larger. When the camp proves unwilling to grant its own government the power to enforce its laws, the possibility looms that Shantung Compound will disintegrate into anarchy. Gilkey arrives at a dilemma: "Two things that apparently contradicted each other had become transparently clear in this experience. First, I had learned that men need to be moral, that is, responsibly concerned with their neighbors' welfare as well as their own, if human community was to be at all possible; equally evident, however, men did not or even could not so overcome their own self-concern to be thus responsible to their neighbor" (162).

Gilkey's final theological position recognizes the truth of both sides of this paradox. His interpretation of Original Sin as the symbol of human self-love follows the tradition of Augustine and

Niebuhr: "The reality to which the symbols of the 'Fall' and of 'Original Sin' point is not really the particular and dubious act of Adam. Rather it is this fundamental self-concern of the total self which, so to speak, lies below our particular thoughts and acts, molds them, directs them, and then betrays us into the actual misdeeds we all witness in our common life" (116). Gilkey uses Tillich's notion of ultimate concern—a person's "deepest spiritual center" or "center of devotion"—to explore connections between religious faith and moral action and to suggest how Christian faith might enable persons to transcend self-concern. When a person gives his ultimate commitment to his own welfare or to that of a group, he cannot be fair when these concerns are threatened. As Niebuhr put it, injustice is the inevitable social consequence of idolatry of one's own interests or group. Gilkey suggests the possibility, however, that an ultimate concern with God might allow humans to be genuinely moral:

> The only hope in the human situation is that the "religiousness" of men find its true center in God, and not in the many idols that appear in the course of our experience. If men are to forget themselves enough to share with each other, to be honest under pressure, and to be rational and moral enough to establish community, they must have some center of loyalty and devotion, some source of security and meaning, beyond their own welfare. . . . Given an ultimate security in God's eternal love, and an ultimate meaning to his own small life in God's eternal purposes, a man can forget his own welfare and for the first time look at his neighbor free from the gnawings of self-concern. (234)

Gilkey argues, as well, that only belief in God's providence allows humans to respond creatively to history's contingencies and to the inevitable frustrations of our intentions and plans. The final sentence of *Shantung Compound* sums up his apology for a reinterpreted understanding of the Christian doctrines of Original Sin and providence: "Only in God is there an ultimate loyalty that does not breed injustice and cruelty, and a meaning from which nothing in heaven or on earth can separate us" (242).

Gilkey's rhetorical strategy for establishing the truth of Christian faith involves a critique of the naturalism, liberalism, and humanism that are the bedrock faith of most of those nonbelievers likely to read his book. The analysis of the ideology of modern social science, for example (93–96), discloses the wishful thinking at work in optimism about technical solutions to moral and political problems. Gilkey's apology is essentially an autobiographical version of Niebuhr's method in *The Nature and Destiny of Man*, whereby the truth of Christianity becomes a matter of relative adequacy to human experience in comparison with other modern myths such as the Marxist vision, Deweyan naturalism, and so forth. Gilkey's perspective also recalls Augustine's insights into the ways that "lesser goods"—all the finite things of creation that are good, but not the supreme good—appeal to humans as centers of meaning and value. When given inordinate commitment, these lesser goods both fail to satisfy our desires and morally corrupt us. Gilkey attempts to show that an ultimate concern may be expressed in any human endeavor and that only an ultimate concern for God provides the possibility—but not the certainty—of a rare transcendence of self-interest.

Another aspect of Gilkey's apologetic strategy is to emphasize the broad applicability of his insights so that readers cannot relegate them to the peculiar circumstances of a unique time and place. In the last chapter, "After It Was All Over," Gilkey describes how he discerned in America's postwar situation the same moral dilemmas he had faced in Shantung Compound. Seeing the response of Americans to the challenges of reconstruction, Gilkey realizes that the human problem remains identical: "Could we summon the moral strength, as well as the wisdom and prudence, to share our wealth with a now famished world? Or would we hoard it to ourselves, stuffing ourselves with surfeit but in doing so demolishing all hopes of achieving a humane and peaceful world community?" (227). At one point a group of suburban ladies seems oblivious to his remarks because they want to hear only about the "spiritual" meaning of his experiences. Gilkey points out that "self-deception, necessary for conscience' sake" (228) explains this audience's failure to appropriate his lesson: "To wish and seek for justice in material things for one's neighbor is perhaps the highest of spiritual attainments, since it is the expression in social relations of what it means to love one's neighbor. . . . So do the material and the spiritual realms, the secular and the religious, not exclude but cry out for each other" (229). The moral problems in the world remain continuous through a variety of situations. Just as C. S. Lewis holds that the reader who has not experienced joy will never understand his autobiography and Dorothy Day speaks of the universality of "the long loneliness" in every human life, so Gilkey generalizes from personal experience so that the reader will discern aspects of the meaning of his or her own life reflected in *Shantung Compound*. These Christian writers present personal experience as representative of the human condition. More specifically, they discern in their own apostasy the contours of a general human tendency to turn away from God.

Together with the other Christian autobiographers under discussion, Gilkey does not simply dismiss or denounce the period of apostasy but uses insights gained from it to present a more self-critical, persuasive, and powerful theological position. Gilkey's alienation from official forms of Christianity enables him to endorse Reinhold Niebuhr's remark that religion is not the place where the problem of human egotism is automatically solved. "It is there that the ultimate battle between human pride and God's grace takes place. Insofar as human pride may win that battle, religion can and does become one of the instruments of human sin. But insofar as there the self does meet God and so can surrender to something beyond its own self-interest, religion may provide the one possibility for a much-needed and very rare release from our common self-concern" (193).

Gilkey brings this theoretical perspective to bear on "Saints, Priests, and Preachers" in two chapters that analyze how certain forms of Christian piety may permit egocentrism and failures of charity. A minister refuses to give up some of his living space because he believes he needs privacy to write his sermons; a family refuses to share living quarters because they wish to provide a "good Christian home" for their children; and legalistic Protestants concentrate so earnestly on petty matters such as smoking and swearing that they entirely ignore the truly serious moral issues concerning justice. In every case rationalization and forms of self-deception distort the judgments of conscience. The pride of most of the missionary families in the camp isolates them from others and makes them victims of a loveless, judgmental mentality. Gilkey does show a few of the missionaries to be capable of genuine self-sacrifice and reveals his deep admiration for the steadfast labor and good humor of the Catholic priests. However, by showing the moral ambiguity of the Christians in the camp and by presenting several cases of self-sacrifice that are not based on any conscious religious commitment, Gilkey shows that religious belief is not a simple panacea for every social conflict. Both as an apology to those outside the faith and as a challenge to fellow believers, Gilkey's autobiography is appealing because it recognizes and shares the moral criticisms of Christianity that move many conscientious persons to reject Christian faith.

Gilkey's presentation of the truth of Christian faith is structured so as to interpret it to the skeptical outsider who wants to know what difference religious belief actually and potentially makes in human society and who therefore asks, "Is there any 'secular' use for religion; does it have any value for the common life of mankind?" (74). This is not to say that Gilkey reduces Christianity to an expedient means of promoting social morality. Gilkey recognizes, as does any good apologist, that he must engage his audience's concerns. As an effective rhetorical strategy for a Christian apology, *Shantung Compound* uses the narrative structure of deconversion and reconversion to demonstrate that Gilkey understands the reasons why many persons reject Christian faith. He presents a reinterpreted and realistic understanding of that faith centered on the symbols of sin and providence as better suited than any available alternative to sustain the moral struggle for justice, the same concern of conscience that motivated his apostasy.

Edwin Muir's *An Autobiography* is as much the story of the growth of a poet's sensibility as it is an account of the vicissitudes of religious faith. Yet Christian themes are central to Muir's poetic vision, and *An Autobiography* meditates at length on matters of faith and doubt, analyzes in detail the religious meaning of symbols in Muir's poems and dreams, and defends the author's belief in immortality. Like Day, Lewis, and Gilkey, Muir presents a period of apostasy as having had a decisive effect on his understanding of Christianity and uses criticisms of traditional belief to reinterpret Christian faith. In Muir's case the influence of apostasy on his apology may be seen in two ways: Muir's devising of an alternative to the traditional form of the conversion narrative and his responses to the modern critiques of religion articulated by Freud, Marx, and Nietzsche.

Muir contrasts two youthful conversions to Christianity with his mature movement toward faith. In his autobiography he undermines the validity of these early conversions, revealing that he shares some of the suspicions that conversions often arouse in skeptics. When he was fourteen, he participated in a revival and declared his acceptance of Christ. Muir discredits this event as a genuine spiritual experience because it was caused primarily by his wish to maintain his closeness to his family: "I felt impelled

towards the only act which would make me one with my family
again; for my father and mother and sister were saved, and I was
outside, separated from them by an invisible wall."[8] Muir qualifies the worth of this conversion experience by presenting it as a
"natural purification" that was temporary, without foundation in
the will or intellect, and too much influenced by others: "A sort
of purification had taken place in us, and it washed away the poi-
sonous stuff which had gathered in me during that year; but it was
more a natural than a spiritual cleansing, and more a communal
than a personal experience, for it is certain that if the whole audience had not risen that night I should never have risen. To pretend
that it was a genuine religious conversion would be ridiculous; I
did not know what I was doing; I had no clear knowledge of sin
or of the need for salvation. . . . I was changed quite beyond my
expectation; but the change did not last long" (87–88). Muir's ambivalence about the public, mass-produced conversions associated
with Christian revivalism is apparent in his description of the
Kirkwall meeting as one of the "communal orgies such as were
probably known long before Christianity came to these islands."
Such movements always had the positive effect of making people
forget their narrow interests for a time, but "the wave passed, and
people returned to their private concerns again and became more
sparing of love" (88). That these communal outbursts have little
in common with Muir's understanding of genuine religious faith
is indicated by his assertion that "like most orgies, they often left
behind them a feeling of shame" (88).

A "second dubious conversion" occurring several years later at
a revival meeting in Glasgow is also repudiated as being largely a
matter of mob psychology. "The time came to summon the saved
to rise in their places; everybody round me rose, and to my great
astonishment I found myself getting up too, although I had had
no intention of doing so: it is very hard to remain sitting when
everybody else has risen" (89). In this instance, too, Muir shows
his skepticism about the worth of much that goes by the name
of Christian conversion. He becomes permanently disillusioned
with this form of religion when he learns about the ways revi-
vals are organized. His final revulsion comes when he discovers
that one of the ministers—an early version of today's television
evangelists—cares primarily about the number of persons "saved."

When Muir presents his firm adherence to Christian belief, he
does so in a way that contrasts markedly with the features of these
spurious conversions. In February 1939 Muir underwent a mysti-

cal experience. He was alone when he had a "realization" of what he had, in fact, always believed. To render the experience of illumination, Muir quotes a diary entry describing how one evening he found himself reciting the Lord's Prayer "with deep urgency and profound disturbed emotion" (246). In reflecting on what had happened to him, Muir realized that he could only see persons as really human when he saw them as immortal souls. He was much preoccupied during this period—and throughout his entire life, as is evident in his poetry—by animal traits in people, and he had frightening moments when he saw humans as nothing but well-trained beasts. What I find most interesting about Muir's turning point is his stress on the recognition that he had *always* been a Christian, even during a period of apostasy: "I had believed for many years in God and the immortality of the soul; I had clung to the belief even when, in horrifying glimpses, I saw animals peeping through human eyes. My belief receded then, it is true, to an unimaginable distance, but it still stood there, not in any territory of mine, it seemed, but in a place of its own. Now I realized that, quite without knowing it, I was a Christian, no matter how bad a one" (246–47). Muir presents this transformative experience not as an ephemeral change of feeling but as the moment of illumination when he first comprehends and conceptualizes his long-term beliefs.

In contrast to his earlier conversions, when "intellectually I despised the man who saved me" (98), this moment of vision involves both overwhelming emotion and intellectual clarity. Unlike his earlier susceptibility to impression, Muir's later conversion (if we may call it that) is a very individual and solitary experience: "I did not turn to any church, and my talks with ministers and divines cast me back upon the Gospels again, which was probably the best thing that could have happened" (247). Furthermore, the changes in self-understanding brought by this experience were lasting, not temporary. Muir's experience of illumination in 1939 is as much a turning toward God as Augustine's incident in the garden or other experiences described in the tradition of Christian spiritual narratives. Yet he does not call it a conversion, and he differentiates it quite distinctly from the earlier episodes he does term conversions. I think he interprets his turning to God in the way he does largely because of his skepticism about revival conversions. He wishes to differentiate his own religious commitment from some of the associations that, because of revivalism, have become attached to the very term *conversion*.

In a similar manner, Muir describes as a "realization" rather than a conversion a second significant religious experience that crystallizes another of his deepest beliefs. The aesthetic beauty of Italy moves Muir in much the same way as it had affected John Ruskin, but Muir interprets his experience in explicitly theological terms. In Rome in 1949 Muir suddenly begins to appreciate the full meaning of the Incarnation. The beauty of Rome and the "splendours of Christendom" offer him an understanding of Christianity that he had never glimpsed in his Calvinist upbringing. In Orkney, "I was aware of religion chiefly as the sacred Word, and the church itself, severe and decent, with its touching bareness and austerity, seemed to cut off religion from the rest of life and from all the week-day world. . . . It did not tell me by any outward sign that the Word had been made flesh" (277). Muir's experience in Italy confirms the vision of the natural world he had always had as a poet. The rendering of Christian truth in pictures and figures drawn from ordinary life—as in a painting of the Annunciation that moves him deeply—shows Muir what he had long believed about God's relation to the world: "That these images should appear everywhere, reminding everyone of the Incarnation, seemed to me natural and right. . . . This open declaration was to me the very mark of Christianity" (278). Once again a visionary moment that turns Muir more consciously toward God is interpreted in a way that distinguishes his turning from the varieties of conversion he rejects. His conversion is a moment of intensification—a deeper realization of what he has always believed on some level of consciousness—rather than a sudden yielding to the momentary force of some external influence. Yet at the same time the incident unmistakably recalls classic Christian scenes of conversion. Though Muir resists the idea of sudden transformation, his insight comes in a flash through responding to a challenge from without. The confrontation with the painting is presented as a kind of epiphany, a recognition of a manifestation of the divine. Thus Muir both resists and adapts conventions of the traditional conversion narrative.

When Muir does refer explicitly to conversion without undermining its validity, it is in an unusual context: not in explaining his religious experience but in a discussion of poetic theory. He uses the term as a verb and quickly qualifies its meaning when speaking of the influence of his friend John Holms: "He held Traherne's and Vaughan's and Wordsworth's theory of childhood, which was bound up with his belief in immortality; in time he converted me to it, or rather made me realize that my own belief was the same as his" (179). Again we see that for Muir conversion means a realization or recognition, as the result of thoughtful reflection, of what one has long believed. I think that Muir's attitude to conversion reflects the influence of his period of apostasy, when he rejected all conversions as temporary emotional outbursts brought about by external pressures. Muir's wish to differentiate his conscious turning toward God from that rejected meaning of conversion explains some of the distinctive features of his autobiography as a first-person Christian apology.

The gradual waning of Muir's faith before his genuine conversion came about for many reasons. He was struck by the inefficacy of his prayers when his father, mother, and two brothers died within several years after the family moved to Glasgow: "If there was a God I told myself that he was dead or indifferent" (103). Muir's considered rejection of Christian faith also reflects the influences of the critiques of religion by Marx, Nietzsche, and Freud. Muir's view of religion was strongly affected by his interest in socialism, his "infatuation" with Nietzsche's philosophy, and his experience of psychoanalysis. These three intellectual involvements either contributed directly to Muir's deconversion or shaped his thinking during what he came to see as a time of apostasy. Muir's apology for Christian faith offers a rejoinder to these three systems of ideas that once kept him from belief.

Muir speaks of a "conversion to socialism" at the age of twenty-one as a "recapitulation of my first conversion at fourteen," in that it was not "the result of an intellectual process, but a sort of emotional transmutation" (113). Muir's socialism expressed his quasi-religious idealism about reforming society. A "purification" of the self inspiring him with a love of all humankind culminated in a visionary experience of "spontaneous attraction to every human being" during a May Day demonstration (114). As in the case of his revivalist conversion, this elation was temporary, a heightened emotional state induced by the crowd. Muir's early socialism was an emotional replacement 'for the religion he had "flung away." Although he affirms his socialist idealism as "a genuine imaginative vision of life," he qualifies it as "false in being earthly and nothing more" (113).

In presenting his mature view of Christian faith, Muir seeks to reconcile it with the socialist ideals that had once led him to reject religion as an impediment to social justice. His basic strategy is similar to Day's, although Muir relies upon the concept of immortality. Muir presents his Christian beliefs and his socialist ideals as not only harmonious but necessarily connected by belief in immortality: "Immortality is not an idea or a belief, but a state of being in which man keeps alive in himself his perception of that boundless union and freedom, which he can faintly apprehend in time, though its consummation lies beyond time. This realization that human life is not fulfilled in our world, but reaches through all eternity, would have been rejected by me some years before as an act of treachery to man's earthly hopes; but now, in a different way, it was a confirmation of them, for only a race of immortal spirits could create a world fit for immortal spirits to inhabit" (170). Muir's hopes of achieving freedom and union with others inspire both his religious and political beliefs. He thus presents his Christian faith as compatible with the idealistic hopes of socialism. At the same time, belief in immortality saved him from the "monstrous simplification that 'religion is the opium of the masses'" (170). Muir rejects the Marxist reduction of religious belief to its social function: "The theory that the soul is immortal was not invented as a pretext for keeping the rich from being made uncomfortable, or to provide texts to quote against the class-conscious workers in the late nineteenth and early twentieth centuries" (170).

Muir's discussion of political movements and ideologies in his autobiography reflects his apologetic interest in integrating Christian belief with certain aspects of socialism while rejecting other aspects.[9] This is especially clear in the chapters of *An Autobiography* added in 1953 to Muir's first version of his autobiography, *The Story and the Fable* (1940). Muir reiterates the theme of the growth of impersonal, dehumanizing power in the twentieth century. P. H. Butter discerns a connection between Muir's belief in immortality and his political themes: "In *The Story and the Fable* the loss and the recovery of his belief in (or, better, experience of) immortality had been treated mainly as a part of his personal history. Now the loss of this experience in so many is seen as one of the things that have made possible the growth of impersonal power."[10] Muir's interpretation of twentieth-century history colors his depiction of socialist thought and action. When he encountered the political poetry of the 1930s, Muir was struck by its simplified categories of right and wrong and its anger unrelieved by compassion. He contrasts this sort of left-wing politics with his own youthful ideals: "I had been a Socialist in my twenties, when we thought more of humanity and brotherhood than of class-war and revolution" (233). Because he holds that communism provides no place for forgiveness, Muir asserts that this political ideology and system betrays the essentially religious hopes that were its original inspiration and deepest source of appeal: "It was as if a conjuring trick had been played with a hope as old as Isaiah, and what the heart had conceived as love and peace had been transmuted into anger and conflict" (234). Muir's witnessing of the communist coup d'état in Prague in 1948 recapitulates his experience of Nazi power: "These shouts, which sounded like the brute response of a huge mass machine and had no resemblance to the spontaneous cheers of a crowd, brought back mean and bullying memories. We seemed to be back in 1939 again, with Europe fearing and preparing for war" (265). When Muir points out the historical consequences of communism, he implies that, lacking belief in the soul's immortality, the socialist is inevitably driven to deny freedom, justice, and compassion. In treating modern political developments, then, Muir emphasizes the compatibility between Christianity and the idealistic hopes of socialism and defends his faith against simplifications and dangers of Marxist ideology.

Muir was strongly attracted to Nietzsche's work for a number of years. What was most appealing was Nietzsche's condemnation of pity, even though this scornful tendency was inconsistent with Muir's socialist ideals. Muir's analysis of his enthusiasm for Nietzsche is much more dismissive and sarcastic than his discussion of socialism or psychoanalysis; there is little in Nietzsche's work that Muir wants to affirm as a Christian. He treats his Nietzschean ideas as a means of psychological "compensation" for the ugliness of his environment in the Glasgow slums and the triviality of his daily work as a clerk in a beer-bottling factory. Nietzsche provided "a last desperate foothold on my dying dream of the future" (126). "My Nietzscheanism was what psychologists call a 'compensation.' I could not face my life as it was, and so I took refuge in the fantasy of the Superman" (127). Nietzsche's philosophy was ill-suited to his basic character, and Muir confesses astonishment that he clung to it for so long. It was only through a form of self-deception that he could ignore his revulsion from the Nietzschean vision of the world. Returning from work in a tram in Glasgow one evening in 1919, Muir had a vision of his fellow passengers as animals. Although he did not believe in the immortality of the soul at this time, he found the vision too frightening to reflect on: "This experience was so terrifying that I dismissed it, deliberately forgot it by that perverse power which

the mind has of obliterating itself. . . . I did not associate it at the
time with Nietzsche. But I realized that I could not bear mankind
as a swarming race of thinking animals" (52). Muir was swayed
by Nietzsche only because he was able to suppress his instinctive
aversion to the implications of Nietzsche's ideas.

Although Muir rejects Nietzsche's ideas as entirely incompatible with Christian faith, his description of his relationship to
the German thinker deploys two crucial Nietzschean ideas, the
concept of ressentiment and the analysis of asceticism. These related ideas interpret certain devious workings of conscience. Muir
shows that he gained significant insights from Nietzsche's analysis, only to turn them against the great critic of the Christian
conscience. Muir describes "a dream about Nietzsche which contained a curious criticism of him and my infatuation with him"
(128). He dreamed of Nietzsche on the cross, staring "round him
with an air of defiant possession." Despite the fact that the dream
is at odds with Nietzsche's philosophy, there seems to Muir a profound naturalness about the image of this man being crucified in
this way. "I slowly began to realize that Nietzsche's life had been a
curious kind of self-crucifixion, out of pride, not out of love" (128).
In effect, Muir turns the concept of ressentiment back against its
originator. He interprets Nietzsche as a "usurper" driven by an
animus toward Christianity deriving from his own frustrated religious longing. Muir's dream reflects the Nietzschean insight that
values may originate in a wish to deny what one is incapable of
achieving in one's own life. Muir perceived that the great critic of
asceticism was himself a victim of deliberate cruelty directed in-
wards and that Nietzsche sought power though the same process
of self-mortification that he rejected in Christianity. Although
Muir does not say as much explicitly, his dream powerfully suggests his intuitive understanding that Nietzsche's suffering and
isolation were a form of asceticism: deliberate self-punishment in
search of transcendence.[11]

Muir goes on to report another dream, strongly resembling a
dream of Nietzsche's, which ends in a disgusting vision of a "black
devouring worm." "The dream was a horrible indication of my
state at a time when I considered myself beyond good and evil"
(128). In both of Muir's dreams a crucial idea or image from Nietzsche's works is turned against the German thinker and against
Muir's early identification with him. Yet even though Nietzsche's
ideas are vehemently rejected, Muir's apology draws on insights
and images garnered from that philosopher. Muir appropriates

these elements from Nietzsche's thought at the same time that he rejects such concepts as the "fantasy of the Superman" and Eternal Recurrence as incompatible with crucial Christian beliefs. Most significantly, he asserts that Christian faith provides answers to the insistent questions of meaning that drew him to Nietzsche but continued to trouble him during his apostasy. In particular, Muir's argument for immortality presents this belief as a far sounder basis for self-respect than Nietzschean contempt for weakness or cultivation of traits that anticipate the Superman.

Muir's many examinations of the symbolism of dreams and literature are indebted to the vocabulary and interpretive strategies of psychoanalysis.[12] At the time of his own analysis in London in 1920, Muir did not consider himself to be a Christian. It is unclear to what extent he saw psychological theory as a challenge to the validity of religious belief, and psychoanalysis was not the direct cause of his deconversion. In composing his autobiography, in any case, Muir confronts the fact that for many modern intellectuals psychology provides an explanation of religious experience that undermines many if not all traditional Christian beliefs by attributing them to unconscious sources within the human psyche. *An Autobiography* responds to this perspective, using the insights of psychological theory not to displace but to supplement and enrich a theological interpretation of symbolism in dreams and literature. A psychological view does not substitute for or discredit religious interpretation, but, as we will see, serves as a partial explanation that incites further thought.

Like Carl Jung's *Memories, Dreams, Reflections*, Muir's autobiography contains extended analyses of vivid dreams that were turning points in the author's life. Many of Muir's most significant religious insights came to him through reflection on his dreams. For example, one dream confirms and clarifies his slowly developing belief in immortality: "After a period of dismissing immortality as an imputation on earthly life and the purity of immediate perception I had tentatively begun to believe in it again. So that the dream did not actually convert me to that belief. But it very much strengthened and at the same time modified it" (167). Muir does not feel that simply because dreams come from the unconscious they have no religious significance. He views the deeper workings of the mind in terms of a human search for religious meaning that is more than conscious. One of the deepest sources of Muir's sense of the universe as a meaningful and coherent whole was the experience of the unconscious mind producing significant patterns.

Of a poem that spontaneously came to him and relieved him of a sense of shame about an incident in his childhood, Muir wrote: "These solutions of the past projected into the present, deliberately announced as if they were a sibylline declaration that life has a meaning, impress me more deeply than any other kind of experience with the conviction that life does have a meaning quite apart from the thousand meanings which the conscious mind attributes to it" (44).

To the skeptic, of course, such an event can hardly count as evidence of an order outside the poet's mind (or, at most, of a collective unconsciousness of the human psyche). Muir, however, consistently links his ideas about the unconscious mind's activity in visions, dreams, and creative writing to his beliefs about the deepest meaning of his life, to what he calls the "fable" as opposed to the "story," or mere facts about one's life. Our dreams, he holds, give us the most important clues to who we are as immortal spirits. He asserts that belief in immortality is, in fact, "connected with the same impulse which urges me to know myself" (54). In a succinct statement of his autobiographical intentions, Muir connects his interest in the psychology of dreams with his belief in immortality, the religious belief for which he is most concerned to offer a modern apologetic: "I shall attend and listen to a class of experiences which the disbeliever in immortality ignores or dismisses as irrelevant to temporal life. . . . If I describe a great number of dreams in this book I do so intentionally, for I should like to save from the miscellaneous dross of experience a few glints of immortality" (54).

What is most notable about Muir's reflection on his own psychoanalysis is the way he juxtaposes his analyst's interpretation of his dreams with his own search for a religious dimension. Neither perspective alone is sufficient; both psychological and theological interpretations are affirmed, even though their disparity produces significant conflicts. For example, his analyst proposes that the animals, dragons, and mythological monsters in Muir's dreams show that he has for many years "suppressed the animal" in himself (56). Muir says the analyst was "right only up to a point," for these monsters aroused no fear. Instead, Muir interprets one crucial dream as a millennial vision of the potential harmony of beasts and humans: "Our minds are possessed by three mysteries: where we came from, where we are going, and, since we are not alone, but members of a countless family, how we should live with one another. . . . In my dream about the animals all three questions are involved; for the dream touches the relation between man and the animals and points to his origin, while in the image of the animal kingdom glorified and reconciled with mankind it points simultaneously to man's end, and with that to the way in which he should live in a society, for that question is inseparable from the question of his end" (56–57). While a psychoanalytic interpretation has partial validity, for Muir it may not fathom a dream's deepest significance, which is often religious.

In another dream the analyst "indicated the sexual symbolism of the dream, which by this time I could read for myself" (163). Muir sees beyond this "obvious" meaning to the dream's significance as a vision of the end of time. Interpreting a "mythological dream" involving falling, Muir is not satisfied with his analyst's view: "The longing to fling myself down from a height . . . is immediately associated with the analyst's exhortations to come down to earth, to accept reality; but it also brings to my mind images of the Fall and of the first incarnation, that of Adam, and another image as well, which is my image of timeless human life as the intersection and interpenetration of a stationary beam falling from heaven and the craving, aspiring dust rising for ever to meet it, in denial or submission, in ignorance or comprehension" (166). In each case that his analyst reduces the meaning of dream symbolism to an illustration of orthodox psychological theory, Muir realizes that there is an alternative interpretation that discerns the dream's religious significance.

Although Muir affirms the partial adequacy of psychological interpretation, he underscores the further insights that arise from pondering his dreams' theological meaning. For example, when Muir's analysis forces him to confront the most unpleasant and contemptible parts of himself, he sees his recognition as a discovery of Original Sin: "At last, by painful stages, I reached a state which resembled conviction of sin, though formulated in different terms. I realized the elementary fact that every one, like myself, was troubled by sensual desires and thoughts, by unacknowledged failures and frustrations causing self-hatred and hatred of others, by dead memories of shame and grief which had been shovelled underground long since because they could not be borne. I saw that my lot was the human lot. . . . It was really a conviction of sin, but even more a realization of Original Sin" (158). The recognition of the truth of this Christian doctrine does not constitute an alternative interpretation to the psychological view, for it comes about in some measure through the methods and assumptions of psychoanalysis. For Muir, self-understanding is not a matter of an either-or choice between these two perspectives but an attempt to integrate the insights of psychological theory and Christian belief. The Christian formulates "in different terms" an understanding of the human condition that may be informed and enriched by the disclosures of psychoanalysis.

Muir's *An Autobiography* is one of the most compelling modern Christian apologies, although it does not emphasize the figure of Christ. Most critics have underestimated the Christian content of Muir's ideas and the extent to which they shape his autobiographies. Finney, for example, holds that Muir "was not prepared to subscribe to any particular sect or church (calling himself 'a sort of illicit Christian') and therefore avoided introducing his specifically Christian beliefs into *The Story and the Fable*."[13] Although Avrom Fleishman analyzes how the myths of Eden and the Fall structure *An Autobiography*, he interprets this narrative pattern as applying only to Muir's personal story, rather than as an element of the "fable," Muir's term for universal religious truths about human experience.[14] Fleishman concludes that "although Muir's religious meditations and personal version of Christianity have come up in the autobiography, they have not been allowed to shape his 'development'—certainly no decisive conversion pattern or pilgrimage has been suggested, even in displaced form."[15]

These two critics are referring to a work that distinguishes between false and genuine conversions and that explores in depth apocalyptic themes, Original Sin, the Incarnation, the Fall, and —again and again—belief in immortality. Muir's understanding of Christian faith does more than just "come up" occasionally. His autobiography is decisively shaped by his wish to present an apology for the convictions that have shaped his life. As much as Augustine's *Confessions, An Autobiography* is a confession of faith and an attempt to discern the mystery of grace in the haphazard events of a life. Muir's closing remarks affirm that the agency of God is the ultimate "fable" beneath the miscellaneous facts of the "story" of his life: "In the infinite web of things and events chance must be something different from what we think it to be. To comprehend that is not given to us, and to think of it is to recognize a mystery, and to acknowledge the necessity of faith. As I look back on the part of the mystery which is my own life, my own fable, what I am most aware of is that we receive more than we can ever give; we receive it from the past, on which we draw with every breath, but also—and this is a point of faith—from the Source of the mystery itself, by the means which religious people call Grace" (281). Grace operates in the "dubious conversions" that prepare Muir to know the meaning of a genuine turning to God and in his involvements with socialism, psychology, and even Nietzsche while he was an apostate. Muir's apology for his beliefs in God and immortality focuses primarily on the period when he lacked faith and is presented largely as a response to his earlier criticisms of these Christian affirmations.

The autobiographical works of Day, Lewis, Gilkey, and Muir are conversion narratives in two senses. In the traditional sense they all describe a transformation of the self that comes about through conscious turning toward God, a turning that alters thoughts, feelings, and purposes. Moreover, these works are conversions of negative experiences in the past into a positive image of religious meaning. In particular, they convert deconversion, the loss of faith, into a significant religious event by interpreting it as apostasy.

Conversion is an apt metaphor for the Christian autobiographer's hermeneutical activity. Inner turmoil, uncertainty, and suffering are transformed into a pattern disclosing the meaning of human experience as understood in the terms of Christian faith. The narrative structure of Christian autobiography often involves reinterpreting the actions and ideas of a period of apostasy; this strategy offers a writer the opportunity and challenge of discerning God's grace even during that time when he or she most decisively rejected religious belief and commitment.

To address nonbelievers, a convincing apology for Christian faith must respond directly to the reasons for which many persons conscientiously reject belief. The autobiographer can say to the unbeliever, "I've been there," taking seriously criticisms of Christianity and yet showing the inadequacies of alternative worldviews in practical life as well as in theory. Probably no systematic theology or theory of religious experience can be as moving and persuasive an apology as the personal testimony of one who has lost faith and regained it. Not all Christian lives, and not all Christian autobiographies, encompass a period of apostasy. But most of those that have been most compelling, to nonbelievers as well as to Christians, have made this pattern the shaping strategy of a first-person apology for faith.

Such autobiographers know, too, what will most affect and challenge fellow believers. Augustine held that Christians rejoice more for the salvation of an endangered soul than for one which was always safe. He asks why this should be the case: "O God, who are so good, what is it that makes men rejoice more for the salvation of a soul for which all had despaired, or one that is delivered from great danger, than for one for which hope has never been lost or one which has been in less peril?" (8.3). Reflecting on Simplicianus' story of the conversion of Victorinus, a professor of rhetoric who had once worshipped idols, Augustine compares our response to such a story to three biblical parables: "We also are overjoyed when we hear that the sheep that was lost is carried home on the happy shepherd's shoulders and that the coin is returned to your treasury, while the neighbours rejoice with the woman who found it. The joy of Mass in your church moves us to tears when we hear the gospel which tells us how the younger son died and returned to life, and how he was lost and found again" (8.3). Augustine goes on to tell three stories about rejoicing after near-calamity, describing the victor of a hard-fought battle, sailors surviving a terrifying storm, and a recovery from a dangerous illness. All of these narratives show that "it is always the case that the greater the joy, the greater is the pain which precedes it." Augustine believes that he has discerned a truth about the losses and gains of human existence. Occasions of threatened or actual negativity can become occasions for the greatest rejoicing.

It is not simply a happy outcome that produces such affirmation but the converting work of interpretation that discerns God's work in human history. Augustine's six tropes not only figure the conversion experience of Victorinus and his own prodigality and return but also describe the interpretive strategy at work in the works of Day, Lewis, Gilkey, and Muir. The negative experiences of a period of apostasy, the ideas and suffering that once produced rebellion or indifference to God, are converted through autobiographical interpretation and come to serve an indispensable role in each writer's apology for Christian belief.

In Christian autobiography at its best, as in *The Long Loneliness, Surprised by Joy, Shantung Compound,* and Muir's *An Autobiography,* the writer's experience of apostasy is not simply a passing phase, dismissed or minimized in comparison with the turning toward God. Instead, apostasy raises issues that force the author to reinterpret Christian faith, and it provides many of the terms in which the writer's final understanding of faith is articulated. The autobiographer reenacts the insights and experiences that led to the repudiation of Christianity and demonstrates the process of reflection and reinterpretation by which faith can be recovered in good conscience. The shaping strategy of Christian autobiography, of apologetic theology in the first-person mode, is the analysis of apostasy from the perspective of faith and the reinterpretation of faith in the light of apostasy.

9

CULTS AND
DEPROGRAMMING

A NEW FORM of deconversion narrative that emerges during the 1970s is the account of defection from a cult. Although this term is sometimes seen as pejorative and replaced by "charismatic group" or "new religious movement," I will follow a number of social scientists who use the term *cult* without negative connotations. One scholar defines a cult as characterized by the following elements: "Members (1) have a shared belief system, (2) sustain a high level of social cohesiveness, (3) are strongly influenced by the group's behavioral norms, and (4) impute charismatic (or sometimes divine) power to the group or its leadership."[1] Those who join cults are often seeking things that they do not find in society's more established churches: intense religious experience, devotion to a charismatic leader, a sense of belonging to a loving community, and absolute certainty about their beliefs. The nature of a devotee's idealism determines the reasons for disillusionment and the form deconversion takes.

In the 1970s many new cults began actively proselytizing in the United States, including the Unification Church, the Divine Light Mission, Hare Krishna, the Children of God, and hundreds of smaller groups. Whether offshoots of Christianity or of more purely Asian origin, such groups share a common "totalistic" character.[2] A cult defines all aspects of a believer's life: not only proper spiritual activities but also social relationships, work, and forms of recreation. Such groups monitor and often prohibit contacts with those outside the faith, especially family relationships, and frequently claim to provide the adherent with a new and "true" family of fellow believers. A cult usually has a charismatic leader who represents or embodies the divine and demands total obedience. Given the total commitment required by this kind of religious group, a deconversion requires a much more radical change than does leaving one of the more mainstream, established Christian churches in the United States. Deconversion from a cult is comparable to abjuring the vows of a nun or monk or to rejecting a Puritan community in New England during the seventeenth century. In this chapter I interpret several versions of deconversion from a cult in relation to the autobiographical tradition traced so far in this book, exploring their continuity and their innovative features in terms of both the substantive reasons for the loss of faith and the metaphors used to explain the loss of faith. Deconversion from a contemporary cult may involve the same criticisms of a religion and similar rhetoric as earlier autobiographies, in addition to new and distinctive factors.

Social scientists have studied these new religious groups intensively. While most early research focused on recruitment strategies and conversion to cults, the subject of deconversion now receives nearly as much discussion.[3] Psychologists and sociologists use varied terminologies for deconversion, including *disengagement, role exiting, disaffiliation, apostasy, defection,* and *withdrawal.* Many of the same issues that arise in conversion research also characterize the study of deconversion, such as whether this process is best understood as a matter of sudden, gradual, or multiple serial change and whether the crucial factors in deconversion are cognitive, emotional, or social. Scholars use alternative analytic frameworks to interpret deconversion, including a "role theory" model that views it as a process of role exiting, and a "causal process model" that proposes a predictable sequence of stages of withdrawal from a cult. Some sociologists favor "organizational models" that explain affiliation and defection in terms of changes in a group's structural elements and dynamics (type of leadership, financial base, delegation of tasks, etc.).[4] These interpretive frameworks suggest important issues for understanding deconversion.

Sophia Collier's *Soul Rush* was written in 1978, when the author was only twenty-two. Collier describes her involvement and break with the Divine Light Mission (hereafter, DLM), a Hindu-oriented group emphasizing meditation practices and commitment to its adolescent leader, Guru Maharaj Ji.[5] In the early 1970s, Maharaj

Ji attracted a large following of mostly young, white, middle-class adherents, including Collier, who learned meditation practices, "received Knowledge," and joined the DLM in 1972. Collier became a writer in the mission's national public relations office and knew the inner workings of the movement well. Her involvement in the DLM, initially based on spiritual searching, soon developed into a career in the movement's executive organization. This combination of motives is reflected in Collier's mixed metaphors, for instance her use of advertising jargon to characterize the DLM's spiritual work: "Even though Knowledge was an excellent product, probably the best on the market, the mismanagement of the business and the ineptitude of the sales force might be too great to overcome."[6] As she begins her work as a "propagandist" for the Divine Light Mission, Collier believes she will never need to compromise herself: "In a situation where I looked at the assets and liabilities of the organization and saw a negative net worth, I thought, knowing me, I wouldn't hang around too long" (151–52).

Her loss of faith in the DLM occurs for two basic reasons. First, she criticizes its leadership for letting concerns of organizational efficiency stifle spontaneity and creativity. Near the end of the book she quotes a long passage from William James's *Varieties of Religious Experience* that contrasts the "spontaneous religious spirit" with "religion's wicked practical partner, the spirit of corporate domination" and with "religion's wicked intellectual partner, the spirit of dogmatic domination" (218). Collier discerns these negative influences at work within the movement as dissent is suppressed, the organization becomes increasingly hierarchical, and its practices are routinized. When Collier's publicity group tries to challenge these tendencies, they are quickly reined in. Collier's disillusionment with the DLM could illustrate the thesis of sociological "organization models" that tie deconversion to changes within a religion's institutional structure.

While Collier's criticisms of the DLM's authoritarian leadership resemble the reasons many autobiographers have given for leaving a religious community, her way of putting matters reflects an intriguing blend of popular psychology, American business jargon, and the rhetoric of spirituality characteristic of the counterculture of the 1970s. She agrees with one friend's description of the destructive effect of the DLM's style of organizational management: "An authoritarian style will naturally inhibit the growth of consciousness" (233). The narrative in the last few chapters of *Soul Rush* involves a great deal of office politics and intrigue reminis-

cent of a story of a corporate takeover. Collier is disillusioned by
the DLM because "the executives were never going to relinquish
their power. There would never be any participatory management
structure in the Mission" (233). For Collier, authentic spirituality
seems necessarily to be expressed in individualistic and unpredictable ways that run counter to an organization's need for efficiency: "By teaching people meditation [the DLM] was encouraging them to be individuals of spirit, but in trying to organize them
to specific tasks, it was not giving them room to be individuals of
action" (235–36).

Collier is finally impelled to leave the movement when several
fellow workers in the Research and Development department are
fired. Her deconversion seems motivated equally by reflections
on her diminished career prospects within the organization and
by religious doubts about Maharaj Ji. A third reason for her deconversion is only mentioned in passing: a developing love affair.
This makes her feel so much "like a *completely* new person" that
she simply loses interest in the internal political maneuvering at
the DLM headquarters: "Suddenly I felt it had nothing to do with
me. . . . [It] was like listening to a family fight among neighbors
that came, muffled, through the walls of an apartment. . . . When
I walked around the office I felt peculiarly free. I had great affection for many of these people, but my destiny was no longer
tied to theirs" (235). This romantic relationship may seem irrelevant to the process of losing faith, and Collier does not explore
it. However, it is often a new interest or attachment outside a
cult's prescribed routines that enables a member to recognize the
narrowness or arbitrary restrictiveness of life within a totalistic
community.

The other primary reason Collier herself gives for leaving the
DLM concerns her skeptical view of Maharaj Ji's divinity. From
the very beginning of her involvement in the DLM, Collier had
been primarily committed to the practice of meditation and to the
ideal of community, not to worshipping Maharaj Ji. She retains
a healthy skepticism during her involvement with the mission:
"Upon joining DLM I did not accept all DLM ideas as my own.
One of the ideas I couldn't go along with was that Maharaj Ji was
the Perfect Master, the current incarnation of a divine lineage"
(124). Her superiors criticize her articles in the cult's newspaper
for being irreverent when she writes that "Maharaj Ji is not only a
Guru but also a premie, a person just like us" (228). A "premie" is
literally a "lover of God" and is the official term to designate the

members of the DLM.[7] Many of the guru's devotees consider him to be a superhuman or divine person. When she is reprimanded for her remark, Collier feels "sorry I'd insulted Maharaj Ji, but, wow, did that sound like ego" (229). Collier wants to learn what the guru thinks about himself: "Had he acquiesced mentally to all the adoration and begun to believe he was the Lord?" (226). If Maharaj Ji does believe he is God, she knows she must leave the mission: "There is no way I could stay around a mission led by a crazy man, no matter how clever, charming, and charismatic that man was" (226–27).

Through his amused response to Peter Sellers's movie *The Mouse that Roared*, Maharaj Ji seems to Collier to indicate that he, too, is engaged in a kind of beneficent deception: "This story indicated to me that Maharaj Ji did not think he was God; he understood that he was a bumbling prince whose claim to power was a placebo called Knowledge" (230). The guru's "gift" of knowledge is a "placebo" in that it gets his followers to develop their unused potential: "Essentially, the guru tricks the people who come to him into doing what they are already able to do" (230). Collier thinks that a time should come when a guru teaches his devotees to move beyond him. She becomes disillusioned when Maharaj Ji allows others to worship him as divine and by the guru's lack of interest in the DLM's organizational problems. Many nineteenth-century agnostics lost their faith in Christianity when they encountered biblical scholarship that interpreted Jesus as a human figure. For many former members of cults, too, perception of the leader as human, and usually all too human, precipitates a deconversion. Collier decides that she can no longer participate in the DLM, no matter how worthy its goal of "consciousness raising," if to do so requires faith that a human being is divine.

Soul Rush ends rather abruptly, with Collier leaving the DLM in March 1976 and returning to live with her mother and write the book. Her concluding thoughts, written only eleven months after she left the DLM, show her still sorting out the value and meaning of her experiences and uncertain about her future plans. She is far from disillusioned or bitter about her involvement in the mission and continues to affirm the value of two aspects of the DLM: the peace and greater awareness attained through meditation and the genuine love and support sometimes realized within the community. Her deconversion does not bring the emotional suffering characteristic of almost all the deconversions examined in this book but rather a "soul rush"—feelings of exhilaration and joy and a desire for more knowledge of both herself and the world—as intense as her original conversion to the DLM. Yet Collier seems to lose interest in specifically religious commitment, and her final resolution to continue "experimenting with living the best life" apparently points toward politics, writing projects, and secular matters.

If Collier's book takes a relatively favorable view of the religious movement she has left, a very different kind of deconversion story can best be called anticult literature. Such narratives are extremely hostile to the rejected religious group and appeal to public fears of cults. Anticult literature is shaped primarily by its conception of the threat a cult poses; it appeals to two basic forms of fear: the threat of violence and the specter of brainwashing. I will first discuss an autobiography that presents cults as a violent menace to American society.

Among the many cults in the United States are a few small, militant apocalyptic groups that see themselves as persecuted. When such a group becomes locked in conflict with the larger society, the consequences can be catastrophic, as in the cases of the black anarchist community MOVE in Philadelphia, the Symbionese Liberation Army that captured Patricia Hearst, or the People's Temple led by Jim Jones. Anticult literature uses autobiographical testimony by ex-members as evidence to persuade popular opinion and public authorities to rescue other members or to suppress the cult. The ex-member's deconversion comes about because he or she realizes that the group's leader is abusing power, threatening or terrorizing members, and exploiting them sexually. Often originating in popular journalism, anticult literature tends to be highly sensational, emphasizing the passivity and helplessness of those "held captive" within the group and the leader's deranged personality and "demonic" capacity for evil. (A literary ancestor of these accounts is thus the captivity narrative of those held prisoner or adopted by American Indians.)[8] While sometimes the presentation of a cult as evil expresses well-founded concern for children or adults prevented from leaving a religious community, an autobiographer's need to come to terms with a deconversion experience plays a crucial role in shaping such documents.

Jeannie Mills's *Six Years with God: Life inside Rev. Jim Jones's Peoples Temple* was published in 1979, soon after the death of 913 people on November 18, 1978 at Jonestown, the apocalyptic commune founded by the Peoples Temple in Guyana. Mills and her husband had been high-ranking leaders in this religious movement when they defected in October 1975. Their deconversion comes about partly because of their anger about punishments their daughter received and partly because of their dissatisfaction with the temple's lack of financial support for a nursing home they ran for the cult. Mills's memoir is a fascinating, frightening, and highly polemical account of how the Peoples Temple, which was originally an idealistic interracial congregation of the Disciples of Christ denomination, degenerated into the violent and apocalyptic community that committed mass suicide. Mills's narrative is intended as a lesson on the potential evil of all cults: "It has been said that more than 3,000 cults exist in the United States alone. I hope, through this record of what happened in one, that people will understand the danger, the depravity of total obedience to one leader. The horror is limitless."[9]

The overall structure of this book is unusual in its arrangement of the chronology of the Millses' involvement in the Peoples Temple. The first half of the book begins immediately after their deconversion and describes their life from the time they left the temple in 1975 until the mass suicide at Jonestown in 1978. Much of the story is an account of incidents of harrassment and threatened violence the family endured after they had left the cult but were still "living under Jim's reign of terror" (25). The second part begins in 1969, at the time of their first involvement in the temple and continues until they defected in 1975. Thus we see first the frightening side of Jim Jones's group as it attacks apostates (the Millses after they left the cult); then the promise and idealism of the temple in its origins; and finally the violence and terror that drove the family out of the movement, as Jim Jones organized ever more sadistic "discipline sessions." The book's finale is not Jonestown, as one would have expected, but the author's deconversion, which saved the Millses from the fate of those who died in the mass suicide.

In contrast to all the other autobiographies discussed in this book, most stories of deconversion from cults are written soon after the loss of faith and express an outpouring of anger, grief, guilt, and moral outrage. Since it was only a year before *Six Years with God* was published that Jones died, along with many entire families, this work involves even more emotional catharsis than most narratives of deconversion. Some of the negative feelings Jeannie Mills has about the Peoples Temple are directed with dubious relevance to the many other small religious groups proselytizing in the United States. One can infer that the lesson of Jonestown announced in part 3 ("Those Who Do Not Remember the Past Are Condemned to Repeat It") and applied indiscriminately to all cults is in part a way of compensating for Mills's frustrated efforts to rescue some of the families who died in Guyana.

Six Years with God represents one extreme on the spectrum of attitudes of ex-believers toward their former faith. Most of the versions of deconversion examined in this book discern some good in the rejected religious community and show continuity between certain former beliefs and the autobiographer's present convictions. Not all defectors see a cult in retrospect as demonic; Collier's *Soul Rush* is highly appreciative of the Divine Light Mission's original purpose of consciousness raising and attaining serenity through meditation practices. Anticult literature, in contrast, exposes fraud, denounces abuse, and expresses deep anger and unrelenting hostility. "Oppositional apostasy" such as this can create bitter conflicts that actually reinforce a cult's self-understanding as a persecuted minority and thus may play a significant role in affecting the cult's eventual fate.[10] Anticult deconversion narratives are not detached, reflective accounts of an ambiguous experience but outraged testimonies about demonic evil or horror stories intended to prove the destructive nature of all cults. Having sacrificed so much for the faith and experienced or witnessed suffering, the authors are embittered by their entire experience within a cult. Writing an autobiography warning others about the cult and similar groups can help an ex-member come to terms with the past and provide a new orientation and activity that fills the vacuum created by abandoning a totalistic religious sect.

Mills's stance as narrator may be compared to the role of the apostate that Max Scheler described in *Ressentiment*. Scheler adopted Nietzsche's concept of ressentiment to explain how strong feelings of hatred and envy can make one wish to destroy something that is also very attractive but is unobtainable. "Thirst for revenge is the most important source of *ressentiment*." Scheler saw the apostate as particularly liable to ressentiment as he engages in "a continuous chain of acts of revenge against his own spiritual past": "Even after his conversion, the true 'apostate' is not primarily committed to the positive contents of his new belief and to the realization of its aims. He is motivated by the struggle against the old belief and lives only for its negation."[11] Scheler's theory explains some of the dynamics at work in many versions of deconversion and seems especially relevant in those accounts that are unrelievedly hostile to their former faith, such as anticult literature.

A particularly interesting type of anticult literature is that written by a person who has lost faith as a result of deprogramming. Deprogramming is a forcible intervention into a believer's life by means of physical abduction, confinement, and intensive confrontation in order to effect a deconversion. The term was coined by one of the leaders of the anticult movement, Ted Patrick. Patrick's *Let Our Children Go!* is an account of the origin and nature of deprogramming that contains an autobiographical account of his own deconversion. Patrick was a "fanatical Bible student" partly because of "the sense of guilt I felt about my responsibility for my speech impediment."[12] He saw his speech impediment as God's punishment for Original Sin until the day he decided that only he could help himself. Patrick, who is an African American, describes his crisis in a passage that recalls Frederick Douglass's similar turn away from prayer to self-reliance: "Somehow I woke up one day and realized how tired I was of not being able to communicate, how inconvenient it was, and how unnecessary. Since everybody had been praying for God to give me normal speech from the time I was old enough to know, I had assumed that a cure was strictly in God's hands, and that if I wasn't cured it was God's will. But that day it occurred to me to say to myself, 'Look, everybody's praying to God and begging God and asking God to cure me. But what is it I'm doing for myself?' " (230). Patrick looks back on his obsession with the Bible as "abnormal and morbid." This personal experience of faith shapes his view of cults in the 1970s: "I'm sure that realization had a lot to do with my feelings about the cults some thirty years later. I had been programmed too; in fact I'd programmed myself, and I knew firsthand how miserable and stunted that kind of life could be" (230).

Patrick became actively involved in fighting against cults as a result of his son's encounter with proselytizers for a group called the Children of God. A good deal of *Let Our Children Go!* depicts his experiences deprogramming members of various cults, including the Children of God, the Divine Light Mission, the Unification Church, Hare Krishna, and a number of smaller groups. A recurring pattern in most of these deconversions is the religious believer's deep feelings of guilt, which drive him to accept a religious doctrine or an authority figure that promises release from guilt while keeping the believer dependent, obedient, and unable to take personal responsibility for decisions. Patrick's involvement and success in deprogramming hundreds of religious devotees reveals both the insights he gained from personal experience and his vicarious reliving of his own religious fanaticism and deconversion.

Deprogramming involves challenging the motives and practices of the cult's leader, marshaling the testimony of former cult members who have deconverted, reestablishing broken contacts with the cult member's family, and demonstrating the harmful consequences of involvement with the cult. Deprogramming is not simply a technique, however, but implies a controversial theory of religious experience propagated by the anticult movement. To understand deconversion as a matter of deprogramming assumes, of course, that the religious believer has been brainwashed. Patrick writes that to deprogram a person is to "counteract the brainwashing he'd undergone" (65). The underlying theory is that the free will of the believer has been vitiated or destroyed by the cult's practice of mind-control techniques. These techniques include deceptive recruitment strategies, relentless criticism of independent thought, authoritarian leadership, isolation from the influences of the larger society, and physical exhaustion from hunger, sleeplessness, and frenetic activity. The theory of brainwashing posits a passive believer who is psychologically manipulated by cult members so as to become, in effect, a willing prisoner of the group.

Because of the cult member's loss of free will, the only way to help him is to forcibly extract him from the cult and try to get him to think critically about it. According to Patrick, "All I want and all I do is to return them their ability to think for themselves, to exercise their free will, which the cults have put into cold storage. I thaw them out, and once they're free of the cult, with very few exceptions, they begin again to lead productive lives" (77). Once the ability to think has been restored, the former devotee is as if resurrected: "It's like turning on the light in a dark room or bringing a person back from the dead" (67).

The assertion that only outside intervention can bring about deconversion makes deprogramming an original and highly controversial theory of the loss of faith. Brainwashing, the idea that attitudes and beliefs can be forcibly replaced, is often used as a simplistic explanation of why others cling tenaciously to beliefs with which one disagrees. Malcolm X uses the metaphor of brainwashing frequently when looking back at his misguided commitment to the Nation of Islam, as well as in describing the faith of Christians and the ways African Americans internalize self-

hatred as a result of racism in the United States. Malcolm X recovered his autonomy and integrity through his own efforts, and
he appeals to his audience to reverse the conditioning that molds
their outlook. The theory of deprogramming, however, assumes
not only the idea of brainwashing but the conviction that an individual cannot recover from mental conditioning through his or
her own efforts. Patrick's book ends, two months after the cap-
ture or rescue of Patricia Hearst from the Symbionese Liberation
Army, with a public plea for the chance to deprogram her: "She
just can't be held responsible for anything she did after the SLA
brainwashed her. . . . She's never going to be herself again. They
can send her to every psychiatrist in the country, it won't do any
good. No psychiatrist can cure what's wrong with her. I know
it. They've taken her mind away. Why don't people understand?"
(284–85). Patrick's claim that only a deprogrammer can restore a
cult member to mental freedom contradicts his own testimony
that he "programmed himself" and that he chose to abandon destructive religious beliefs.

In spite of the evidence of countless cult members who voluntarily leave their group, however, the theory of deprogramming
has not only advocates but true believers. A particularly large
number of deconversion stories have come from ex-members of
the Reverend Sun Myung Moon's Unification Church, and many
of these are by individuals who have undergone some sort of coercive intervention designed to undermine their religious commitment.[13] Christopher Edwards's *Crazy for God: The Nightmare
of Cult Life* (1979) describes his involvement in the Unification Church and deprogramming by Ted Patrick. Edwards's book
"is about the rapid near-destruction of a human being—myself"
through a cult's "deceit, manipulation, and terror."[14] The first
paragraph sets up a parallel between his own experience and Jonestown: "Although a different group was involved, I believe it is
also a story which may help to explain the paranoia and absolute
obedience which led to the recent horror of the Peoples Temple
murders and mass suicide." *Crazy for God* dramatizes a form of
psychological violence that is as destructive of human autonomy
as Jim Jones's more overt domination: "the sinister indoctrination
process by which I was transformed from an intelligent, independent human being into a completely subservient disciple of my
new Messiah—terrified of questioning, dependent on my leaders
for my every move, ready and willing to die or even kill to restore
the world under the absolute rule of Reverend Moon" (ix–x).

Immediately after his graduation from Yale in 1975, Edwards

became involved with the Unification Church. His account of his seven months in this group describes the church's recruiting practices, including such ethically questionable practices as "love bombing" and "heavenly deception." Love bombing means offering a targeted individual promises of unlimited love and care; heavenly deception is the church's justification for temporarily misleading potential converts, such as keeping secret the proselytizers' identity as "Moonies." Edwards describes how pressure from other believers, sleeplessness, hunger, and prolonged chanting and prayer keep a believer in an exhausted state that inhibits critical thinking. Rapidly indoctrinated in the cult's beliefs, he suppresses his doubts, loses his ability to concentrate or read, and offers God "the ultimate sacrifice," his mind (201).

In January 1976 Edwards is kidnapped and deprogrammed by Ted Patrick, whom his father had hired. At first Edwards views Patrick as Satan and chants continuously to block out his words. But gradually the deprogramming works, and Edwards returns to "doing what I had always treasured most—questioning and thinking about life situations, especially my own" (227). Three strategies are most effective in undermining Edwards's faith. First, Patrick appeals strongly to Edwards's feeling of guilt for having hurt his parents in rejecting them. He forces Edwards to admit that he would kill his father if commanded by the "Heavenly Father," Moon:

> "Wouldn't you kill for Moon? Wouldn't you? Answer me you mindless zombie!"
>
> "Yes, I'd gladly lay down my life for Father," I shouted.
>
> "You see that man over there?" Satan pointed to my father, slumped in a chair. "That's your father, your *real* father, the man who birthed you, and raised you and gave you everything he could. . . . You'd kill him, admit it!"
>
> I turned and stared at my father. His face was ashen. What had he seen in mine? (221–22)

Edwards's deconversion culminates in an emotional reunion with his father. The interconnections between religious affiliation and issues of family enmeshment and separation are as evident and complex here as in the case of many of the autobiographers we have discussed, especially Augustine, Mill, Ruskin, and Gosse. The stories of Collier, Mills, and Edwards confirm Janet Jacobs's thesis that charismatic new religions engage in "ideological indoctrination and spiritual practices that are geared toward the development of a religious family consciousness that replaces the family of origin as the source of needs gratification."[15] Especially significant is the idealization of the male leader of the group, given the paternalistic family ideology of post-World War II America. Deconversion follows the religious group's failure to fulfill its promise to create the perfect family.

The second deprogramming tactic that breaks through Edwards's defenses is helping him to understand the process of brainwashing in other situations, such as in other religious groups and in communist countries. Edwards meets two young men who were deprogrammed from cults, and although he first denies any relevance to his own experience, he finally sees parallels. When an ex-member of the Scientology cult recounts his story, Edwards is struck by undeniable similarities: "From what I heard about visions and voices the leaders claimed to experience, I was startled at how closely his tales matched the mystical experiences of Family members. But they *couldn't* both be true!" (217–18). Edwards has to learn how other believers join and disengage from a cult before he can apply these insights directly to his own situation. Ted Patrick's third basic strategy is to point out inconsistencies between Moon's book *The Divine Principle* and the Bible, as well as ethical criticisms of the Unification Church's practices. Edwards's internal conflict between dogmatic faith and critical questioning feels like "two minds struggling, Old and New. One that looked and thought and examined, the other reciting Family revelation. Both of them *mine*" (226). He does not immediately reject his faith when confronted with inconsistencies, but the crucial turning point in his deconversion is his commitment to "examine Family practices and ideology" (227), to begin to think for himself again.

In a brief epilogue, Edwards warns his readers about the danger of cults and explains their appeal to young Americans of his generation. The success of groups like the Unification Church is made possible by "the development of a technology to influence and control the mind" (230), which he says is best explained by psychiatrist Robert Lifton's *Thought Reform and the Psychology of Totalism*. Edwards asserts that his generation is rebelling against American culture's "overemphasis on science and technology" and that young people's hunger for friendship and love is exploited by cults claiming to form a new and better family. He concludes with a warning about the danger of permanent, irreversible psychological damage in those who have been "acculturated." He claims that it is all but impossible to escape from brainwashing without forcible deprogramming: "There seems to be no escape from cult madness for many members, as evidenced by the fact that in my seven months in the Moonies I only saw one follower able to openly reject the beliefs and leave on his own" (233). This assertion is controverted by many social scientists, including a statistical study of the Unification Church showing that "the majority of members seem to leave voluntarily within two years of joining."[16] Edwards again appeals to the tragedy of Jonestown as the most horrifying possible consequence of involvement in cults. Even short of such an outcome, he urges concern for the psychological suffering of those caught up in these religious groups. His deepest hope is that his autobiography will warn others about "the threat of cult madness."

Anticult literature has played a crucial role in shaping public opinion about new religious movements. Autobiographies by ex-members have been a powerful influence in creating the largely negative public view of most new religious groups as relying heavily on brainwashing to control the minds of adherents. In the 1970s much of the general public's knowledge of cults, especially of the Unification Church, came from newspaper and magazine accounts of successful deprogrammings. One social scientist speaks of the anticult movement's use of a "subversion myth" that postulates a conspiracy endangering an entire society and of its role in creating a "social scare" that supposedly requires "a remedial agenda that must be followed if catastrophe is to be avoided."[17] Deconversion narratives are ideological weapons in conflicts involving substantial financial interests of both deprogrammers and religious groups. They are a form of sensational journalism shaped by the mass media's efforts to appeal to an audience. These narratives provide evidence in legal disputes involving the free expression of religion and the separation of church and state. Many scholars express concern that the brainwashing argument offers a dangerous precedent for governmental repression of unconventional forms of religion and for the use of medical and psychiatric rhetoric to suppress deviance.[18] We need to consider not only these texts' literary form and religious significance but also the politics of deconversion, the role of stories of lost faith in various struggles for power.[19]

Ted Patrick and Christopher Edwards often describe individuals as passive objects determined by social forces. Their interpretation of deconversion as deprogramming is very different from the other autobiographies studied in this book, which give a much greater emphasis to choice and agency. The deprogramming paradigm tends to interpret the loss of faith not as an individual choice but as a social process that bypasses a deciding center of the person. This model of deconversion is oddly similar in this respect to Christian stories of conversion that stress self-surrender to the power of grace. Whereas most deconversion stories differentiate themselves from Christian conversion by insisting on the autobiographer's active role in bringing about a movement away from faith, deprogramming narratives are similar to traditional conversion stories in their emphasis on the self's submission to forces beyond its control. For Edwards, though, it is not God but humans—first the Moonies and then Ted Patrick—who mold his beliefs.

An irony of those versions of deconversion that assume the theory of deprogramming is the way they mirror the very aspects of cults that they most criticize in their reliance on forcible abduction, isolation, intensive group pressure on an individual, and sometimes sleeplessness, hunger, and exhaustion. A few researchers suggest that deprogramming may actually inflict greater harm than involvement in cults, damaging a person's attempt to become independent and autonomous in relation to parents: "In so far as the brainwashing thesis is believed, it also leaves deprogrammees with the feeling that twice in their lives they have been incapable of controlling their own destiny, not just in the way that all of us feel blocked by circumstances, but in a more fundamental way, which can severely threaten their sense of personal identity. . . . How can they have any confidence in their ability to conduct their own lives in the future?"[20] Deprogramming may make a person feel helpless and irresponsible, unable even to learn from making mistakes. The process may defeat its essential purpose of restoring independence and individual responsibility.

Sociologists and psychologists have compared the ways voluntary defectors from a cult differ from persons who have been deprogrammed. Ex-cult members who have been deprogrammed are far more alienated from the beliefs of their former faith and from individuals still in the group. The process leads to much greater animosity toward the cult and often to an ex-member's participation in the deprogramming of other members. "Those who are successfully deprogrammed will almost inevitably express profound gratitude to their rescuers and, usually, feelings of guilt for having cost their parents so much suffering and so many thousands of pounds. They are also likely to assert that they would never have left without the intervention of the deprogrammer."[21] Another researcher concludes that "deprogrammed persons are more likely than voluntary defectors to claim they were brainwashed, to demonstrate greater feelings of anger and hostility toward their former groups, to reflect a greater degree of alienation from former associates in the group, to feel their involvements were harmful or dangerous to their mental well-being, and to exhibit a greater need for a safe, conflict-free emotional affiliation with others."[22] These generalizations are borne out in the autobiographical literature by deprogrammed cult members such as Christopher Edwards. The theory of brainwashing and deprogramming provides a way to absolve both ex-cult members and their families of any responsibility for their actions, and a convenient way to explain a confusing and often humiliating series of transformations. Deprogramming produces a highly pejorative view of all cults, and, since the distinction between a cult and a "normal" religious community is difficult to delineate, implicitly suggests that much of religious experience involves the believer's abdication of critical thinking and moral responsibility.

The deprogramming narrative is significant in its challenge to concepts of the self's freedom and integrity. The metaphor of deprogramming presents deconversion not as a matter of individual rational choice but as a causal process determined by social pressures. This view has enough genuine insight into the reality of social conditioning, and enough practical success, to pose a credible interpretation of religious experience and deconversion. Yet it is finally incoherent, for at the same time that deprogrammers try to restore an individual's agency they deny personal responsibility for beliefs, assuming an inability to change without outside intervention. The process of deprogramming, which is supposed to restore the individual's free will, in fact duplicates the coercive practices of cults. The most thorough social-scientific study of the brainwashing controversy concludes that there is "little evidence in support of the brainwashing thesis." In her study of the Unification Church, Barker points out that thousands of members defect voluntarily, while the success rates claimed by deprogrammers are highly exaggerated.[23]

In a significant aside, Edwards says that in his book he changed the names of everyone in the Unification Church (except Moon) "to protect the guilty, among whom are some of the most innocent victims of all" (x). This confusion about guilt and innocence indicates the dissolution of the concept of responsibility. If even the leaders of the Unification Church have been brainwashed, deprogramming becomes necessary on a truly massive scale. How society would determine the limits of such forcible intervention into religious life is a deeply troubling issue that deprogrammers avoid. It is probably this unwelcome implication of the theory of deprogramming that has led to its demise. Courts in both the United States and Great Britain have ruled that while trying to dissuade persons of their faith is not against the law, abduction and confinement are illegal. Although the circumstances authorizing parents' temporary legal custody of their adult children continue to be controversial, the practice of deprogramming has been severely curtailed since the early 1980s.[24]

Accounts of deconversion from cults, especially deprogramming narratives, provide striking evidence of how radically individuals can be transformed under the influence of coercive social pressure. These narratives juxtapose a reductive type of social-scientific perspective that explains action solely in terms of determining social causes and the individualistic orientation of autobiography, which usually assumes a certain amount of choice and agency even in a religious believer's positive or negative response to God. Their challenge to traditional concepts of free will, integrity, and responsibility is a primary source of these narratives' power to disturb and fascinate a large audience. Far more than deconstructionist or postmodern theories of the subject, which are so obscure as to mystify the general public, these versions of deconversion present a vivid picture of the self's fragility. In deprogramming narratives in particular, the plot centers on the narrator's recovery of integrity and independent judgment, but the way this comes about undermines the very values at stake. Such a narrative calls in question central concepts associated with the Western idea of the self—its freedom, integrity, identity, and responsibility—even as it supposedly defends these values. In the deprogramming version of deconversion, the author's final position is deeply ambiguous, for he has been restored to free thought against his own will.

10

GENDER AND
DECONVERSION

ONE'S UNDERSTANDING OF gender can make a significant difference both as a causal factor in the loss of faith and in the portrayal of deconversion, shaping the possibilities for depicting the
loss of faith in narrative. In accordance with much recent work
in women's and gender studies, *gender* in this chapter refers to
the cultural experience of being male or female, the social differences and expectations that become attached to the biological
fact of one's sex.[1] So deeply formative of personal identity are
conceptions of one's gender and religious convictions that a radical change in either usually requires significant change in the
other. We can neither reduce religious thought to being merely
a disguised expression of gender (or to any other single cause)
nor discuss religious experience abstracted from the factor of gender. The analysis of gender assumptions and rhetoric may disclose
significant meaning in any discourse or text, including all those
previously discussed in this book. This chapter focuses on autobiographies that explicitly make issues of gender identity central
to the account of deconversion. I reflect on the implications of
extensive recent scholarship on gender and autobiographical self-
representation and show in five recent works by American women
how the writer's account of deconversion is affected by questions
about gender identity.

The reasons why both men and women lose religious faith are
often closely related to issues of gender identity. Feminist criticism has explicated how pervasively, if usually unconsciously, the

writing and religious thought of male authors are influenced by their gender. The experience of deconversion, too, often reflects men's concerns about gender identity. For instance, Augustine's dissatisfaction with Manicheism and certain forms of philosophy was based partly on their failure to help him understand his anxieties about his sexual life. There are intimate connections between an autobiographer's attempt to define his masculinity and the search for an ultimate commitment in John Stuart Mill's struggle for independence from his father, in Malcolm X's criticisms of Elijah Muhammad's sexual misconduct, and in the experience of those who reject a form of Christianity because of its Puritanical sexual morality. However, it is only recently that male autobiographers have discerned and articulated explicitly some of the connections between male sexuality and masculine spirituality, including the reasons men lose faith in a tradition. A particularly moving group of autobiographies, sometimes called "AIDS memoirs," reflects the experiences of those who have contracted AIDS or are HIV infected or have lost loved ones to disease, and some of these documents record a rejection of a religious faith because of its inadequacy in helping the writer deal with suffering.[2]

The issue of whether women's autobiographies have a distinctive literary form has been much discussed in recent years, and scholars have demonstrated ways that women's gender affects the construction of identity and its textual representation.[3] Some attempts to define a basic form of women's autobiographies seem oversimplified: for example, the claim that women write in more discontinuous, fragmented forms such as the diary; that women disclose the self not in isolation but in relationship to some "other"; or that women must find oblique or displaced ways to assert themselves. If the issue of gender's role in autobiography is conceptualized in terms of defining specifically female structures that express women's identities, the critic quickly falls into the trap of perpetuating traditional stereotypes of essential male and female characteristics. Even as generalizations, such theories are dubious, for they are "based on a preselected corpus of male autobiographies and a preestablished set of common traits."[4] Countless men have also written diaries, explored their private lives in relationships with others (including God), or expressed themselves indirectly, obliquely, or covertly. Nonetheless, we need not posit some essentially female autobiographical form to appreciate that gender often makes a crucial difference in writing about the self. Specifically, the forms of women's deconversion narratives have sometimes been decisively influenced by the author's conception of the relationships between gender, personal identity, and religious faith.

There are few women's autobiographies before the twentieth century that describe a deconversion. In fact, argues Linda Peterson, there are few spiritual autobiographies of any sort by women before the twentieth century because of prohibitions that prevented them from this kind of writing: "In general, they did not compose retrospective accounts of spiritual or psychological progress, they did not use principles derived from biblical hermeneutics to interpret their lives, and they did not attempt to substitute another system of interpretation to create a secular variant of the form."[5] Women encountered not only the general prohibition against female self-expression but a specific exclusion from the traditional basis of British spiritual autobiography: the interpretation of one's life in terms of biblical typology. In Victorian times, the prohibition of women from engaging in biblical hermeneutics led them to develop alternative forms of self-expression.

It is not surprising that before the twentieth century there are few texts by women in the tradition I have traced. In addition to cultural prohibitions against self-assertion, assumptions about the limited female intellect, and exclusion from biblical hermeneutics, a woman writing a version of deconversion would have had to overcome tremendous social pressures demanding that women be the guardians of religious piety. During the nineteenth century the notion that women are naturally religious and responsible for the preservation of religion was asserted frequently and forcefully. This did not prevent the expression of doubts and even denunciations of Christian authorities in women's diaries, letters, novels, and poetry. African American autobiographers such as Jarena Lee and Julia Foote found ways to criticize the male structures of power that tried to prevent them from preaching the gospel.[6] During the second half of the nineteenth century, American women involved in spiritualism wrote autobiographies expressing their rejection of harsh Calvinist doctrines and searching for spirit manifestations of loved ones.[7] Harriet Martineau's autobiography "makes a man's refusal to explain a theological dilemma the crisis of her autobiography and the impetus for her search for a non-theological hermeneutics."[8] But in the vast majority of works by women, criticisms of Christianity were either disguised, displaced into the voices of fictional characters, or presented as a rebuke to an aberration of Christianity rather than shown as causing a loss of faith. Women's autobiographies are similar to those by writers such as Frederick Douglass and Charles Eastman in the oblique ways that loss of faith in Christianity is intimated but not publicly avowed.

In the twentieth century, as prohibitions against women writing about their loss of faith broke down, there arose both newly perceived reasons for deconversion and innovative literary strategies to explain the loss of faith. The grounds for deconversion include such events as the perception of a church's misogyny, a decision to have an abortion, or an experience of sisterly solidarity with other women that discloses by contrast the deficiencies of a religious community. In the four autobiographies by women discussed previously in this book, gender-related conflicts were crucial aspects of the process of deconversion. For Mary McCarthy, the events in "C'est le Premier Pas Qui Coûte" take place amidst adolescent uncertainties about the transition between girlhood and womanhood. McCarthy's initial claim to have lost her faith is motivated by desires for intellectual independence and social recognition and shows an early attempt to assert her own identity as other than a conventionally good Catholic girl. Dorothy Day's apostasy from Christianity was justified partly by her wish to affirm her freedom from Christian sexual morality, and she returns to the church largely because she feels the need to offer praise and thanksgiving for her experiences of giving birth and being a mother. For Sophia Collier, leaving the Divine Light Mission occurs partly because she can no longer accept its rule that "premies" be celibate, and for Jeannie Mills, a primary reason for defection from the Peoples Temple is the sexual abuse and exploitation she witnesses. Questions about their identity as women and about sexual morality influence these writers' deconversions in explicit and self-conscious ways.

A common and crucial issue for women deconverting from the new religious movements examined in the previous chapter is rejection of the prescribed sex roles and exploitation fostered by many of these groups. "At the deepest levels of commitment and love, rejection of the spiritual father symbolizes the failure of a morality that is grounded in the theology of dominance and control."[9] A similar pattern may be traced in many recent criticisms of Christianity as "patriarchal," justifying the subordination of women to male authority. The argument of these women's autobiographies parallels that in the works discussed in chapter 5, "Christianity and 'the White Man's Religion,'" but for these women the emphasis falls not on *white* but on *man*. Such works utilize the author's experiences to deconvert readers from the belief that Christian faith requires the normative conceptions of masculinity and femininity defined as patriarchy. Women of color, forming a tradition sometimes called "womanist" thought, explore the relationship between their twofold oppression and religious beliefs. We can further distinguish reformist critiques from those put forward by a smaller group of radical feminist thinkers who insist that oppressive tendencies are not just corruptions of Christianity but are inherent in its myths, theology, and institutions.

Four recent spiritual autobiographies by Kathleen Norris, Terry Tempest Williams, China Galland, and Patricia Hampl dramatize a religious search underway and assert their conclusions or convictions with more tentativeness than many works of religious autobiography. These writers emphasize uniquely personal experience rather than acceptance of dogma, doctrine, or ecclesiastical authority. Their autobiographies are this-worldly and antidualistic, seeking the holy or the sacred in areas of life often viewed as secular or profane by the official institutions of Christianity. An experience of deconversion is an important part of each author's religious development, and for all of them questions about gender identity are crucial aspects of both their deconversion and their further search. These works are also similar to each other and differ from the last work I will consider, Mary Daly's *Outercourse*, in that they distinguish between the patriarchal form of Christianity that they reject and a reinterpreted form of Christianity that they affirm.

In *Dakota* (1993), Kathleen Norris writes of her return to the isolated town in which her grandparents lived, rediscovering there the religious heritage she had abandoned. Norris's ambivalence about her Presbyterian upbringing emerges in her reflections on her female ancestors, especially two grandmothers, who represent "two very different strains of American Protestantism that exist in me as a continual tension between curse and blessing, pietism and piety, law and grace, the God of wrath and the God of love."[10] One grandmother "implanted the seed of fundamentalism within me, a shadow in Jungian terms, that has been difficult to overcome." As a feminist, for many years Norris could not accept much of the church's language. She also rejected the tyrannical "Monster God" of some Calvinists in her family, a God she feared but could not trust. Another female relative who shapes her view of Christianity is her Aunt Mary, whose death was partly attributable to a moralistic, judgmental form of Protestantism: "She died of lots of things: sex and fundamentalist religion and schizophrenia and postpartum despair. She was a good girl who became pregnant out of wedlock and could make no room for the bad girl in herself. She jumped out of a window at a state mental hospital a few days after she had her baby" (100–101). Norris must abandon a harsh Presbyterian creed before she can come to a richer appreciation of Christian faith, largely through worship experiences with a community of Benedictine monks and meditation on the wilderness conditions of the Great Plains, which she compares to the desert sought out by monks. *Dakota* is a "spiritual geography" that interprets the author's deepening relationships to a particular landscape and the people who dwell there.

While the process of deconversion is not the central focus of *Dakota*, the overall movement of Norris's spiritual journey is a return to a faith once rejected. She endorses Flannery O'Connor's remark that "most of us come to the church by a means the church does not allow" (95). Although she stayed away from the church for many years, her return to South Dakota was a religious pilgrimage back to her family's sources of strength: "On the ground of my grandmother's faith I would find both the means and the end of my search" (93). Like the Christian writers discussed in chapter 8, Norris returns to Christian faith after having passed through a deconversion. However, unlike Lewis, Day, or Muir, she does not criticize her rejection of her childhood beliefs as apostasy. Leaving the "hard religion" of Calvinist Protestantism is a necessary stage in the formulation of her own personal faith. The way Norris defines conversion reflects this gradual return to a former point of view but with a new perspective: "Conversion . . . connotes not a change of essence but of perspective, as turning round; turning back to or returning; turning one's attention to" (145–46).

Norris's loss of faith reflects questions about women's identity, especially her sense that the church oppresses women, as well as such issues as her conception of religious language. When she refused to go to church she "exemplified the pain and anger of a feminist looking warily at a religion that has so often used a male savior to keep women in their place" (94). Her return to Christianity centers on her revised understanding of the issues that drove her away. In using Christian ideas and metaphors—such as sin, grace, or asceticism—to express her spiritual search,

Norris distinguishes between the meanings she affirms and those she rejects. She shows that a Protestant background may be both bane and gift, even for her Aunt Mary: "The church was music for her, and she sang all her life in church choirs" (101). Norris traces to Mary her intention to become a writer: "I believe I became a writer in order to tell her story and possibly redeem it. . . to make sure she was forgiven and at peace" (101). For Norris to "redeem" her aunt's suicide, she must describe what might drive a feminist, "a thinking and questioning person" (96), out of the church. The reasons for Norris's earlier deconversion must be included along with her discovery of positive resources in the Christian tradition if the whole truth about her experience of Christianity is to be rendered. The end of her religious journey is, in T. S. Eliot's words, "to arrive where [she] started / And know the place for the first time." She finds her spiritual home in the church she had once rejected for feminist reasons: "Against all the odds, I rediscovered the religion I was born to, and found in it a home" (134).

In a different way, deconversion is an equally crucial element in Terry Tempest Williams's *Refuge* (1991). This work describes the author's responses to two "unnatural" events that began simultaneously in 1983: her mother's slow death from cancer and the overflowing of Great Salt Lake, which threatens the Bear River Migratory Bird Refuge and the birds to which Williams is devoted. Autobiographical writing is Williams's attempt to heal the wounds caused by these losses: "Perhaps, I am telling this story in an attempt to heal myself, to confront what I do not know, to create a path for myself with the idea that 'memory is the only way home.'"[11]

Much of *Refuge* explores parallels between the author's experience of loss, grief, and healing and the natural cycles of disorder and recovery evident among the many species of birds in the environment of Great Salt Lake. Only a few passages before the last chapter suggest that Williams is critical of the Mormon church, of which she is a member. The most significant criticism occurs in the context of a discussion of the ecosystem of pelicans. Williams contrasts the diversity within any natural ecosystem with the ideal of self-sufficiency sought by the Mormon community: "There is an organic difference between a system of self-sufficiency and a self-sustaining system. One precludes diversity, the other necessitates it. Brigham Young's United Order wanted to be independent from the outside world. The Infinite Order of Pelicans suggests that there is no such thing" (103). Williams observes that had Brigham Young focused his attention "more on Earth than 'heaven on earth' his vision for managing the saints in the Great Basin might have been altered" (107). This passage recalls Edmund Gosse's use of biological metaphors to interpret religious behavior and his analogies between natural phenomena and the survival, adaptation, flourishing, and vulnerability of religious communities. Through most of *Refuge*, however, Williams's doubts and criticisms of Mormonism are subordinated to her observations of the natural world and to her recounting the family's ordeal as her mother suffered from cancer until her death in January 1987.

In the last chapter, "The Clan of One-Breasted Women," Williams makes a discovery that calls her Mormon faith into question. She learns that the reason why so many women in her family (her mother, both grandmothers, and six aunts) have had mastectomies may be linked to atomic testing in Utah during the 1950s. The final analogy between human life and the behavior of birds is that both Williams's family and the birds of Great Salt Lake are residents of what the Atomic Energy Commission described as "virtually uninhabited terrain." Habits of uncritical deference to authority may have been a factor in these deaths: "In Mormon culture, authority is respected, obedience is revered, and independent thinking is not. I was taught as a young girl not to 'make waves' or 'rock the boat'. . . . For many years I have done just that—listened, observed, and quietly formed my own opinions, in a culture that rarely asks questions because it has all the answers. But one by one, I have watched the women in my family die common, heroic deaths. We sat in waiting rooms hoping for good news, but always receiving the bad. . . . The price of obedience has become too high" (285–86). Williams attributes to her Mormon tradition a habit of submissiveness and obedience that may have contributed to both the "unnatural disasters" of her story. At the close of *Refuge* her religious faith seems about to dissolve.

Williams also shows that Mormon tradition can empower women in important ways, for instance in women's rituals of blessing and healing each other. She repeatedly demonstrates the paradox that her extremely patriarchal community produces many exceptionally strong and independent women. In her acknowledgments, speaking of her family, she states that "the Mormon community we are a part of also healed us" (295). Because she shows the positive side of her Mormon background and traces to it some of her love of nature (for instance, citing the examples of Jesus and Joseph Smith sojourning in the wilderness), I see Williams as

wanting to salvage certain aspects of her tradition rather than reject it completely. Yet her memoir concludes rather ambiguously
just at the point where deconversion seems to be the logical next
step: "As a Mormon woman of the fifth generation of Latter-Day
Saints, I must question everything, even if it means losing my
faith, even if it means becoming a member of a border tribe among
my own people. Tolerating blind obedience in the name of patrio-
tism or religion ultimately takes our lives" (286).

The question of whether Williams will remain a Mormon is
not clearly resolved within the book, and we leave the author on
the brink of either deconversion or a decision to try to reform
her religious tradition from within. Williams seems to prefer the
roles of prophetic critic and political activist to simply dropping
out of unjust institutions. Yet, depending partly on the response
of the authorities she challenges, she may soon become an alienated outsider. In the final paragraph of *Refuge*, Williams and several other women engage in civil disobedience, protesting nuclear
tests in the desert. They find themselves stranded in the desert
by government officials who do not realize "that we were home,
soul-centered and strong, women who recognized the sweet smell
of sage as fuel for our spirits" (290). The natural world and relationships with other women are "home," providing solace and
inspiration for Williams.

Facing death, Williams's mother experienced a form of spiritual
comfort outside the confines of the Mormon church. She feels a
new openness and confidence in herself when "personal revelation
replaces orthodoxy" (136). As Williams's grandmother is dying she
looks at a tumor from her body and thinks: "Finally, I am rid of the
orthodoxy" (246). Her foremothers' examples suggest where Williams's own path will lead. The natural world, with its marshes,
birds, and harsh yet comforting beauty, may henceforth provide
Williams with "refuge" not only from her grief but from officially
sanctioned religious institutions.

China Galland's *Longing for Darkness* (1990) describes a search
for dark images of female divinity. Her story begins with a repudiation of her church because of its treatment of women. Raised
a strict Roman Catholic, Galland finds herself at twenty-one, with
one child and expecting a second, seeking a divorce for her own
safety and that of her children. It is suggested that she send a canon
lawyer to Rome to expedite her case, which might otherwise take
seven years: "I made my first adult decision and left the Church.
I was unwilling to let a group of celibate men who had never had

families have this kind of power over my life. With no money of my own and no enforceable order for child support, the suggestion that I fly a priest to Rome, however well intended and practical, was a cruel joke."[12] Galland is drawn to the figure of the Virgin Mary but finds her "impossibly good, inhumanly pure" (15). Such perfection and purity leave Galland, conscious of her own faults, feeling despair and utterly remote from the church.

Turning outside the Christian Church for spiritual direction, Galland discovers Zen Buddhism but is unhappy with the traditional Buddhist belief that a person can only be enlightened in a man's body. Then she learns of Tara, a female Buddha in the Tibetan tradition. She begins to search more widely for female divinities, especially dark images of goddesses, and travels to Nepal, India, Switzerland, France, Yugoslavia, Poland, and Texas. At first looking only outside Christian traditions, Galland soon learns about the many black madonnas within Roman Catholicism and makes pilgrimages to Einsiedeln, Switzerland, to Czestochowa, Poland, and to the Rio Grande Valley in Texas.

Galland affirms that darkness has symbolic meanings that are important to many religious communities and that the longing for darkness is a deeply felt human need. Dark female images can symbolize numerous things repressed or denigrated by patriarchal traditions: the earth, the body, the unconscious, matter, the feminine, darker races, the womb, and the unknown, including all we do not know of divinity. She discovers a political dimension of dark images of Mary when she sees how reverence for a black madonna is linked to Polish nationalism and Lech Walesa's Solidarity Movement, and how in El Salvador a black madonna is represented as Madre de los Desaparecidos, the Mother of those who disappeared at the hands of death squads. Galland contrasts this representation of a powerful Mary with the passive, suffering one: "This is a Mary that we need now, a fierce Mary, a terrific Mary, a fearsome Mary, a protectress who does not allow her children to be hunted, tortured, murdered, and devoured" (275). This fascinating and moving spiritual autobiography explores the ways in which the imagery and symbols of deity in various religious traditions diminish or affirm women.

An experience of deconversion initiated Galland's spiritual search for dark female deities. Deconversion is itself a form of darkness, a frightening wilderness of the soul, that can bring new light and life. Galland's first loss of faith and her subsequent doubts about all the traditions that she encounters are crucial parts of her search and continue to influence her as she assesses religious symbols and communities. In particular, her partial return to Catholic tradition—understood not as an authoritarian institution but as a community responding to the inexhaustible wealth of meaning in symbols—is explicated through contrasts with forms of Christianity that she argues no longer have the spiritual vitality to empower women. Galland's work, too, shows deep connections between a loss of faith, a struggle with models of gender identity, and spiritual searching that leads to a reinterpretation of certain aspects of Christianity.

As a final instance of a woman's spiritual autobiography in which deconversion figures significantly in the author's reinterpretation of her faith, consider Patricia Hampl's *Virgin Time* (1992). Hampl's story is cast as three journeys to Assisi, Lourdes, and a Cistercian monastic retreat on the coast of northern California. She begins her quest somewhat uncertainly and bristles when Donnie, a friend who is a sister in a monastery, suggests she is going on a pilgrimage: "Something about the word set my teeth on edge. *Pilgrimage.* I wince at the eau-de-cologne language of spirituality, but the whole world as I first understood it comes rushing back on the merest scent. I still want to embrace it—so, of course, when it dares to draw close, I slap it clean across the mouth. Love and loathing, those old partners."[13] Hampl can neither embrace wholeheartedly her Catholic heritage nor abandon it. Like Mary McCarthy, who also spent her childhood years in St. Paul, Hampl interweaves "memories of a Catholic girlhood" with later experiences shaped by this past, even when they involve rebellion or flight from Catholicism.

Hampl left the church for many years: "I had *fallen away*, a figure of speech utterly Catholic in its cosmic reach, obliterating the notion of personal choice. To have fallen away suggested you were not a person but a dislodged fragment of a larger eternal structure. You were a particle which had teetered off the edge of the universe and dropped into limitless black space, where you drifted aimlessly in the thin air of your own vain disbelief" (15). Two actions symbolize this defection and suggest reasons for her rejection of the church. The first is a brief vignette of a solitary meal in a restaurant, after a visit to a gynecologist, when she polishes off her lunch with her first birth control pill (13). A second revealing turning point is the Sunday morning when she tells her father, "I'm not going to Mass anymore." Hampl reconstructs her response to her mother's assertion that she broke her father's heart: "*Good*. That rotten killer instinct of the young which also happens to be the life instinct. The strange thing was, my heart was broken, too. But I was glad it was broken. I was expressing myself. Self-expression had become my true faith" (17). Hampl indicates that leaving the church was bound up with her need for autonomy in relation to her parents and with the need for "self-expression" at the center of her sense of identity.

Most of *Virgin Time* is set two decades after her deconversion, as she searches for "the contemplative life," the sources of wonder, and both understanding and experience of prayer. She finds most of what she is looking for in Catholic communities of worship and feels able to ignore what she does not like about the church. The repressive and restrictive institution "deconstructed," leaving the senses of wonder and yearning that for Hampl are the core of the religious life:

> The legalisms of the Church fell away from me. In a sense, the Church deconstructed. It ceased to be the imprisoning cell of catechized thought and repressive habit, with its egregious insults to common sense. It became, simply, my most intimate past. It returned to its initial state, it became poetry. . . . I wasn't fallen away anymore; now, magically, the Church had fallen away. What remained of its colossal architecture was a frail structure of wonder, long forgotten. Hence, the return to Mass, the visits to Donnie. And now, the Road to Assisi, which I had difficulty calling a pilgrimage but which certainly felt like an act of fascination. (16)

Hampl's return to Catholicism constantly recalls her past deconversion. The symbolism of the book's title both epitomizes the motif of returning to what was once rejected and reveals one of the ways that Hampl's meditations reflect her experience as a woman. The title comes from Thomas Merton's notion of the "point vierge," which he called "the virgin point between darkness and light, between nonbeing and being . . . when creation in its innocence asks permission to be once again, as it did on the first morning that ever was" (206). In the central epiphany of the book, Hampl uses the symbol of the virgin to interpret the moment when she offers her first real prayer. She had for years rejected virginity, and every other symbol of innocence, as a barrier to adulthood and "the real world":

That old monster, innocence. My ingenue life which had been clutched even more fiercely in the stranglehold of willful Catholic naïveté than James Joyce's furious Irish artist lads—who at least were boys and meant to break the rules. I had done everything I could think of to wrestle free: broke my parents' hearts, hardened my own, mixed it up every way I could, tried to be a furious artist myself. My methods had been many: sex as freedom; books as tactical missiles; the outward mobility, away from the soul, of intellectual life; passionate politics; and a string of wrong romances—I suited up in all the knightly armor I could find to ride against the convent school ingenue who refused to convert to the secular faith of the real world. (206)

In a moment of recognition and self-acceptance, at dawn in a California meadow, Hampl realizes that a kind of innocence resulting from her Catholic background is indelibly ingrained in her character. She had started out her pilgrimage with the knowledge that "there was something Catholic about this virginal self, with its stubborn habit of trust and its taste for finding meaning in everything" (56). But for much of her life, and through much of *Virgin Time*, Hampl struggles with the "Catholic" qualities she associates with virginity and innocence: "What was remarkable 'back there' was the endlessness of girlhood, the sheer tenacity of my naïveté. Twenty-five, thirty, thirty-five, still a girl, propelled by a fierce ingenue heart. Which I wished to cut out, I suppose. Innocence gets vicious in the long run" (55). She repeatedly feels ashamed of being Catholic and yet also tries to understand "what prompts shame, what is *under* it" (40). Underneath the shame is a deep attachment to the past that, for better and for worse, but in any case undeniably, makes her who she is.

Hampl's spontaneous act of prayer in the California meadow involves accepting that element of her upbringing from which she had desperately sought to escape. Whereas for years she had seen innocence as only "an absence, a vacancy," she finally finds "a *use* for innocence, after all":

Tears spiked my eyes. *I can't help it, its how I am.* Like the hot metal of a Linotype, these ordinary words cast themselves across my mind.

The words could have been "Lord, have mercy," or "Forgive me, for I have sinned." They *were* those words, in fact, those prayerful

words of old, but neatly camouflaged in my modern voice that can't
resist ripping the religious art off the walls; *I can't help it, its how
I am.* Finally, prayer. After all my running away from it, and then
running after it to Assisi and Lourdes. (207–8)

In this climactic experience Hampl embraces as a symbol of innocence the Catholic icon that she had scorned for many years:
virginity. Virginity is reinterpreted as not simply the absence of
sexual experience but the symbol of the positive qualities of innocence and openness to experience, which she can now accept as
part of her character. At last she can pray, and she discovers that
prayer is "a plain submission of fact. An admission of existence. . . .
Surrender of intention into the truth of a life" (208). Yet her prayer
is registered in the "modern voice that can't resist ripping the religious art off the walls," a voice that shows the effect of the author's
past deconversion.

Hampl's reconciliation with the faith of her childhood is presented with constant reminders of a past deconversion that, while
not described in detail, still shapes her life, including her religious
experience. The meaning of "virgin time" in the book epitomizes
how Hampl finds "a use for innocence, after all," discerning a positive meaning in the "monster" she had hated as an impediment
to becoming a mature woman, and living a life. "You don't get to
live Life—that thing I feared I was missing. You just live a life.
This one" (208). Innocence does not mean simply "to be marked
by an absence, a vacancy. By nothing at all" (207). Nor is it primarily a moral command or rule imposed by the church. Hampl
reinterprets innocence, purity, and virginity as symbols that nour-
ish the imagination and help her understand aspects of her life,
such as the "immaculate moment" of time, the "virginal morning
instant," when she encounters "the anonymous presence of being
itself."

An aspect of deconversion is incorporated into the contemplative life insofar as an element of mystery, of not knowing, is necessary to experience the crucial religious experience of wonder.
The epigraph to *Virgin Time* is part of an Emily Dickinson poem:

Wonder is not precisely Knowing
And not precisely Knowing not—
A beautiful but bleak condition
He has not lived who has not felt.

Loss of faith does not in itself produce wonder but rather the kinds of emotional suffering we have seen throughout this book. However, a loss of faith is sometimes prerequisite for the "beautiful but bleak" condition of striving to know, or to be related to, an ultimate reality that is finally mysterious and that cannot truly be known with the kind of clarity and certainty that many Christians claim. Although deconversion need not lead to wonder, prayer, or the contemplative life, Hampl's work reveals one way in which the loss of faith may influence later religious experience and provide insights with theological significance.

In these four spiritual autobiographies, deconversion is an important theme that is significantly related to gender issues. Each author rejects a religious tradition partly because of its normative image of women or its actual treatment of women. Norris, Galland, and Hampl return to the faith they left, rejecting certain elements and affirming others. Williams emphasizes rejection more than retrieval of her tradition and represents a midpoint between the other three writers and the final author to be considered, Mary Daly. These women jettison the theological doctrines and moral rules of the institutional church and emphasize the mystery of Christian symbols, reinterpreting their meaning in the light of personal experience. Although they differ in important ways, and each explores many other religious ideas not related to gender issues, I see them all as revisionists or reformers of traditional Christian assumptions about women. In each, an experience of the loss of faith is central to the autobiographer's portrayal of her spiritual journey and demonstrates the inadequacy of some traditional Christian attitude, belief, or interpretation of a symbol. Like the Christian apologists discussed in chapter 8, their return to Christian faith centers on a transformed understanding of the issues that once drove each writer away. This is not to say that Hampl or any of these writers sees herself primarily as an apologist for any fixed religious position.[14] They all stress spiritual searching and leave the reader with a sense of the search being still underway, open-ended, incomplete.

Deconversion is central in each work as the pain and spiritual hunger following a loss of faith motivates and orients the author's search for religious experience both inside and outside the institutions of the church. The way each author's faith is lost, especially as this is connected with issues of gender identity, conditions the way she experiences a moment of grace or a new understanding of her religious search. When they move beyond deconversion, all four finally gain something that has been associated with women, as Norris finds a mystical relationship to the landscape, Williams turns toward nature for healing, Galland seeks the darkness of female imagery for the divine, and Hampl reappropriates virginity and innocence as parts of her identity.

Among those women who reject Christianity as unreformable is Mary Daly, whose recent autobiography dramatizes a life-long process of deconversion. Daly's *Outercourse: The Be-Dazzling Voyage* (1992) recounts the author's repudiation of Christianity and presents her "Radical Feminist Philosophy." The structure of Daly's narrative is determined by her continuing flight from the confinements of male authority. "My true course was and is Outercourse—moving beyond the imprisoning mental, physical, emotional, spiritual walls of patriarchy, the State of Possession."[15] The plot of her life story involves "voyaging" through four "spiral galaxies" representing periods of Daly's life, culminating in "Momentous Moments" of Be-Speaking, Be-Falling, Be-Witching, and
· embracing "the Be-Dazzling Now."

Outercourse represents a version of deconversion in both of the senses in which I have used that term. That is, it involves a deconversion in the narrower sense of a loss of faith in a historical religious tradition and also in the larger metaphorical way that deconversion is used to interpret other forms of identity transformation. After Daly loses faith in Christianity during the period of writing *Beyond God the Father* (1973), her further voyage involves not only an intensely spiritual search for full awareness of "Being" in the present but a continued effort to decode, demystify, and debunk all the institutions and ideology of patriarchy. In Daly's *Websters' First New Intergalactic Wickedary of the English Language*, she defines patriarchy as "the prevailing religion of the entire planet, whose essential message is necrophilia."[16] She sees Christianity as but one expression of male domination and oppression and devotes her life to overthrowing every form of patriarchy. Thus deconversion provides the paradigm for interpreting not only loss of faith in Christianity but the rest of Daly's life as well. Daly's autobiography dramatizes the experiences and intellectual development that led her to reject Christianity and the many other manifestations of patriarchy and argues for the philosophical inadequacy and ethical injustice of all expressions of male power and domination.

Outercourse brings together several themes from earlier versions of deconversion. Daly is similar to the African American and Native American writers discussed in chapter 5 in her strongly didactic determination to challenge aspects of the reader's faith. Deconversion is not simply an aspect of the writer's personal experience but a publicly avowed agenda, an indispensable part of the program of abolishing patriarchy. For Mary Daly, in contrast to almost all the other writers examined in this book, deconversion is more than a past experience and a theme for the autobiographer's present reflections. Only Sartre presents himself, as does Daly, as still working to undo the residual effects of a former faith. Deconversion is not only past event and present subject matter but projected future task. Given Daly's commitment to constant revision of ideas, her "spiraling outwards" to new galaxies, and the goal of "coming into the fullness of the Expanding Now," she anticipates and envisages future deconversions as necessary stages of the ongoing journey beyond patriarchy's mental and spiritual walls.

The literary form of Daly's work reflects this understanding of her life as involving successive deconversions. Daly plots her voyage as a spiraling outwards, away from patriarchal attempts to circumscribe her course. *Outercourse* is "a Voyage of Spiraling Paths, Moving Out from the State of Bondage" (3). The spiral shape of her journey reflects the way that the past is never left behind completely as she returns to old problems and questions with a fresh perspective. On the more local level of the text, Daly's style is marked by constant punning, unorthodox capitalizing, redefinition of terms, and invention of "New Words," as she calls attention to language's pervasive reflection of gender ideologies. It is only by "ReNaming" experience that women will escape "mindbinding" and effect their own liberation. *Outercourse* carries on the work of the "webster" in reweaving webs of connection that women have repressed and in spinning new connections. Another distinctive hallmark of Daly's work is her embracing and redefining of traditional female caricatures, especially those pertaining to lesbians and older women. She recovers the elements of wisdom and power that men fear in witches, crones, and spinsters, and she dubs herself a "Nag-Gnostic" and a "Positively Revolting Hag." The need for constant criticism of patriarchal thinking embedded in language is expressed in Daly's creative wordplay, which exposes and undercuts the ways language perpetuates the oppression and marginalization of women. Continuing deconversion from the many forms of patriarchy is both subject matter and formal principle of *Outercourse.*

Daly's earlier works contain extensive autobiographical reflection, including such reinterpretations of previous writing as the "Autobiographical Preface," "Feminist Postchristian Introduction by the Author," and "New Archaic Afterwords" in the most recent edition of *The Church and the Second Sex*, and the "Original Reintroduction by the Author" in the latest version of *Beyond God the Father*.[17] *Outercourse*, too, demonstrates Daly's method, so reminiscent of Nietzsche, of reaching new insights by reinterpreting her past writings. She speaks of her autobiography as not a mere recalling of memories but itself a further voyaging: "Although the events described Originally happened 'back then,' in the earlier Galaxies, the Re-Calling of them is occurring Now, and the result is utterly Other than a simple collection of memoirs. It is participating in New Spiraling Movement. This is not quite like any writing that I have done before. It is a series of Acts of Momentous Remembering of my own Voyage" (11).

This general remark about the energizing (or "Gynergizing") effect of Re-membering applies especially, I think, to the recalling of the loss of faith. Reconstructing the crucial choice to break with discredited beliefs may help an author to revitalize the fundamental values that justified deconversion, linking present with past in a way that discerns new meanings and orientation in each. The autobiographical act of interpreting a deconversion may help one break free from present confinements: "It is my Hope that these Re-Callings will be helpful to women—mySelf included—in overcoming the time warps that mark the Age of Dis-memberment— the foreground 'present' that impedes our Living a true Present / Presence. It is my Hope also that the Re-membering will generate more Gynergy for further Be-Dazzling Voyaging" (12). Daly conceptualizes what I think is one of the primary if usually unarticulated incentives for an author to focus the autobiographical act on deconversion: the hope that the interpretation of a loss of faith will bring positive meaning and direction for the future. She hopes that spinning a web connecting past and present will encourage further deconversion from the worldwide religion of patriarchy and (to use Daly's language) encourage participation in the Now of ever Unfolding Be-ing.

Like *Outercourse*, the autobiographical works of Norris, Williams, Galland, and Hampl make central each author's rethinking and reassessment of the issues that led her to reject a religious tradition. In each the interpretation of deconversion reveals a continuing search for meaning in that event and a fresh discernment of sources of strength and value that orient the writer toward the future. These authors demonstrate the rich potential of women's autobiographies for illuminating the relationships between one's gendered identity and one's religious views and between deconversion and spiritual searching.

11

CONCLUSION

The Literary and Religious Significance of Deconversion Narratives

SOME LITERARY THEORISTS have claimed that every autobiography reflects a conversion: "One would hardly have sufficient motive to write an autobiography had not some radical change occurred in his life—conversion, entry into a new life, the operation of Grace. If such a change had not affected the life of the narrator, he could merely depict himself once and for all, and new developments would be treated as external (historical) events. . . . It is the internal transformation of the individual—and the exemplary character of this transformation—that furnishes a subject for a narrative discourse in which 'I' is both subject and object."[1] This view makes the distinction between the author as protagonist and as narrator the basis for a claim that autobiography as a genre is either overtly or covertly a form of conversion narrative. I could make a similarly sweeping assertion that deconversion is equally central in autobiography, that the author's transformation from protagonist to narrator necessarily entails a rejection of certain beliefs, moral practices, and communal loyalties. The starting point from which he or she deconverts is as inescapable and decisive an influence on an autobiographer's writing as any subsequently discovered truth. In this concluding chapter, however, I want to make a more modest claim: while deconversion is not inevitable or universal in autobiography, it continues to be of crucial significance both as an influence on literary structure and as a religious theme.

Many autobiographies explore how particular commitments and beliefs came to be seen as mistaken. For instance, in *A Leg to Stand On* (1984), Oliver Sacks describes how a severe injury to his leg undermined his dualistic view of the self and led to a radical reorientation in his understanding of his profession as a neurologist. Commenting on this work, Paul John Eakin compares it to several other works that also depict the disconfirmation of a theory by personal experience:

> This disjunction between theory and experience that structures Sacks's story of his injury and his quarrel with "classical" neurology is an insistent theme in a number of twentieth-century autobiographies. I am thinking here not only of Jean-Paul Sartre's *The Words* (1964) and Andre Gorz's *The Traitor* (1959), but also of . . . Ronald Fraser's *In Search of a Past* (1984), and Roland Barthes's *Roland Barthes by Roland Barthes* (1975). All of these autobiographers report that they reached a point in their lives when the theories to which they were committed—in Sartre's sense of life-informing "project"—simply did not square with the affective reality of their experience.[2]

A "disjunction between theory and experience" often generates the elements constitutive of deconversion: intellectual doubt, moral criticism of an inadequate way of life, emotional upheaval, and rejection of a community or a conception of society. This is especially so when the disconfirmed theory is not simply a philosophical perspective but approximates a Sartrean project of a lifetime. Such an identity-forming theory is in effect a faith commitment, and rejecting such a worldview and project is tantamount to a loss of religious faith. The theme of identity transformation, which becomes more and more prominent in twentieth-century autobiography, often involves a form of deconversion. The faith that is lost is less frequently in a historical religious tradition and increasingly a matter of devotion to some secular substitute, an ideology or commitment that claims to provide the final and normative terms for understanding one's life and determining one's conduct. And the literary structures used to interpret such a transformation are less likely to be recognizable permutations of the essentially Christian narrative tradition traced in this book.

The literary significance of deconversion narratives is, then, the continuing prominence in autobiography of the experience of losing faith and the formal innovations devised to render such experiences. The coherence of this species of autobiography is partly a matter of direct influence, as the Christian tradition I have traced exerts its vitality and power even on writers such as Sartre who reject Christian beliefs. Autobiographers will undoubtedly continue to use biblical metaphors, an Augustinian crisis scene, or the example of earlier autobiographers as they construct their own stories. Deconversion narratives form a distinctive species of autobiographical writing not only because of this direct literary influence but also because individuals respond in analogous ways to common circumstances, such as the claim of a religious group or philosophical ideology to provide certain knowledge, a moral way of life, and a community worthy of commitment. When autobiographers find the promises broken or the ideals on which they have built their lives disconfirmed, they describe and reflect upon the meaning of experiences of disillusionment or despair. The affinities and family resemblances among such works call for comparison and interpretation in terms of the hermeneutic perspective I have proposed in this book.

In the future, versions of deconversion will undoubtedly be written that resemble the basic types this book has explored. For example, Ingmar Bergman's *The Magic Lantern* depicts his rejection of a gloomy theology and an oppressive religious upbringing and his exhilarating discovery of the beauty and truth-telling power of theater and cinema.[3] Bergman offers an indictment of Protestant tradition similar to Ruskin's and Gosse's aesthetic critique, which I discussed in chapter 4. We can expect new versions of flight from the totalistic claims of a cult and Christian apologetic works in which the author reassesses an early loss of faith as a mistake and as apostasy. Writers will undoubtedly censure Christianity for authorizing racial or sexual injustice or for perpetuating divisions by social class. Autobiographers inspired by liberation theology may contrast their understanding of true Christianity with "the rich man's religion" and call on readers to abandon the latter. Reformers will uphold the possibility of authentic Christian faith; more radical voices will reject all forms of Christianity, since, as Mary

Daly insists with regard to patriarchy, "oppressive tendencies are not aberrations but the very stuff of christianity, since its symbols are inherently oppressive" (135).

As traditional forms of deconversion narrative continue to be written, autobiographers will search for new metaphors and plot structures to express the uniqueness and particularity of their personal struggle with a faith. While we cannot predict the shape of future narratives of deconversion, I hope that this book helps readers to recognize them as they come. A recent work that does not fit any of the thematic rubrics organizing previous chapters is Thomas Simmons's *The Unseen Shore: Memories of a Christian Science Childhood* (1991).[4] Simmons explores his ambivalent feelings about his religious upbringing and the insights leading to his withdrawal from the Church of Christian Science. He especially criticizes the church's sanctioning of cruelty by denying medicine to children in agonizing pain—for instance, when he suffers recurring ear infections and a broken arm. He explores, too, how religious doctrines created emotional distance between his mother and father, and between them and their children. Simmons felt torn between commitment to the spiritual abstractions his faith told him were alone real and desire for all the undeniable physical presences and people he loved. *The Unseen Shore* is similar to Ruskin's and Gosse's works in its analysis of the entanglement of religious beliefs with family loyalties; the book also resembles stories of deconversion from cults in its tracing of a movement from a sectarian outlook to a larger, freer world. Chapters on "Mourning" and "Ghosts" explore the painful "hangover identity" inherent in his "ex-role" (as I defined this term in chapter 3). Mourning is a process "in which one lays pieces of oneself and one's faith to rest when they can no longer serve," yet memories of past religious beliefs retain, even after decades, "the capacity to detonate" (116), creating guilt or feelings of meaninglessness. Simmons's work is continuous with the narrative traditions I have traced, yet its weaving together of different themes and its probing exploration of his religious experience and doubts make *The Unseen Shore* a rich and innovative version of deconversion deserving much fuller analysis. The literary forms of autobiography will surely continue to reflect writers' creative new strategies for exploring the events and effects of deconversion.

The theme of deconversion is central in so many autobiographies, I think, because the loss of faith and the writing of autobiography both involve a search for individuality and autonomy. The autobiographical act and the rejection of one's religious community alike represent an attempt to choose personal identity rather than being defined by a social authority. Sometimes it is the organized, institutional form of a religious tradition that an individual experiences as oppressive and constrictive. The large number of versions of deconversion that involve a struggle for autonomy in relation to the writer's parents (for instance, those by Augustine, Mill, Ruskin, Gosse, and many apostates from cults) indicates that the loss of faith is often closely related to the task of forming personal identity in the context of one's family.

Autobiographical writing and deconversion alike require an effort to define one's individuality and values, and both processes involve detaching the self from formative communities. This is not to deny that a person's subjectivity is deeply related to collective and relational identities or that individuality must be defined partly in terms of commmitment to community if it is not to end in isolation and estrangement. While no one can be free of social conditioning and participation in a culture, individuals may strive for greater self-consciousness and choice about which communities within their social world are most worthy of commitment. Before a person can make a mature commitment to a community, or arrive at a defensible form of religious faith, he or she needs to move beyond uncritical identification with a group and—at least imaginatively, for an interval—doubt its system of belief. Thus I see a written narrative of deconversion as a public, self-conscious, and highly articulated version of a more general process of individuation in modern Western cultures.

This is not to say that individuation can be achieved only by the person who ends in atheism or a secularized worldview. When a person returns to the original faith community and the crucial transition appears in retrospect as a crisis of faith rather than a loss of faith, doubt and criticism of traditional authority have played an important role in individuation. As we saw in the case of the Christian autobiographers discussed in chapter 8, a doubting believer may return to the original faith community with a new view of the church and a critically tested theology. The Christian apologies by Day, Lewis, Gilkey, and Muir present an early loss of faith as a moment in the individuation process and indicate the possible place of deconversion within a lifelong journey of faith. A similar process of rebellion and selective retrieval of Christian elements characterizes the spiritual autobiographies of Norris, Williams, Galland, and Hampl analyzed in chapter 10.

I have distinguished deconversion in the narrower sense of rejecting a historical religious tradition from the use of deconversion as a metaphor for interpreting some other emotion-wrought transformation involving a change of belief, morality, and community. With the exception of chapters 3 and 7, this book has looked at deconversion primarily in the narrower sense of loss of faith in a religious tradition, usually some form of Christianity. Yet in closing I also want to suggest that deconversion is a subtle yet pervasive impulse and theme not only in autobiographies but in a great deal of modern and postmodern thinking. Deconversion is a metaphor for our times that expresses modernity's search for authenticity, which so often takes the form of a flight from authority, from inherited paradigms of thought, and from various forms of pressure to conform. The theme of deconversion is a latent autobiographical dimension of a great deal of the dissenting and debunking tone of art and argumentation in the twentieth century. Nietzsche first discerned that deconversion from all inherited beliefs could become a systematic program reflecting a scrupulous intellectual conscience: "Christianity *as a dogma* was destroyed by its own morality; in the same way Christianity *as a morality* must now perish, too: we stand on the threshold of *this* event. After Christian truthfulness has drawn one inference after another, it must end by drawing its *most striking inference,* its inference *against* itself; this will happen, however, when it poses the question *'what is the meaning of all will to truth?'* "[5] The literary theory of deconstruction exemplifies deconversion become a program, for it demands systematic critique of all forms of belief, which are seen as determined by the nature of language. The deconstructionist seeks to undermine not simply our confidence in God and religious ideas but also the concepts of self, text, goodness, and truth. The theory of deconstruction reveals the loss of conviction that any intellectual position could attain truth—except perhaps that of the skeptic who has been deconverted from belief in the possibility of attaining any fixed conclusions. The concept of deconversion may illuminate not only autobiographies but other forms of discourse in which the loss of faith is not an explicit theme but a subtext, an undercurrent, a dimension of meaning not fully articulated.

Deconversion narratives have several kinds of religious significance. The loss of faith and writing about that loss are momentous events that reflect both the religious tradition rejected and the search for new values. We have seen that the way an author casts a story of deconversion reflects the characteristic emphases of a particular faith commitment. For example, the decisive impact of Ruskin's and Gosse's reinterpretations of the Bible on their faith reveals the preoccupation with Scripture of what would now be called Protestant fundamentalism. The reasons for McCarthy's and Kenny's deconversions reflect the high priority given by Roman Catholicism to public avowals of creedal assent. The form of Sartre's disillusionment is conditioned by the nature of his vision of the literary artist's mission in society. Native American and African American autobiographers criticize that belief which was so greatly stressed to people of color: the equation of Christian faith with assertion of the superiority of the white man's ways. The loss of faith reflects the religious tradition abandoned: "Only a person with a firm faith can lose it in a problematic fashion, and he or she will lose it in a manner directly related to the character and expectations of the faith itself. In that respect the loss of faith or the modification of faith are inherently religious acts largely conditioned by and channelled through the spiritual categories and social expectations of the original community of faith."[6]

The religion that is rejected deeply influences both the way the story is told and the author's present commitments. A central theme of this book is that deconversion is rarely if ever a total transformation of character and religious concern. We can see the impress of a former faith on every one of the autobiographers studied here, and the degree of each writer's continuity with early beliefs is one of the principal issues debated by scholars. Specialists on individual figures continue to discuss, for example, how much Augustine's mature theological and ethical views were influenced by his Manichee background, which Protestant beliefs Ruskin and Gosse retained, and the degree to which Frederick Douglass distanced himself from the Christian beliefs of his upbringing. Every author considered here can be shown to have been permanently marked by the faith he or she supposedly rejected. Thus one aspect of the religious significance of deconversion narratives is the deep and pervasive influence of religious commitments and ways of thought even on those who have abandoned a historical religious tradition.

In addition to these works' reflection of historical traditions, the religious significance of deconversion narratives may be formulated in other terms. Many of these books reveal the impulse and imperative to criticize idolatry. Very often an autobiographer

attacks what he or she sees as a confusion between the truly ultimate and some human institution, doctrine, or symbol that is
supposed to represent the divine but comes to usurp its place. Deconversion rarely means the rejection of faith itself and is always
experienced in relationship to a particular commitment. Early
Christians were seen as atheists by the Romans because of their
refusal to worship Roman deities. Like any usage of the term *atheism*, any particular deconversion is conditioned by the particular
form of faith it negates. What from one perspective looks like a
radical loss of faith may be seen from another view as a denunciation of idolatry. An autobiographer often interprets a deconversion
in retrospect as a stage in a long spiritual journey. In recounting
his loss of faith in Elijah Muhammad and the Nation of Islam,
Malcolm X explains that he came through this crisis because he
realized that "there was something—one thing—greater than my
reverence for Mr. Muhammad. It was the awesomeness of my
reason to revere him. . . . I silently vowed to Allah that I never
would forget that any wings I wore had been put on by the religion
of Islam."[7] For the theists among the autobiographers examined
here, the shattering of an earlier faith is later seen as an existential correlative of the theological principle that God transcends all
symbols, representations, and institutions.

Deconversion narratives are also religiously significant in that
nearly always a loss of faith is justified by reasons of conscience.
This is so whether the autobiographer is a prophetic voice recalling a corrupt tradition to its true character, like Douglass, Day,
and Gilkey, or whether the writer has become an outsider rejecting a religious faith as inherently destructive of human integrity
and responsibility, like McCarthy, Sartre, or Daly. When the primary reason for deconversion is cognitive doubt about a theology's
adequacy (as in the case of Anthony Kenny) or about its fidelity
to Christian tradition (Newman), considerations of the ethics of
belief determine the point at which uncertainty becomes the compelling ground for rejecting a creed. Even when a deconversion
is largely motivated by a desire to reaffirm the world's beauty
and goodness and to turn to aesthetic values for primary meaning
(Ruskin and Gosse), here, too, ethical concerns justify the author's
negative assessment of a world-denying stream of Protestantism.

The term *deconversion* mirrors Christian conversion narratives
and orients my study in a certain direction. My conclusions about
the loss of faith in autobiography are based largely on texts challenging Christian beliefs and reflect my own interests and limi-

tations. Very different insights would be garnered were one to approach the loss of faith from the perspective of other religious and literary traditions, for instance Jewish, Native American, Islamic, or Buddhist ones. Consider, for instance, narratives of deconversion from Judaism emerging from the Holocaust. The implications of the Holocaust for religious faith are extremely varied, shattering some persons' faith, augmenting it for others, and for some confirming their earlier belief or nonbelief.[8] In the diverse body of autobiographical documents by survivors, victims, and executioners, the best-known account of a loss of Jewish faith as a direct consequence of the Holocaust is Elie Wiesel's *Night* (1958). Wiesel describes his arrival in Auschwitz: "Never shall I forget those flames which consumed my faith forever. Never shall I forget that nocturnal silence which deprived me, for all eternity, of the desire to live. Never shall I forget those moments which murdered my God and my soul and turned my dreams to dust. Never shall I forget these things, even if I am condemned to live as long as God Himself. Never."[9] In this passage, God is said to have been "murdered" and yet, more ambiguously, may go on living. Wiesel stops praying but argues with God, in the manner of Job: "I did not deny God's existence, but I doubted His absolute justice" (56). He feels himself "stronger than the Almighty" (79), accuses God of injustice on Rosh Hashanah, and refuses to fast on Yom Kippur, the Day of Atonement. When he sees a child executed, he feels that God is hanging on the gallows (76). Is *Night* a decisive rejection of faith in God, or does Wiesel's challenge, doubt, rebellion against, and accusation of God signify a continuation of the covenant by means of actions comprehensible in terms of similar quarrels with God by Abraham, Moses, Job, and the prophets?

Differing interpretations of *Night* reflect a larger debate among Jews about the implications of the Holocaust for Jewish faith. Some, such as Richard Rubenstein, argue that the Holocaust signifies that "God is dead," that in the aftermath of the Holocaust traditional monotheistic faith is impossible for Jews. Other Jewish thinkers interpret the Holocaust as not a unique event but one analogous to earlier tragedies in Jewish history such as the Exile or persecutions by Romans, Inquisitors, and Cossacks. Martin Buber uses the metaphor of an "eclipse" of God to interpret the possible presence-in-absence of God in the events of the Holocaust. Emil Fackenheim proposes a new commandment: "Jews are forbidden to hand Hitler posthumous victories."[10] Analysis of Jewish Holocaust autobiographies needs to interpret them in the light of this theological discussion. Such a study should also locate Jewish responses to the Holocaust within distinctive literary traditions rather different from the largely Christian ones traced in this book.[11] The example of Jewish autobiographical responses to the Holocaust suggests that my findings in this book need to be supplemented and extended by interpretations of a broader range of literary texts and religious traditions, a project requiring considerable attention to problems of literary theory, definition of terms, and cross-cultural comparison.

In the course of this book I have frequently noted the difficulty of separating the analysis of deconversion from the topic of conversion (or reconversion) to an author's subsequent vision of truth. An autobiographer's present commitments are evident in his analysis of mistaken beliefs, even when he tries to focus only on the process of loss, as in the case of Gosse. Almost all of these autobiographers are deeply religious in their ongoing search for meaning, although many of them become wary of institutional commitments. Some writers, such as Augustine and Malcolm X, have radical conversion experiences after their deconversions, but the majority of them, including such Christians as Dorothy Day and Edwin Muir, distinguish their own gradual deepening or redirection of religious commitment from the claim of a sudden and radical transformation brought about by supernatural intervention. Among those who leave a cult, a sociologist finds a continued quest for faith: "Among the 40 respondents who participated in the study, not one spoke of atheism in response to their disillusionment, and few expressed an interest in returning to mainstream religion, which, according to the majority of respondents, had previously failed to meet their spiritual needs. The evidence strongly suggests that those who choose a spiritual path in life will stay on that path, even if it is hurtful, troubling, and disappointing."[12] Similarly, in the autobiographies examined here, the death of one god usually brings not the end of spiritual searching but its reorientation.

The decision to write an autobiography focusing on deconversion indicates religious seriousness, the conviction that religion *matters*. In contrast to a person for whom faith simply dwindles away, leaving a secular outlook indifferent to the deepest sources of life and meaning, writers of deconversion narratives view the loss of faith as a crucial matter of choice and commitment, and in describing this event they articulate their ultimate concerns. The rejection of a particular religious faith usually reveals a writer's ongoing search for truth, moral goodness, and a community that will nurture understanding and solidarity or love.

These autobiographies show the dynamic relationship between faith and doubt in the spiritual life. Paul Tillich concisely explains the way certainty and doubt are not mutually exclusive but structurally related elements in the "dynamics of faith" in human existence: "Faith is certain in so far as it is an experience of the holy. But faith is uncertain in so far as the infinite to which it is related is received by a finite being. This element of uncertainty in faith cannot be removed, it must be accepted. And the element in faith which accepts this is courage. Faith includes an element of immediate awareness which gives certainty and an element of uncertainty. To accept this is courage. In the courageous standing of uncertainty, faith shows most visibly its dynamic character." [13] Our study of ways in which deconversion has been interpreted as part of the spiritual life discloses the potentially productive roles of doubt and disillusionment in religious experience. If religious faith meant the end of doubt and of longing for further understanding of God, it would be better not to have faith. Doubt and the loss of faith can drive one to renewed searching, and without the element of seeking, religious commitment becomes either dogmatic or dormant.

Autobiographical versions of deconversion elaborate an insight metaphorically conveyed in a passage in Herman Melville's *Moby-Dick*. In chapter 85, Ishmael reflects on the rainbow that sometimes appears in "the fountain" of the whale's spouting. The vapor is then "glorified by a rainbow, as if Heaven itself had put its seal upon his thoughts. For, d'ye see, rainbows do not visit the clear air; they only irradiate vapor. And so, through all the thick mists of the dim doubts in my mind, divine intutions now and then shoot, enkindling my fog with a heavenly ray. And for this I thank God; for all have doubts; many deny; but doubts or denials, few along with them, have intuitions. Doubts of all things earthly, and intuitions of some things heavenly; this combination makes neither believer nor infidel, but makes a man who regards them both with equal eye." [14] This passage suggests that skepticism and doubt are crucial experiences that, in combination with the faith that endures, can give rise to insights and intuitions with their own unique beauty and value. Studying versions of deconversion helps me to understand my own spiritual searching, as I doubt, discard, and rediscover aspects of my own version of Christian faith.

The process of writing an autobiography offers an opportunity for religious growth, as a writer reflects on the ultimate concerns that required him or her to reject a particular community and its beliefs. I argued in an earlier book that autobiography is not simply a description or report on how an author's conscience operated in the past but itself represents an act or exercise of conscience, and sometimes an occasion for a transformation or renewal of religious commitment.[15] Similarly, the assessment of a past loss of faith is an action with deep significance in a writer's present. Making this experience central in autobiographical writing engenders reflection on the ultimate powers, values, and standards by which the old faith is judged deficient. A deconversion narrative may thus be motivated by a desire for, and in turn lead to, a firmer grounding or a reorientation in relation to the fundamental values a person trusts and seeks to live by. Writing the story of a loss of faith leads one to consider which aspects of the past can be reclaimed as still meaningful and what new loyalties or concerns brought one through a crisis. For a Christian autobiographer, writing a version of deconversion may provide an occasion for discerning God's providence at work in suffering, for reinterpreting a painful event as a Fortunate Fall or a stage in a Pilgrim's Progress, or for exemplifying the *via negativa* by which the demolition of idols clears the ground for authentically monotheistic faith.

The religious significance of deconversion narratives lies in the examples of such writers as Augustine, Newman, and Malcolm X as they responded to a loss of faith with courage, integrity, and renewed searching for meaning. Religious meaning is disclosed, too, in the ways autobiographical writing itself reenacts, continues, and extends in new directions the essentially religious quest for truth and human community. Latent in the act of retracing one's loss of faith is the search for future direction in one's life and the hope for renewed and justifiable faith. These versions of deconversion have, potentially, deep significance for readers who may never record their lives in a literary text but who struggle in similar ways to find meaning in the loss of faith and in the uncompleted search for a better understanding of what is truly ultimate.

NOTES

INDEX

NOTES

1. Introduction

1. All quotations from Augustine's *Confessions* are from the translation by R. S. Pine-coffin (Harmondsworth: Penguin, 1961). Subsequent references to book and chapter number appear in text.
2. For example, see A. D. Nock, *Conversion: The Old and the New in Religion from Alexander the Great to Augustine of Hippo* (Oxford: Oxford Univ. Press, 1933), 7: "By conversion we mean the reorientation of the soul of an individual, his deliberate turning from indifference or from an earlier form of piety to another, a turning which implies a consciousness that a great change is involved, that the old was wrong and the new is right." See also Eugene Gallagher, *Expectation and Experience: Explaining Religious Conversion* (Atlanta: Scholars Press, 1990) and Karl Morrison, *Understanding Conversion* (Charlottesville: Univ. Press of Virginia, 1992).
3. For criticisms of how Paul's example of sudden conversion has dominated and distorted studies of conversion, see Alan Segal, *Paul the Convert: The Apostolate and Apostasy of Saul the Pharisee* (New Haven: Yale Univ. Press, 1990), 285–300, and Morrison, *Understanding Conversion.*
4. William James, *The Varieties of Religious Experience* (New York: Macmillan, 1961), 174. The phrase James quotes is taken from E. D. Starbuck's *The Psychology of Religion.*
5. This book grows out of my *The Conscience of the Autobiographer: Ethical and Religious Dimensions of Autobiography* (London: Macmillan; New York: St. Martin's, 1992). As in that work, here, too, I focus on conscience as an aspect of autobiographical writing, that is, on how ethical and religious concerns are expressed not only in the loss of faith but also in writing about that loss.
6. On the relationship of faith and doubt, see Paul Tillich, *Dynamics of Faith* (New York: Harper and Row, 1958), 16–22.
7. For a useful anthology of philosophical criticisms of theism, see J. C. A. Gaskin, ed., *Varieties of Unbelief from Epicurus to Sartre* (New York: Macmillan, 1989). Also see James Thrower, *A Short History of Western Atheism* (London: Pemberton Books, 1971).

8. Philippe Lejeune, *On Autobiography*, trans. Katharine Leary, ed. Paul John Eakin (Minneapolis: Univ. of Minnesota Press, 1989), viii.

9. A problematic case for my study is Thomas Carlyle's *Sartor Resartus*, which by Lejeune's definition would not be an autobiography. *Sartor* is discussed in chapter 3 because Carlyle affirmed the autobiographical dimensions of its account of deconversion and because of its influence on later autobiographies and William James's theory of conversion. An extensive discussion of the issue of referentiality in autobiography is Paul John Eakin's *Touching the World: Reference in Autobiography* (Princeton: Princeton Univ. Press, 1992).

2. Three Christian Versions of Deconversion:
Augustine, Bunyan, and Newman

1. See H. G. Keppenberg, "Apostasy," *Encyclopedia of Religion* (New York: Macmillan, 1987).

2. Avrom Fleischman, *Figures of Autobiography: The Language of Self-Writing* (Berkeley: Univ. of California Press, 1983), 55.

3. Paul Delany, *British Autobiography in the Seventeenth Century* (New York: Columbia Univ. Press, 1969), 31. Delany speculates that the reasons for Augustine's negligible influence were mainly sociological: "Conservatives in religion, who would have known Augustine's works, tended to write restrained autobiographies in which Augustinian fervour and self-accusation were carefully avoided. The Baptists and other enthusiastic sects were closer to the spirit of the *Confessions*; but his works were probably too scholarly and expensive for them, since he is very rarely mentioned in their writings" (32).

4. Lewis R. Rambo, "Conversion," *Encyclopedia of Religion*.

5. John Bunyan, *Grace Abounding to the Chief of Sinners*, ed. with an introduction by W. R. Owens (Harmondsworth: Penguin, 1987), 13. Subsequent references appear in text.

6. Fleishman, *Figures of Autobiography*, 85.

7. Anne Hunsaker Hawkins, in *Archetypes of Conversion: The Autobiographies of Augustine, Bunyan, and Merton* (Lewisburg, Pa.: Bucknell Univ. Press, 1985), uses James's distinction between sudden and gradual types of conversion to develop her own theory of a *crisis* and a *lysis* form. Hawkins argues that these can be distinguished by the author's positioning of the two phases of struggle away from sin and longing for the positive ideal. "In a *crisis* conversion, negative reality and positive ideal coalesce and occur at the same time. But in a *lysis* conversion, these two motions (the turning away from sin and the turning toward God) are not only separated, but the space between them is extended and prolonged" (98).

8. Charles Lloyd Cohen, *God's Caress: The Psychology of Puritan Religious Experience* (Oxford: Oxford Univ. Press, 1986), 104.

9. Ibid., 108.

10. See ibid., chap. 8, for an interpretation of John Winthrop's diary and "Christian Experience" as illustrating the Puritan procedure for duplicating one's original conversion in repeated acts of reconversion.

11. See Delany, *British Autobiography*, 171.

12. See Owen C. Watkins, *The Puritan Experience: Studies in Spiritual Autobiography* (New York: Schocken, 1972), chaps. 10 and 11. See also Hugh Barbour, *The Quakers in Puritan England* (New Haven: Yale Univ. Press, 1964) and Daniel Shea, *Spiritual Autobiography in Early America* (Madison: Univ. of Wisconsin Press, 1968), 3–84.

13. Patricia Caldwell, *The Puritan Conversion Narrative: The Beginnings of American Expression* (Cambridge: Cambridge Univ. Press, 1983), 26.
14. Ibid., 66.
15. On Franklin's distant relation to the Christian autobiographical tradition, see Shea, *Spiritual Autobiography*, 234–48.
16. See Rambo, "Conversion," 74.
17. John Henry Newman, *Apologia Pro Vita Sua*, ed. David J. DeLaura (New York: Norton, 1968), 168. Subsequent references appear in text.
18. See Robert A. Colby, "The Structure of Newman's *Apologia Pro Vita Sua* in Relation to His Theory of Assent," 465–80 in DeLaura's edition of the *Apologia*. An interpretation of the *Apologia* as embodying Newman's "theory of consciousness" is Jonathan Loesberg, *Fictions of Consciousness: Mill, Newman, and the Reading of Victorian Prose* (New Brunswick: Rutgers Univ. Press, 1986).
19. Linda Peterson, *Victorian Autobiography: The Tradition of Self-Interpretation* (New Haven: Yale Univ. Press, 1986), 104–5.
20. Ibid., 105. Heather Henderson, in *The Victorian Self: Autobiography and Biblical Narrative* (Ithaca: Cornell Univ. Press, 1989), disputes this point and argues that Newman uses Job and Paul as typological figures of himself responding to accusers by telling his own life story. Interestingly, Avron Fleishman makes the same point about Bunyan's use of biblical reference—that it is not true typology—as does Peterson about Newman (see above, note 6). Scholars differ significantly about when a pattern of biblical metaphors becomes "systematic" or "consistent" rather than simply "occasional" or "rhetorical."
21. In the *Apologia* Newman cites only part of Augustine's sentence, and in Latin.
22. Peterson, *Victorian Autobiography*, 111.

3. Deconversion as a Metaphor
for Personal Transformation

1. John N. Morris, *Versions of the Self* (New York: Basic Books, 1966), 6. "The experiences recorded in nineteenth-century autobiography are, I suggest, secular counterparts of the religious melancholy and conversions set down in the autobiographies of earlier heroes of religion" (5).
2. Jean-Jacques Rousseau, *Confessions*, trans. J. M. Cohen (Harmondsworth: Penguin, 1953), 65.
3. Ibid., 68.
4. Ibid., 74.
5. Ibid., 327.
6. Ibid., 328.
7. M. H. Abrams, *Natural Supernaturalism: Tradition and Revolution in Romantic Literature* (New York: Norton, 1971), 80.
8. Ibid., 96.
9. Cited in Harrold's notes to Thomas Carlyle, *Sartor Resartus: The Life and Opinions of Herr Teufelsdröckh*, ed. Charles F. Harrold (Indianapolis: Bobbs-Merrill, 1937), 166. On the autobiographical dimensions of *Sartor*, see Ian Campbell, *Thomas Carlyle* (New York: Scribner, 1974).
10. References in text are from Harrold's edition of *Sartor Resartus*, cited in the previous note.
11. Jerome H. Buckley, in *The Victorian Temper: A Study in Literary Culture* (Cambridge: Harvard Univ. Press, 1951), 95, asserts: "*Sartor Resartus* dramatized the general states of mind through which Mill, Newman, and Carlyle

himself passed in achieving their assent, and it supplied useful categories to many other Victorians concerned with the common regenerative process. The 'Everlasting No' fitly characterized the despair that regarded the material world as a dead mechanism and the spiritual as an impotent abstraction."

12. See Harrold's Introduction to *Sartor*, xxxiii–xxxvii. Similarly, the definitive study of *Sartor*, G. B. Tennyson's *Sartor Called Resartus: The Genesis, Structure, and Style of Thomas Carlyle's First Major Work* (Princeton: Princeton Univ. Press, 1965), speaks of Carlyle's "fundamental but no longer dogmatic Christian orientation" (303) and concludes that "because Carlyle conceived of a higher force outside space and time, his orientation remained basically Christian" (318).

13. Basil Wiley, *Nineteenth Century Studies: Coleridge to Matthew Arnold* (New York: Harper, 1949), 115.

14. See A. O. J. Cockshut, *The Unbelievers: English Agnostic Thought 1840–1890* (New York: New York Univ. Press, 1966), 136: "Carlyle undoubtedly discovered the will to believe. Whether he found more cannot perhaps be known for certain, but the best verdict would seem to be that he did not. It was an experience of great importance, but it was not a modern version of a Calvinist conversion."

15. See Walter Reed, "The Pattern of Conversion in *Sartor Resartus*," *ELH* 38 (1971): 411–31.

16. Carlisle Moore, "*Sartor Resartus* and the Problem of Carlyle's 'Conversion,'" *PMLA* 70 (1955): 681. Moore analyzes in detail the parallels and contrasts between Teufelsdröckh's and Carlyle's own conversion experiences. In contrast, Campbell, *Carlyle*, 51, treats "the Centre of Indifference" as based primarily on Carlyle's year (1825–6) at Hoddam Hill.

17. James, *Varieties*, 177.

18. John Stuart Mill, *Autobiography* (New York: Columbia Univ. Press, 1924), 94. Subsequent references appear in text.

19. See Fleishman, *Figures of Autobiography*, 152: "The conversion traced in the *Autobiography* is to the ideal of human potentiality to which his previous authority figure, with its concomitant sense of the autonomous self, was incapable of binding him."

20. See Janice Carlise, *John Stuart Mill and the Writing of Character* (Athens: Univ. of Georgia Press, 1991), 65: "An examination of Mill's crisis, not from the later perception from which he views it, but in relation to the earlier events that actually preceded it, suggests that the famous upheaval was less a crisis of emotion than a crisis of vocation."

21. Although Mill said Carlyle's writings seemed to him "a haze of poetry and German metaphysics," he admits he read *Sartor Resartus* "with enthusiastic admiration and the keenest delight" and that the good Carlyle's writings did him "was not as philosophy to instruct, but as poetry to animate" (123). *Sartor* must have exerted a large influence on Mill's version of the crisis scene.

22. For this argument, see Martin Warner, "Philosophical Autobiography: St. Augustine and John Stuart Mill," in *Philosophy and Literature*, ed. A. Phillips Griffiths (Cambridge: Cambridge Univ. Press, 1984). See also James Olney, *Metaphors of Self: The Meaning of Autobiography* (Princeton: Princeton Univ. Press, 1972), 243: "In its rational clarity, in its high and dry thinness, Mill's prose is quite emptied of affective feeling; in its emotional poverty, it offers no hook, no variation of texture, for the reader's sensory imagination. . . . Mill very infrequently makes a total—i.e., more than intellectual—appeal."

23. *The God That Failed*, ed. Richard Crossman (New York: Harper, 1949), 62. The editor classifies the six authors as "Initiates" (Arthur Koestler, Ignazio Silone, and Richard Wright) and "Worshipers from Afar" (André Gide, Louis Fisher, and Stephen Spender). Koestler's analogy between the break with totalitarian

political ideology and religious deconversion also shapes his novel *Darkness at Noon* (New York: Macmillan, 1941).

24. Helen Rose Fuchs Ebaugh, *Becoming an Ex: The Process of Role Exit* (Chicago: Univ. of Chicago Press, 1988).

25. Helen Rose Fuchs Ebaugh, *Out of the Cloister: A Study of Organizational Dilemmas* (Austin: Univ. of Texas Press, 1977).

26. Ebaugh, *Becoming an Ex*, 149.

27. Ibid., 123.

28. Ibid., 143.

29. See Peter Brown, *Augustine of Hippo* (Berkeley: Univ. of California Press, 1967); Carlisle Moore, "*Sartor Resartus* and the Problem of Carlyle's Conversion"; Jack Stillinger, Introduction to *The Early Draft of John Stuart Mill's "Autobiography,"* ed. Stillinger (Urbana: Univ. of Illinois Press, 1961); and Ann Thwaite, *Edmund Gosse: A Literary Landscape* (Oxford: Oxford Univ. Press, 1985). Stillinger says that Mill's experience of mental crisis "lasted, with relapses, for at least three years" (19).

4. Ruskin, Gosse, and the Aesthetic Critique

of Protestantism

1. See J. Hillis Miller, *The Disappearance of God* (Cambridge: Harvard Univ. Press, 1963); James Thrower, *A Short History of Western Atheism* (London: Pemberton Books, 1971); Cockshut, *The Unbelievers*; Bernard Lightman, *The Origins of Agnosticism: Victorian Unbelief and the Limits of Knowledge* (Baltimore: Johns Hopkins Univ. Press, 1987); James Turner, *Without God, without Creed: The Origins of Unbelief in America* (Baltimore: Johns Hopkins Univ. Press, 1985); Susan Budd, *Varieties of Unbelief: Atheists and Agnostics in English Society, 1850–1960* (London: Heinemann, 1977); Richard J. Helmstadter and Bernard Lightman, eds., *Victorian Faith in Crisis: Essays on Continuity and Change in Nineteenth-Century Religious Belief* (Stanford: Stanford Univ. Press, 1990); and David Jasper and T. R. Wright, *The Critical Spirit and the Will to Believe: Essays in Nineteenth-Century Literature and Religion* (New York: St. Martin's, 1989).

2. See James Livingston, *The Ethics of Belief: An Essay on the Victorian Religious Conscience* (Tallahassee, Fla.: Scholars Press, 1974).

3. From an unpublished portion of Darwin's "Autobiography," quoted in William Irvine, *Apes, Angels, and Victorians: Darwin, Huxley, and Evolution* (New York: World, 1955), 61.

4. See George Landow, *The Aesthetic and Critical Theories of John Ruskin* (Princeton: Princeton Univ. Press, 1971), 265.

5. Mrs. Humphrey Ward, in *Macmillan's Magazine* 52 (May–October 1885): 134, cited in David L. Wee, *The Forms of Apostasy: The Rejection of Orthodox Christianity in the British Novel, 1880–1900*, (Ph.d. diss., Stanford, 1966), 6.

6. See Bernard Lightman, "*Robert Elsmere* and the Agnostic Crises of Faith," in Helmstadter and Lightman, *Victorian Faith in Crisis*, 283–311.

7. Budd, *Varieties*, 106.

8. Ibid., 111. For a similar argument, see Howard Murphy, "The Ethical Revolt against Christian Orthodoxy in Early Victorian England," *American Historical Review* 60 (1955): 800–817, which discusses the works of Francis Newman, George Eliot, and James Anthony Froude.

9. A. O. J. Cockshut, *The Art of Autobiography in 19th and 20th Century England* (New Haven: Yale Univ. Press, 1984), 187–88.

10. Frank Turner, "The Victorian Crisis of Faith and the Faith That Was Lost," in Helmstadter and Lightman, *Victorian Faith in Crisis*, 17.

11. Budd, *Varieties*, 105.

12. Peterson, *Victorian Autobiography*, 150.

13. John Ruskin, *Praeterita*, (Oxford: Oxford Univ. Press, 1949), 1. Subsequent references appear in text.

14. George Landow, *Aesthetic and Critical Theories*, 243–65, describes the distinctive doctines and attitudes of the evangelical movement. An excellent general biography is John Dixon Hunt, *The Wider Sea: A Life of John Ruskin* (New York: Viking, 1982).

15. See Fleischman, *Figures of Autobiography*, 174–88; Peterson, *Victorian Autobiography*, 60–90; and Henderson, *The Victorian Self*, 65–115.

16. On Ruskin's loss of religious faith in 1858 and recovery of belief in 1875, see Landow, *Aesthetic and Critical Theories*, 265–317.

17. On Ruskin's insanity and its effect on his work, see John Rosenberg, *The Darkening Glass: A Portrait of Ruskin's Genius* (New York: Columbia Univ. Press, 1961).

18. Elizabeth Helsinger, "The Structure of Ruskin's *Praeterita*," in *Approaches to Victorian Autobiography*, ed. George Landow (Athens: Ohio Univ. Press, 1979), 94.

19. See Ruskin's letter to his father defending Veronese in Tim Hilton, *John Ruskin: The Early Years* (New Haven: Yale Univ. Press, 1985), 256. Veronese's "Solomon and the Queen of Sheba" is reproduced in Raymond Fitch, *The Poison Sky: Myth and Apocalypse in Ruskin* (Athens: Ohio Univ. Press, 1982), 305.

20. See Landow, *Aesthetic and Critical Theories*, 292–93, and Hilton, *Ruskin*, 254: "The turning-points Ruskin identified were often over-precise. . . . We must not believe that Ruskin changed his mind about religion as abruptly as this."

21. See Landow's *Aesthetic and Critical Theories*, especially chap. 5, "Ruskin and Allegory." See also Fitch, "A Religion of Humanity," in *The Poison Sky*, 295–323, on Ruskin's interest in Greek religion during his period of apostasy, 1858–75.

22. Landow, *Aesthetic and Critical Theories*, 284–85.

23. Ruskin, *Fors Clavigera*, quoted in Landow, *Aesthetic and Critical Theories*, 284.

24. Henderson, *The Victorian Self*, 94, says that Ruskin's conversion to the work of social criticism, which resulted in failure in his own eyes, is the "repressed subtext" of *Praeterita*.

25. Ruskin, in 1845, cited in Peterson, *Victorian Autobiography*, 61.

26. Elizabeth Helsinger, "Ulysses to Penelope: Victorian Experiments in Autobiography," in Landow, *Approaches to Victorian Autobiography*, 12: "Ruskin shares the poets' distaste for solitary self-discovery in print, and for very similar reasons. *Praeterita* . . . portrays introspective journeying as isolated, self-involved, and finally fruitless: incapable of yielding a confident sense of self, or an exhilarating view of a purposeful life."

27. James, *Varieties*, 171.

28. Ibid., 150.

29. Ibid., 165.

30. Edmund Gosse, *Father and Son* (New York: Norton, 1963), 30. Subsequent references appear in text.

31. Augustine furthermore claimed that when Manes was "proved wrong by genuine scientists" his religious "insight into more abstruse matters" was discredited (*Confessions*, 5.2).

32. James D. Woolf, in "The Benevolent Christ in Gosse's *Father and Son*," *Prose Studies* 3 (1980): 165–75, interprets Gosse's theological position as that of the English liberal tradition. The emphasis on benevolence is certainly central to

Father and Son, but I see no evidence that the figure of Christ plays a role in Gosse's thinking.

33. Peterson, *Victorian Autobiography,* 186. Peterson interprets *Father and Son* as "a work that both embodies an attempt at scientific autobiography and self-consciously critiques it" (169).

34. My view differs from Henderson, *The Victorian Self,* 119–58, as well as from most other critics, in seeing Gosse as not simply subverting biblical tradition but using it skillfully to make fundamentally Christian criticisms of certain religious practices.

35. On comic dimensions of *Father and Son,* see R. Victoria Arana, "Sir Edmund Gosse's *Father and Son:* Autobiography as Comedy," *Genre* 10 (1977): 63–76, and William R. Siebensusch, *Fictional Techniques and Factual Works* (Athens: Univ. of Georgia Press, 1983), 28–52. However, Arana undervalues Gosse's interest in evoking sympathy for the pathos of his father as well as Gosse's concern to bring out the tragic aspects of the estrangement.

36. Peterson, *Victorian Autobiography,* 173.

37. Ibid., 175.

38. See Ann Thwaite, *Edmund Gosse: A Literary Landscape* (Oxford: Oxford Univ. Press, 1985), 77. Gosse's mature religious convictions are subject to considerable debate. Peterson, citing a letter Gosse wrote to his father affirming "the Godhead of Christ" (*Victorian Autobiography,* 221, n. 53), holds that Gosse "maintained a belief in God, Christ, and the Christian 'scheme of the world's history.'" However, this letter was written in 1873, and to his father, so it can hardly represent Gosse's final religious beliefs. Thwaite quotes a letter of 1907 to Sydney Holland that suggests an agnostic position at the time Gosse wrote *Father and Son:* "What I should like to think my book might be . . . is a call to people to face the fact that the old faith is now impossible to sincere and intelligent minds, and that we must consequently face the difficulty of following entirely different ideals in moving towards the higher life. But what ideals, or (what is more important) what discipline can we substitute for the splendid metallic vigour of an earlier age?" (432).

5. Christianity and "the White Man's Religion"

1. The term *multicultural autobiography* is somewhat ambiguous, but the alternatives, such as "minority autobiography," are worse. The term is used with increasing frequency for the works of persons of color, and in an even broader sense by James Robert Payne, ed., *Multicultural Autobiography: American Lives* (Knoxville: Univ. of Tennessee Press, 1992).

2. Henry Bibb, *Narrative of the Life and Adventures of Henry Bibb, An American Slave, written by himself,* in Gilbert Osofsky, ed., *Puttin' On Ole Massa* (New York: Harper and Row, 1969), 170–71.

3. William Wells Brown, *Narrative of William Wells Brown, a Fugitive Slave,* in Osofsky, *Puttin' On Ole Massa,* 211.

4. Harriet Jacobs, *Incidents in the Life of a Slave Girl,* in Henry Louis Gates, Jr., *The Classic Slave Narratives* (New York: Penguin, 1987), 402.

5. Jacobs, *Incidents,* 403.

6. Frederick Douglass, *Narrative of the Life of Frederick Douglass, An American Slave, Written by Himself* (New York: New American Library, 1968), 67. Subsequent references appear in text.

7. On Douglass's *Narrative* as part of the jeremiad tradition, see William Andrews, *To Tell a Free Story: The First Century of Afro-American Autobiography, 1760–1865* (Urbana: Univ. of Illinois Press, 1986), 123–32, which draws on Sacvan Berkovitch's *The American Jeremiad.*

8. Page numbers refer to Frederick Douglass, *My Bondage and My Freedom*, ed. William Andrews (Urbana: Univ. of Illinois Press, 1987).

9. Andrews, *To Tell a Free Story* 229.

10. Henry Louis Gates, Jr., *The Signifying Monkey: A Theory of African-American Literary Criticism* (New York: Oxford Univ. Press, 1988).

11. For a fuller analysis of Douglass's revisions of the 1845 narrative in *My Bondage*, see Andrews, *To Tell a Free Story*, 214–39.

12. Evidence from his last autobiography, *The Life and Times of Frederick Douglass*, written long after the Civil War, presents still more explicitly the nature of Douglass's religious doubts while he was a slave. Douglass wrote that his doubts arose "partly from the sham religion which everywhere prevailed under slavery" and partly from "the conviction that prayers were unavailing and delusive" (135). William Van Deburg, in "Frederick Douglass: Maryland Slave to Religious Liberal," *Maryland Historical Magazine* 69 (1974): 27–43, traces Douglass's religious development to show how Douglass gradually lost his faith that God would destroy slavery and by 1870 had come to reject belief in God, insisting that only human efforts could reform society. See also Donald Gibson, "Faith, Doubt, and Apostasy: Evidence of Things Unseen in Frederick Douglass's *Narrative*," in Eric Sundquist, ed., *Frederick Douglass: New Literary and Historical Essays* (Cambridge: Cambridge Univ. Press, 1990), 84–98, for further extratextual evidence of Douglass's "apostasy," such as his refusal to thank God for the deliverance of his race from slavery. In contrast, David Blight, *Frederick Douglass' Civil War: Keeping Faith in Jubilee* (Baton Rouge: Louisiana State Univ. Press, 1989) presents Douglass's views of the Civil War throughout his life as deeply religious (and within the millennialist and apocalyptic traditions), although Douglass was scornful of the institutional church and the clergy.

13. I follow Arnold Krupat's distinction between "Indian autobiographies," in which a white editor records the life story of a preliterate Native American, and "autobiographies by Indians," in which the author takes primary responsibility for writing. See Krupat's *The Voice in the Margin: Native American Literature and the Canon* (Berkeley: Univ. of California Press, 1989), 141.

14. Arnold Krupat's view is typical of many critics who see early autobiographies by Christian Indians as entirely dominated by the language and worldview of European Christian culture, and as evidence of complete assimilation. "Apes proclaims a sense of self, if we may call it that, deriving entirely from Christian culture. . . . There is the implication as well that when the Native lost his land, he lost his voice as well. . . . Inasmuch as Apes's autobiography is constructed in terms of its author's progress to full permission to speak the language of salvationism, we may see it as documenting a struggle for monologism" (*The Voice in the Margin*, 145, 147–48).

15. William Apes, *A Son of the Forest: The Experience of William Apes, a Native of the Forest* (New York, 1829), 131. The copy of the text I used is in the Newberry Library in Chicago. See also Arnold Krupat's interpretation of Apes's later writings in "Native American Autobiography," in Paul John Eakin, ed., *American Autobiography: Retrospect and Prospect* (Madison: Univ. of Wisconsin Press, 1991), 180–85.

16. After I finished this manuscript I discovered a modern edition of all of Apes's works: *On Our Own Ground: The Complete Writings of William Apess, a Pequot*, ed. with an introduction by Barry O'Connell (Amherst: Univ. of Massachusetts Press, 1992). O'Connell's introduction is an outstanding analysis of how Apess (as he later spelled his name) used not only Christian rhetoric but also American republican theory to assert the equality and dignity of his people.

17. On Copway's work, see A. LaVonne Brown Ruoff, "George Copway: Nine-

teenth-Century American Indian Autobiographer," in *a/b: Auto/Biography Studies* 3 (1987): 6–17. Analysis of the historical accuracy of Copway's writings documents that he was neither a Methodist preacher nor an Ojibway chief when he presented himself as such in his autobiography; see Donald Smith, "The Life of George Copway or Kah-ge-ga-gah-bowh (1818–1869)—and a review of his Writings," *Journal of Canadian Studies* 23 (1988): 5–38.

18. Charles Alexander Eastman, *From the Deep Woods to Civilization: Chapters in the Autobiography of an Indian* (Lincoln: Univ. of Nebraska Press, 1916), 138. Subsequent references appear in text.

19. Eastman's ideas about the inevitable passing of Indian culture reflect Social Darwinist assumptions of his time. See the interpretation of Eastman's earlier autobiography *Indian Boyhood* by H. David Brumble III in *American Indian Autobiography* (Berkeley: Univ. of California Press, 1988). Hertha Dawn Wong discusses Eastman's works in *Sending My Heart Back across the Years: Tradition and Innovation in Native American Autobiography* (New York: Oxford Univ. Press, 1992).

20. Malcolm X, *The Autobiography of Malcolm X*, with the assistance of Alex Haley (New York: Ballantine Books, 1964), 340. Subsequent references appear in text.

21. See "*Ressentiment,* Public Virtues, and Malcolm X," in Barbour, *The Conscience of the Autobiographer.*

22. John (Fire) Lame Deer and Richard Erdoes, *Lame Deer: Seeker of Visions* (New York: Simon and Schuster, 1972), 186. Subsequent references appear in text.

23. William Apes, *The Experience of Five Christian Indians of the Pequod Tribe; or An Indian's Looking-Glass for the White Man* (Boston, 1833).

24. James Axtell, *The Invasion Within: The Contest of Cultures in Colonial North America* (New York: Oxford Univ. Press, 1985).

6. Hypocrisy and the Ethics of Disbelief

1. See Livingston, *The Ethics of Belief.*

2. See especially Van Harvey, *The Historian and the Believer* (New York: Macmillan, 1966) and "The Ethics of Belief Reconsidered," *Journal of Religion* 59 (1979): 406–20.

3. Mary McCarthy, *Memories of a Catholic Girlhood* (New York: Harcourt Brace Jovanovich, 1957), 13. Subsequent references appear in text.

4. For an interpretation of McCarthy's treatment of experiences of shame, see "Shame in the Autobiographies of Mary McCarthy," in Barbour, *The Conscience of the Autobiographer.*

5. For an interpretation of Leslie Stephen's deconversion in these terms, see Jeffrey von Arx, "The Victorian Crisis of Faith as Crisis of Vocation," in Helmstadter and Lightman, *Victorian Faith in Crisis,* 262–82.

6. See Monica Baldwin, *I Leap over the Wall* (New York: Rinehart, 1950); Kathryn Hulme, *The Nun's Story* (Boston: Little, Brown, 1956); M. Griffin, *The Courage to Choose: An American Nun's Story* (Boston: Little, Brown, 1975); Mary G. Wong, *Nun: A Memoir* (New York: Harper, 1983); Rosemary Curb and Nancy Manahan, *Lesbian Nuns: Breaking the Silence* (Tallahassee: Naiad Press, 1985).

7. Helen Rose Fuchs Ebaugh, "Leaving Catholic Convents: Toward a Theory of Disengagement," in David Bromley, ed., *Falling from the Faith: Causes and Consequences of Religious Apostasy* (Newbury Park, Calif.: Sage Publications, 1988), 114.

8. Newman, *Apologia Pro Vita Sua,* 136.

9. Anthony Kenny, *A Path from Rome* (New York: Oxford Univ. Press, 1986), 71. Subsequent references appear in text.

7. Sartre's Ambiguous Atheism:
"A Cruel and Long-range Affair"

1. Jean-Paul Sartre, *The Words*, trans. Bernard Frechtman (New York: Vintage, 1964), 97–98. Subsequent references appear in text.

2. Ronald Hayman quotes Sartre on his desire to destroy the bourgeois myth of the family: "Above all I detest the well-worn myth of childhood perfected by the adults. I'd like this book to be read for what it really is: the attempt to destroy a myth" (*Sartre: A Life* [New York: Simon and Schuster, 1987], 395). Paul John Eakin sees the critical thrust of the autobiography differently: "*The Words* records a pivotal moment in the secularization of Western culture: Sartre's life enacts, and his autobiography indicts, the pervasive function of nineteenth-century historicism as a surrogate religion. The lesson of *The Words* is the loss of narrative salvation; teleological history is dead" (*Fictions in Autobiography: Studies in the Art of Self-Invention* [Princeton: Princeton Univ. Press, 1985], 164). And for Germaine Bree, the primary myth Sartre attacks is that of the romantic genius: "He is hammering at a concept firmly rooted in his own mind and which he wants to eradicate, the romantic concept of the writer as a man set apart and accountable only to his own genius, just such a man as he has been" (*Camus and Sartre: Crisis and Commitment* [New York: Delta, 1972], 56).

3. Lejeune, *On Autobiography*, 77.

4. For accounts of Sartre's political development, see the biographical works by Hayman, *Sartre: A Life;* Annie Cohen-Solal, *Sartre: A Life* (New York: Pantheon, 1987); Philip Thody, *Sartre: A Biographical Introduction* (New York: Scribners, 1971); and Hazel Barnes, *Sartre* (Philadelphia: Lippincott, 1971).

5. Further evidence that Sartre saw this as the dominant plot in his life comes from an unpublished manuscript quoted by Cohen-Solal: "I realize that literature is a substitute for religion. . . . I felt the mysticism of words. . . . little by little, atheism has devoured everything. I have disinvested and secularized writing. . . . I have systematically undermined the bases, yanked religion away from literature: no more salvation, nothing can save" (*Sartre: A Life*, 356–57).

6. See Eakin, *Fictions in Autobiography*, 153: "Sartre's analysis of the shape and shaping of his life takes the form of the case history of an illness in which the cherished myth of the writer as hero and saint is the principal symptom." Sartre sometimes views his work according to this pattern, as in *Sartre by Himself*, trans. Richard Seaver (New York: Urizen Books, 1978), 88: "I came to the realization that ever since I had first begun to write I had been living in a real neurosis—longer, actually, from the time I was nine till I was fifty. My neurosis . . . was basically that I firmly believed that nothing was more beautiful than writing, nothing greater, that to write was to create lasting works."

7. For analysis of the continual and insistent use of religious themes throughout Sartre's work, see Stuart Charmé, *Meaning and Myth in the Study of Lives: A Sartrean Perspective* (Philadelphia: Univ. of Pennsylvania Press, 1984) and Thomas King, *Sartre and the Sacred* (Chicago: Univ. of Chicago Press, 1974).

8. Stuart Charmé referred me to this footnote on p. 412 of Sartre's *Being and Nothingness* (New York: Philosophical Library, 1956).

9. Hayman, *Sartre: A Life*, 400.

10. Eakin, *Fictions in Autobiography*, 152.

11. Thody, *Sartre*, 14.

12. For the latter view, see Jane Tompkins, "Sartre Resartus: A Reading of *Les Mots*," in Robert Wilcocks, ed., *Critical Essays on Jean-Paul Sartre* (Boston: G. K. Hall, 1988), 277, 280: "One cannot take him altogether seriously. His exaggerations involve clowning as well as self-reproach, and are a game he enjoys

playing, not for masochistic reasons but for the glee that accompanies skillful satire. . . . Superb entertainer, relentless moralist, he can recognize his love of show and damn it, but his theatrical denunciation only confirms the rejected trait. This paradox lies at the center of his book. 'I was *nothing*,' proclaims Sartre at the the top of his lungs, but the egotistical style of his assertion denies what its content affirms."

13. Catharine Savage Brossman, *Jean-Paul Sartre* (Boston: Twayne, 1983), 13.

14. King, *Sartre and the Sacred*, quoting Sartre's work on Flaubert, 52. Also see p. 20: "The theological complex is the result of a choice whereby another's consciousness is preferred to one's own. It is this choice that establishes the sacred world. Every object that is associated with the judgment of the foreign consciousness appears hallowed with a religious value."

15. See Charmé, *Meaning and Myth*, 124–25: "Sartre uses theological categories, purged of their supernatural reference, to explore the dynamics of human consciousness and self-identity. . . . He desacralizes the Christian model of salvation in order to resacralize the existential task of self-discovery / creation. . . . For Sartre . . . the life of the self is the real arena for the theological drama of cosmogony, death, and rebirth. When the traditional theological model is internalized, the 'fundamental project' of every person becomes that of self-creation and protection of the ever-changing boundaries of the self where chaos and order meet."

16. See Dominick La Capra, *A Preface to Sartre* (Ithaca: Cornell Univ. Press, 1978), 185: "The myth relatively protected here is that of self-genesis, related to a notion of pure and total freedom. In terms of this potent myth, Sartre identifies autonomy with self-creation *ex nihilo* and attempts to become his own genitor."

8. Apostasy and Apology in Christian Autobiography

1. See Kippenberg, "Apostasy," *Encyclopedia of Religion:* "Early Christians were less anxious about apostasy to foreign religions than the Jews in Maccabean times had been. They were much more anxious about teachers of a false doctrine. . . . Here the Jewish and Christian views of apostasy diverge. The apostate abandoning Christian belief is not an ally of the external enemy but the follower of an internal adversary."

2. For a convenient anthology of Christian autobiographical narratives, see *Conversions*, ed. Hugh T. Kerr and John M. Mulder (Grand Rapids: Eerdmans, 1983). The focus on conversion takes in only one, though arguably the most important, phase of the Christian life, and there are many other kinds of Christian autobiography.

3. Many accounts of deconversion basically illustrate the Marxist, Freudian, Nietzschean, or feminist critiques of Christian belief and practice, dramatizing the loss of faith as a liberation from oppressive ideology. I assume the reader's familiarity with these modern criticisms of religion in my focus on how twentieth-century Christians have responded to challenges to belief.

4. Leo Tolstoy, *Confession*, trans. David Patterson (New York: Norton, 1983), 14. Subsequent references appear in text.

5. Dorothy Day, *The Long Loneliness* (New York: Harper and Row, 1952), 43. Subsequent references appear in text.

6. C. S. Lewis, *Surprised by Joy* (New York: Harcourt Brace Jovanovich, 1955), 64. Subsequent references appear in text.

7. Langdon Gilkey, *Shantung Compound* (New York: Harper and Row, 1966), 71. Subsequent references appear in text.

8. Edwin Muir, *An Autobiography* (London: Hogarth Press, 1954), 85. Subsequent references appear in text.

9. For a contrary view of Muir's political perspective, which sees *An Autobiography* as simply a conservative reaction against socialism, see Sheila Lodge, "The Politics of Edwin Muir's Autobiographies," in *Modern Selves: Essays on Modern British and American Autobiography,* ed. Philip Dodd (London: Frank Cass, 1986), 97–117. Lodge presents Muir's devotion to the role of "apolitical mystic" as incompatible with his earlier political commitments.

10. P. H. Butter, *Edwin Muir: Man and Poet* (Edinburgh: Oliver and Boyd, 1966), 248.

11. See Ronald Hayman's biography, *Nietzsche: A Critical Life* (New York: Viking Penguin, 1980), for evidence supporting this interpretation of the religious significance of Nietzsche's asceticism.

12. For a fuller discussion of Muir's use of myths and dreams, see Brian Finney, *The Inner Eye: British Literary Autobiography of the Twentieth Century* (London: Faber and Faber, 1985), 197–206.

13. Ibid., 199.

14. Fleishman, *Figures of Autobiography*, 371.

15. Ibid., 386.

9. Cults and Deprogramming

1. Marc Gallanter, in *Cults: Faith, Healing, and Coercion* (Oxford: Oxford Univ. Press, 1989), 5. A contrasting definition of cults, stressing devotion to a leader and simple organizational structure, is David Bromley and Anson Shupe, Jr., *Strange Gods: The Great American Cult Scare* (Boston: Beacon Press, 1981), 23–24.

2. The concept of totalism originates in Robert Jay Lifton, *Thought Reform and the Psychology of Totalism: A Study of "Brainwashing" in China,* (New York: Norton, 1961). Lifton discusses the extent to which the concept can be applied to cults in "Cult Processes, Religious Totalism, and Civil Liberties," in Thomas Robbins, William Shepherd, and James McBride, eds., *Cults, Culture, and the law: Perspectives on New Religious Movements* (Chico, Calif.: Scholars Press, 1985), 59–70.

3. See, for instance, the bibliography of 276 works in David G. Bromley, ed., *Falling from the Faith: Causes and Consequences of Religious Apostasy* (Newbury Park, Calif.: Sage Publications, 1988).

4. For discussion of this research, see Stuart A. Wright, "Leaving New Religious Movements: Issues, Theory, and Research," in Bromley, *Falling from the Faith,* 143–65.

5. On the Divine Light Mission, see James V. Downton, *Sacred Journeys: The Conversion of Young Americans to the Divine Light Mission* (New York: Columbia Univ. Press, 1979).

6. Sophia Collier, *Soul Rush: The Odyssey of a Young Woman of the '70s* (New York: Morrow, 1978), 193. Subsequent references appear in text.

7. Downton, *Sacred Journeys*, 2.

8. In "Experience / Narrative Structure / Reading: Patty Hearst and the American Indian Captivity Narratives," *Religion* 18 (1988): 255–82, Gary Ebersole argues that the American Indian captivity narratives provide a helpful paradigm for interpreting Patty Hearst's identity transformations in relation to the Symbionese Liberation Army. Hearst's story might also be interpeted as a version of a double deconversion, as her "faith" in two quasi-religious understandings of American society is twice forcibly undermined.

9. Jeannie Mills, *Six Years with God: Life inside Reverend Jim Jones's Peoples Temple* (New York: A & W Publishers, 1979), 10. Subsequent references appear in text.

10. See John R. Hall, "The Impact of Apostates on the Trajectory of Religious Movements: The Case of Peoples Temple," in Bromley, *Falling from the Faith*, 229–50.

11. Max Scheler, *Ressentiment*, trans. William Holdheim (New York: Schocken, 1961), 46, 66.

12. Ted Patrick with Tom Dulack, *Let Our Children Go!* (New York: E. P. Dutton, 1976), 229. Subsequent references appear in text.

13. Stories of deconversion by ex-"Moonies" include C. Elkins, *Heavenly Deception* (Wheaton, Ill.: Tyndale House, 1979); E. Heftmann, *Dark Side of the Moonies* (Harmondsworth: Penguin, 1980); Susan Swatland and Anne Swatland, *Escape from the Moonies* (London: New English Library, 1982); Barbara and Betty Underwood, *Hostage to Heaven* (New York: Clarkson Potter, 1979).

14. Christopher Edwards, *Crazy for God: The Nightmare of Cult Life* (Englewood Cliffs, N.J.: Prentice-Hall, 1979). ix. Subsequent references appear in text.

15. Janet Liebman Jacobs, *Divine Disenchantment: Deconverting from New Religions* (Bloomington: Indiana Univ. Press, 1989), 39–40. For an interpretation of the relationship between involvement in cults and issues of psychological development, see Saul Levine, *Radical Departures: Desperate Detours to Growing Up* (New York: Harcourt Brace Jovanovich, 1984).

16. Eileen Barker, "Defection from the Unification Church," in Bromley, *Falling from the Faith*, 167. See also Barker's *The Making of a Moonie: Brainwashing or Choice?* (New York: Blackwell, 1984).

17. David G. Bromley, "Deprogramming as a Mode of Exit from New Religious Movements: The Case of the Unificationist Movement," in Bromley, *Falling from the Faith*, 186–87. See also Bromley and Shupe, *Strange Gods*.

18. See, for instance, Stuart Wright, *Leaving Cults: The Dynamics of Defection* (Washington, D.C.: Society for the Scientific Study of Religion, 1987).

19. For example, see Anson Shupe, Jr., and David Bromley, *The New Vigilantes: Deprogrammers, Anti-cultists, and the New Religions* (Beverly Hills, Calif.: Sage Publications, 1980).

20. Barker, "Defection," in Bromley, *Falling*, 175–76.

21. Barker, *Making of a Moonie*, 252. See also Gallanter, *Cults*, 177.

22. Wright, "Leaving New Religious Movements," 160, and see Bromley, "Deprogramming," 185–204, both in Bromley, *Falling*.

23. Barker, "Defection," in Bromley, *Falling*, 182. Also see Barker, *Making of a Moonie*, 252.

24. On the legal status of deprogramming, see David Bromley and J. Richardson, eds., *The Brainwashing / Deprogramming Controversy* (New York: Mellen Press, 1983) and Robbins et al., ed., *Cults, Culture, and the Law*.

10. Gender and Deconversion

1. See Caroline Walker Bynum, Stevan Harell, and Paula Richman, eds., *Gender and Religion: On the Complexity of Symbols* (Boston: Beacon Press, 1986), 7: "*Sex* is the term scholars use to designate the differences between men and women that can be attributed to biology. . . . *Gender* is the term used to refer to those differences between male and female human beings that are created through psychological and social development within a familial, social, and cultural setting." Also see Mary Stewart Van Leeuwen, Annelies Knoppers, Margaret L. Koch, Douglas J. Schuurman, and Helen M. Sterk, *After Eden: Facing the Challenge of Gender Reconciliation* (Grand Rapids: Eerdman's, 1993), 1: "The term *gender* refers to the social construction of what, in any given culture, is taken to be properly masculine or feminine."

2. See Susan Henking, "The Legacies of AIDS: Religion and Meaning in AIDS-

Related Memoirs," in Michael Stemmeler and J. Michael Clark, eds., *Gay Men's Issues in Religion* (Dallas: Monument Press, forthcoming) and Susan Henking, "Beyond the Wrath of God: Evangelical Christianity and the Making of Identities in the Age of AIDS," unpublished manuscript.

3. Estelle Jelinek, *The Tradition of Women's Autobiography: From Antiquity to the Present* (Boston: Twayne, 1986); Sidonie Smith, *A Poetics of Women's Autobiography: Marginality and the Fictions of Self-Representation* (Bloomington: Indiana Univ. Press, 1987); Françoise Lionnet, *Autobiographical Voices: Race, Gender, Self-Portraiture* (Ithaca: Cornell Univ. Press, 1989); Felicity Nussbaum, *The Autobiographical Subject: Gender and Ideology in Eighteenth-Century England* (Baltimore: Johns Hopkins Univ. Press, 1989); Carolyn Heilbrun, *Writing a Woman's Life* (New York: Ballantine, 1988); Domna Stanton, ed., *The Female Autograph: Theory and Practice of Autobiography from the Tenth to the Twentieth Century* (Chicago: Univ. of Chicago Press, 1987); Shari Benstock, ed., *The Private Self: Theory and Practice of Women's Autobiographical Writings* (Chapel Hill: Univ. of North Carolina Press, 1988); Bella Brodzki and Celeste Schenck, eds., *Life / Lines: Theorizing Women's Autobiography* (Ithaca: Cornell Univ. Press, 1988); and Sidonie Smith and Julia Watson, eds., *De / Colonizing the Subject: The Politics of Gender in Women's Autobiography* (Minneapolis: Univ. of Minnesota Press, 1992).

4. Domna Stanton, "Autogynography: Is the Subject Different?" in Stanton, *The Female Autograph*, 11.

5. Linda Peterson, "Gender and Autobiographical Form: The Case of the Spiritual Autobiography," in James Olney, ed., *Studies in Autobiography* (New York: Oxford Univ. Press, 1988), 212.

6. See William Andrews, ed., *Sisters of the Spirit: Three Black Women's Autobiographies of the Nineteenth Century* (Bloomington: Indiana Univ. Press, 1986).

7. See Ann Braude, *Radical Spirits: Spiritualism and Women's Rights in Nineteenth-Century America* (Boston: Beacon Press, 1989).

8. Peterson, *Victorian Autobiography*, 132.

9. Jacobs, *Divine Disenchantment*, 132.

10. Kathleen Norris, *Dakota: A Spiritual Geography* (New York: Ticknor and Fields, 1993), 95. Subsequent references appear in text.

11. Terry Tempest Williams, *Refuge: An Unnatural History of Family and Place* (New York: Vintage, 1991), 4. Subsequent references appear in text.

12. China Galland, *Longing for Darkness: Tara and the Black Madonna: A Ten-Year Journey* (New York: Penguin, 1990), 13. Subsequent references appear in text.

13. Patricia Hampl, *Virgin Time* (New York: Farrar, Straus and Giroux, 1992), 6. Subsequent references appear in text.

14. In a reading of *Virgin Time* at St. Olaf College in January 1993, Patricia Hampl registered her deep dismay that the Library of Congress cataloguing data on the copyright page classifies her book as "Apologetics—20th Century."

15. Mary Daly, *Outercourse: The Be-Dazzling Voyage: Containing Recollections from my "Logbook of a Radical Feminist Philosopher" (Be-ing an Account of My Time / Space Travels and Ideas—Then, Again, Now and How* (San Francisco: Harper San Francisco, 1992), 1. Subsequent references appear in text.

16. Mary Daly, with Jane Caputi, *Websters' First New Intergalactic Wickedary of the English Language* (Boston: Beacon Press, 1987), 88.

17. Mary Daly, *The Church and the Second Sex* (Boston: Beacon Press, 1985) and *Beyond God the Father: Toward a Philosophy of Women's Liberation* (Boston: Beacon Press, 1985). For interpretation of the autobiographical dimensions of these and later works, see Susan E. Henking, "The Personal Is the Theological: Autobiographical Acts in Contemporary Feminist Theology," *Journal of the American Academy of Religion* 59 (1991): 511–25.

11. Conclusion: The Literary and Religious

Significance of Deconversion Narratives

1. Jean Starobinski, "The Style of Autobiography," in James Olney, ed., *Autobiography: Essays Theoretical and Critical* (Princeton: Princeton Univ. Press, 1980), 78. See also Henderson, *The Victorian Self*, 9: Augustine's "autobiography illustrates the way in which the telling of every life 'story' requires a conversion for its climax—otherwise the story has no plot, and the telling of it no point."

2. Eakin, *Touching the World*, 186.

3. Ingmar Bergman, *The Magic Lantern: An Autobiography*, trans. Joan Tate (New York: Penguin, 1988).

4. Thomas Simmons, *The Unseen Shore: Memories of a Christian Science Childhood* (Boston: Beacon Press, 1991).

5. Friedrich Nietzsche, "Genealogy of Morals" (Third Essay, section 27), in *"On the Genealogy of Morals" and "Ecce Homo,"* trans. and ed. Walter Kaufmann (New York: Vintage, 1967), 161.

6. Turner, "The Victorian Crisis of Faith and the Faith That Was Lost," in Helmstadter and Lightman, *Victorian Faith in Crisis*, 15.

7. Malcolm X, *The Autobiography of Malcolm X*, 287.

8. See Reeve Robert Brenner, *The Faith of Holocaust Survivors* (New York: Free Press, 1980).

9. Elie Wiesel, *Night* (New York: Avon, 1958), 44. Subsequent references appear in text.

10. Richard Rubenstein, *After Auschwitz* (New York: Bobbs-Merrill, 1966); Martin Buber, *The Eclipse of God* (New York: Harper and Row, 1952); Emil Fackenheim, *God's Presence in History* (New York: New York Univ., 1970), 84.

11. For instance, Alan Mintz discusses Hebrew literature in terms of both the theme of response to historical catastrophe and the theme of loss of faith, in *Hurban: Responses to Catastrophe in Hebrew Literature* (New York: Columbia Univ. Press, 1984) and *"Banished from Their Father's Table": Loss of Faith in Hebrew Autobiography* (Bloomington: Indiana Univ. Press, 1989). See also Joseph Sungolowsky, "Holocaust and Autobiography: Wiesel, Friedlander, Pisar," in Randolph L. Braham, ed., *Reflections of the Holocaust in Art and Literature* (Boulder, Col.: Social Science Monographs, 1990), 131–46. There has been considerable reflection on the role of anti-semitism as a pressure for Jewish apostasy, the ambiguity of forced or "pragmatic" conversions to Christianity, and the question of how to interpret modern movements "from a nominal Judaism to a nominal Christianity." See Todd M. Endelman, Introduction, in *Jewish Apostasy in the Modern World* (New York: Holmes and Meier, 1987), 9. If the majority of Jewish conversions to Christianity were for pragmatic reasons of social assimilation or survival, under what conditions would one consider an account of such a change of identity to be a deconversion? For a medieval autobiographical account of a conversion from Judaism to Christianity, see Morrison's analysis and reproduction of Herman-Judah's *Short Account of His Own Conversion*, in *Conversion and Text*.

12. Jacobs, *Divine Disenchantment*, 123.

13. Tillich, *Dynamics of Faith*, 16. See also Geddes MacGregor, "Doubt and Belief," *Encyclopedia of Religion*.

14. Herman Melville, *Moby-Dick* (New York: Norton, 1967), 314.

15. Barbour, *The Conscience of the Autobiographer*.

INDEX